NAPOLEON'S 'LITTLE PEST'

Naples: A Palimpsest
Vernon Lee
The Companion Guide to Southern Italy
My Dearest Augusta
A Concise History of Italy
Byron's Prose (ed.)
Normandy: Landscape with Figures
Burgundy: Landscape with Figures
The Actons

NAPOLEON'S 'LITTLE PEST'

The Duchess of Abrantès
1784–1838

PETER GUNN

HAMISH HAMILTON

LONDON

First published in Great Britain 1979
by Hamish Hamilton Ltd
Garden House 57-59 Long Acre London WC2E 9JL

Copyright © 1979 by Peter Gunn

British Library Cataloguing in Publication Data
Gunn, Peter
  Napoleon's 'Little Pest'.
  1. Abrantès, Laure Permon, *duchesse d'*
  2. Historians—France—Biography
  3. Napoleon I, *Emperor of the French—*
  Friends and associates—Biography
  I. Title
  944'.007'2024   DC198.A3
  ISBN 0-241-10183-2

Printed in Great Britain by
Western Printing Services Ltd, Bristol

CONTENTS

LIST OF ILLUSTRATIONS

(between pages 134 and 135)

PREFACE

No historical personage or period perhaps have received from historians such detailed documentation as the Emperor Napoleon and the era which goes by his name. History, however, has its own methods, dealing impersonally as it does with men and events. Yet for living portraits and for that colour and texture that bring life to the canvas of the period one looks elsewhere than to history proper— to novelists, rather, to diarists or the writers of memoirs. It is in Stendhal's *La Chartreuse de Parme* that the very sensation of what it was like to be living in the Napoleonic age is brought home most vividly to the reader. It is the same with memoirs; there it is an individual person who is face to face with other persons and an eye-witness of events. History, indeed, is the touchstone of the veracity of such novelists and memoir-writers alike. Against it may be judged the inaccuracies of Bourrienne's accounts of the young Bonaparte or the prejudices of Las Cases' reports of the exiled Emperor on Saint Helena. If memoirs are part of the material of history, they resemble novels in their vital immediacy. How much we owe to the *Mémoires* of Mme de Rémusat for our intimate knowledge of court life at the Tuileries and Malmaison and of the personalities of Napoleon and Josephine. What would have been gained had Mme Récamier, like Stendhal, kept a journal? General Thiébault and President Pasquier, in their *Mémoires*, reveal, each in his way, the existence of an officer serving through the Napoleonic campaigns and the practical nullity of a lawyer and politician, when one man guided the destiny of France.

Laure Permon, married to the First Consul's closest friend Andoche Junot, later to become one of Napoleon's generals and as Duke of Abrantès Governor of Paris, was in a particularly privileged position to watch the unfolding of the Napoleonic drama, both from the audience and as a leading actress in it. Placed so favourably as she was to observe, she was not one to let the opportunity slip, and has left an incomparable record of court and society, of public glamour and private intrigues, written with verve and spiced with a certain malice, in thirty volumes of personal recollections. And what is more, it is she herself who has drawn back the curtain to reveal some of the most intimate scenes of a life in which love and violence and despair went hand in hand.

If the Revolution acted as a solvent on French society, the seizure of supreme power by General Bonaparte was followed by the consolidation of the nation in the Empire and by the fusion of classes to form a new imperial society that far outshone the *ancien régime* of the court of Versailles in its outward brilliance and *parvenu* splendour. The French, by the very rapidity of change, became only too conscious that they were living in exceptional times. The ever-present possibility of death on the battlefield served the young as a stimulant to whet the appetite for a frenetic enjoyment of living, however ephemeral. Never was *carpe diem* so apt a rule of life. The rewards were commensurate with the dangers undergone. Bravery, military initiative and dash, the qualities in which Murat excelled, led to fame, titles, unheard-of riches. Like the heroes and heroines of Stendhal, ordinary Frenchmen and French women discovered within themselves unsuspected resources, the potentiality of a metamorphosed, more heroic, self. Glory was the spur, pleasure the prize. If Paris was the gayest, the most brilliant capital of Europe, the scene of a display of quite dazzling luxury and uninhibited sexuality, after Waterloo it was said that black, for mourning, was the French national colour.

As spectators, or as participants in those momentous events, the memoir-writers convey with all the cachet of personal involvement the impact produced on French society by this Titan among men—for such was the Emperor Napoleon. But none of them, not even Bourrienne, who was at military school with him and equivocally served him until his disgrace in 1810, was able to write from personal knowledge of Napoleon at all stages of his incredible career—and Bourrienne is far from reliable. Few were so advantageously, so uniquely, placed to observe and report on the Emperor and the society that he created as the Duchess of Abrantès. And fewer still among the writers of memoirs could rival her gifts of self-expression, her conversational powers and literary ability. Possessed of a remarkable memory, she had the foresight to appreciate the future value of her inside knowledge. Many a night, or rather early morning, returning home from the Tuileries or Saint-Cloud, from a ball at the Grand

Duchess of Berg's or at a foreign embassy, or from the Hôtel de Ville, where as wife of the Governor of Paris she had been hostess at a reception for the élite of official Parisian society, before she retired to bed she would jot down her impressions of scenes that she had witnessed or of conversations overheard or carried on with distinguished persons, or with the Emperor himself. Years later, encouraged by Balzac, she set herself to recall for a Restoration society avid for such details the glories of the fallen Empire. Between 1831 and 1834 appeared her *Mémoires* in eighteen volumes; and these were followed by *Histoires contemporaines* (two volumes, 1835), *Scènes de la vie espagnole* (two volumes, 1836), *Histoire des salons de Paris* (six volumes, 1837-8), and *Souvenirs d'une ambassade en Espagne et en Portugal* (two volumes, 1837)—in all thirty volumes of personal recollections.

In these works she undertook, as she expressly declared, to record public events; of her private life she was for the most part silent. It was first for Balzac alone that she wrote her *Journal intime*, in which she recounted her affair with Metternich and Caroline Murat's and Junot's revenge. In 1902 was published *La Générale Junot, Duchesse d'Abrantès* by Joseph Turquan, the Napoleonic scholar, who had access to the mss. of the *Journal intime* but not to those letters and papers that related to her tempestuous affair with Maurice de Balincourt, which were still in the possession of his descendants. All this material was at the disposal of Robert Chantemesse, who published in 1927 *Le roman inconnu de la Duchesse d'Abrantès*, and of Henri Malo, who brought out in the same year *Les années de bohème de la Duchesse d'Abrantès*, which deals with her affair with Balzac and her last years. However, it is to her own *Mémoires* that the reader will chiefly turn for a revelation of the life and character of this remarkable woman and for an inimitable picture of an age whose magnificence can perhaps never be repeated. The only English translation of these, in a much abridged edition in three volumes, was published as long ago as 1883. For English readers only a portion of her private life is available: *The Secret Memoirs of the Duchess of Abrantès* by Robert Chantemesse, translated and with an introduction by Eric Sutton, which was published by Jonathan Cape in 1927. The present book is an attempt to make good this lack.

PETER GUNN
Swaledale, Yorkshire
August 1978

ONE

The Corsicans

IT WAS the month of Vendémiaire 1795 in the Revolutionary calendar. The Permon family, who had returned to Paris from Bordeaux, was installed in a suite of rooms at the Hôtel de l'Autruche, ex-Autriche, in the Section (or Quarter) of Pelletier, in the rue de la Loi, today rue Richelieu. The family, with their two servants, a *valet de chambre* and a chamber maid, consisted of Monsieur and Madame Permon, their son Albert, aged twenty-seven, and their daughter Laure, who was then nearly eleven. M. Permon was seriously, dangerously ill. The state of Paris at the period was that almost of continuous insurrection against the Convention, which had lost control of the situation, so that it failed to ensure even the necessities of life. The Permons became more and more alarmed every day by the dangers which were apparent around them. Paris rang with the tumults of the factions, who were in possession of arms, and each faction hoisted its own standard. Against the Convention, then the only legal authority, were opposed the Sections, which for some days past had declared war against it. Paris resembled a garrison town. At night they heard the sentries calling to and answering one another, as in a besieged city; the strictest search was made for arms and ammunition; and the Section was furnished with lists of all the men capable of having arms in defence of the country. Paris was on the brink of civil war.

On the 11 Vendémiaire (3 October) there was a domiciliary visit by the authorities of the Section. They wanted to know why Citizen Permon, whose arrival in Paris had been notified by the hotel, had not reported to the Section. Their behaviour was rude and ominously threatening, and they went off only when General Buonaparte, who called every day or sent his aide-de-camp Junot to enquire after the sick man, offered to go himself and explain matters to the president. Amid the violence of these scenes, at times in the house itself and constantly in the streets, the condition of the patient worsened. Laure was to remember these fateful days. She wrote in her *Memoirs:* 'On the morning of the 12th, Bonaparte, who had called according to custom, appeared to be lost in thought; he went out, came back, went out again, and again returned when we were at our dessert. I recollect that he ate a bunch of grapes, and took a large cup of coffee. "I break-fasted very late," he said, "at Bourienne's"—I think he said. "They talked politics there until I was sick of the subject. I will try to learn the news, and if I hear anything interesting I will come and tell you." We did not see him again. The night was stormy, especially in our Section. The whole rue de la Loi was studded with bayonets. General d'Agneau, who commanded the Sections, had called to see someone in the next house to ours, and one of the officers who were with him had expressed the most hostile disposition. Barricades were already set up in our street, but some of the officers of the National Guard ordered them to be removed. The National Guard was the principal force of the Sections. These were the elements opposed to the troops of the line commanded by experienced generals such as Brune, Berruyer, Montchoisy, Verdier, and lastly Bonaparte.'

On the morning of the 13th the condition of M. Permon gave rise to grave concern. Owing to the turmoil in the streets, they feared that the doctor, M. Duchannois, would not be able to come; but he arrived, and let his fears be known that the patient might not survive the shock of the commotion that was brewing in the city. At the moment all was quiet. Laure wrote in her *Memoirs*: 'For some hours we flattered ourselves that matters would be adjusted between the Convention and the rebels; but about half-past four the firing of cannons began. Scarcely was the first discharge heard before it was answered from all quarters. The effect upon my poor father was terrible and immediate. To no purpose did we administer the draughts prescribed for him by M. Duchannois. All the scenes of the Revolution passed in review before him, and every discharge that he heard was a blow that struck him personally. What a day! what an evening! what a night! Every pane of glass was broken in pieces. Towards evening the Section fell back upon our quarter: the fighting was carried on almost under our windows; but when it reached Saint Roch, and particularly the Théâtre de la République, we imagined that the house was tumbling about our ears.' Barricades were run up in the rue de la Loi; the tumult was indescribable, bells pealing, drums beating, frenzied cries, the rattle of musketry, the booming of guns, and noise of glass shivering on the pavement. Towards dawn the clamour died away, and the firing was only heard in the distance. Next day tranquillity was restored in the city. Buonaparte called in briefly. The Permons did not know till afterwards that he was the hero of the hour; his 'whiff of grapeshot' had dispersed the rebels and thereby saved the Convention. Three days later, on 17 Vendémiaire (8 October) M. Permon died.

Nicholas-Auguste-Charles-Martin Permon (it was only later, when a rich man, that he affected the *particule*, to which as a commoner he had no right) had as a young man of twenty served as a commissary to the French forces in Corsica. He was distinguished both by his elegant manners and his accomplishments; he fenced well, performed delightfully on the violin, and was thoroughly versed in the ways of the world. He was ambitious. At Ajaccio he met and fell in love with the fourteen-year-old Panoria Stephanopoulos Comnena, of a patrician family of Greek origin. Doubt has been cast on the family's claim to be directly descended from the imperial family of Comnena, the rulers of Constantinople and Trebizond; but it may well have been a fact. Napoleon and Talleyrand seemed to have smiled at the pretension. But the young General Buonaparte, when looking for a wife well placed in society, had proposed to the widowed Madame Permon, and it was on her laughing refusal that he married Josephine de Beauharnais. The Bonapartes (or Buonaparte, as they were known in Corsica), as gentry in Ajaccio, would have been aware of the social standing of the Stephanopoulos family. Much later Count Armand Marquiset remarked of the then celebrated Duchess of Abrantès, '*Commère* (gossip), *oui; Comnène, non.*' It was said, that Count Charles de Vergennes, Louis XVI's minister, having formed a mésalliance with a Greek lady, had obtained for her relations a brevet of nobility. Nevertheless, there was published in Amsterdam in 1784 a book, bearing the cumbersome title: '*Historic Précis of the Imperial House of Comnena, where one finds the origin, customs and usages of the Maniotes, preceded by the direct filiation, recognized by letters patent of the King in the month of April 1782, from David, last Emperor of Trebizond, to Demetrius Comnena, now captain of cavalry in France.*' This Captain Demetrius Comnena was Madame Permon's brother, who, with another brother, the Abbé Comnena, emigrated at the outbreak of the Revolution. He styled himself Prince Comnena, and was, one does not know with what complaisance, recognized as such by Louis XVIII.

When the Emperor David II was put to death by order of Mahomet II, his family escaped first to Persia, and from there migrated to Greece,

to the Peloponnese, where the senior member of the clan was acknowledged as the Protogeras of Mania. On 3 October 1675 the clan, with
other adherents, quitted Greece and sought lands from the Genoese,
who assigned to the new colonists districts in Corsica, then under the
rule of Genoa. It was not sold to France until 1768. Constantine
Stephanopoulos Comnena, the head of the family, was granted the
title of Privileged Chief. In 1729, when the Corsicans rose to throw off
Genoese suzerainty, the Greeks sided with Genoa. The lands of the
colonists were invaded by the Corsicans, their houses and property
destroyed or pillaged, and the survivors found a refuge mostly in
Ajaccio. It was from the house of one of the families resident there that
Charles Permon sought his bride, Panoria Comnena. Husbands were
difficult to come by in Corsica, and the Comnenas did not think they
were demeaning themselves, when they allowed their daughter to
marry the handsome, well-to-do Frenchman. Panoria was regarded
as the most beautiful girl in the island, her nearest rival being a girl of
about her own age, Laetizia Ramolini, who married Charles Buonaparte. The two girls were close friends in Ajaccio, but they lost sight
of each other, when Charles Permon returned to France, taking his
bride with him.

In France, where the affairs of the young couple prospered, two
children were born to them, Albert, the elder, and Cecile, some seven
years his junior. When the boy was eight, Permon took him with him
to America, where he was a contractor to the army of General Roch-
ambeau, commander of the French forces assisting the revolt of
American colonists. Panoria Permon, with the baby Cecile, returned
to Ajaccio, to await her husband's return. There she renewed her
acquaintance with Laetizia Buonaparte, who now possessed a growing
family of her own. It was then that she saw Napoleon for the first
time; Cecile played with the younger Buonaparte children. Many
years later Napoleon told Laure a story of his childhood, at a time
when she was not yet born. She relates how: 'He was one day accused
by one of his sisters of having eaten a basketful of grapes, figs and
citrus fruits, which had come from the garden of *his uncle the Canon*.
None but those acquainted with the Buonaparte family can form any
idea of the enormity of this offence. To eat fruit belonging to the
uncle the Canon was infinitely more criminal than to eat grapes and
figs which might be claimed by anyone else. An enquiry took place.
Napoleon denied the fact and was whipped. He was told that if he
would beg pardon he should be forgiven. He protested that he was

innocent, but he was not believed. If I recollect rightly, his mother was at the time on a visit to M. de Marbeuf, the French Resident, or some other friend. The result of Napoleon's obstinacy was that he was kept three whole days on bread and cheese, and that cheese was not *broccio* [an excellent Corsican cheese]. However, he would not cry: he was sombre but not sulky. At length, on the fourth day of his punishment, a little friend of Marianna Buonaparte returned from the country, and on hearing of Napoleon's disgrace, she confessed that she and Marianna had eaten the fruit. It was now Marianna's turn to be punished. When Napoleon was asked why he had not accused his sister, he replied that though he suspected that she was guilty, yet out of consideration to her little friend, who had no share in the falsehood, he had said nothing. He was then only seven years of age.'

On the conclusion of the American War M. de Permon, as he now styled himself, set up house in Languedoc, in Montpellier, where he had purchased the post of receiver-general of departmental taxes. He and his wife were received in the best society. One of their friends was the governor of Languedoc, the Comte de Périgord, M. de Talleyrand's uncle. There on 6 November 1784, after supping with Mme de Moncan, the wife of the under-commandant of the province, Mme Permon was delivered of a baby girl, Laure. The birth left her paralysed on the right side and part of the left. She spent three months in agony, the doctors of Montpellier, famous for its medicine, being unable to cure her; it was only after she had been administered herbal poultices by a wise man from Gilles, a nearby village, that she recovered. Meanwhile the child, which had been put out to nurse, was kept out of its mother's sight, and she seemed to have forgotten its existence, until the day, seeing by chance a child being carried by a nurse, she gave a shriek. 'Charles,' she cried, 'I have a baby. Where is it?' Her brother, who was then sixteen, afterwards told Laure that nothing could have described the delight the mother had when her child was restored to her. She vowed that she would make up in maternal affection for her long neglect.

Meanwhile, Charles Buonaparte, having secured recognition of his French nobility, successfully applied, pleading his poverty, for places for his eldest children at schools in France: Joseph, the eldest, at the College of Autun, Napoleon at the military school in Brienne, and Marianna at the convent in Saint-Cyr. He seems to have been of a somewhat feckless, contriving character, but he was latterly in ill-health and had a large family to provide for. In 1784, the year of

Laure Permon's birth, he was in France, with his son Joseph, then aged sixteen who had just left college, and his brother-in-law, the Abbé Joseph Fesch, to seek advice from the doctors of Montpellier on his chronic abdominal pains. It was found that he was suffering from cancer of the stomach. The Buonapartes were so poor that they had put up in a miserable inn, and there Charles Buonaparte, taken seriously ill, was confined to bed. Mme Permon, hearing from friends that three Corsicans were living in poverty in the town, one very ill, sent her husband to seek them out. To her astonishment she found that they were relatives of her old friend Laetizia Ramolini. She straightway took them into her own house and personally cared for the now dying Charles Buonaparte. He died in her arms. It was with money supplied by the Permons that the funeral was carried out, a tombstone raised to his memory, and that Joseph and the Abbé were enabled to return to Ajaccio.

In the following year, 1785, M. Permon, who was negotiating the purchase of the post of farmer of the public revenue, left Montpellier with his family for Paris, where they took a house on the fashionable Quai Conti. One of Mme Permon's first thoughts on arriving in the capital was to look up Napoleon Buonaparte, who had left Brienne in the preceding September and was then in the military school in Paris. Her brother Demetrius Comnena had met the boy—he was just turned fifteen—on his arrival in the city, and thought that he looked like a newcomer fresh from the country, gaping and staring about him in bewilderment. He considered that he would have been an excellent victim for pickpockets—if he had had anything worth taking. Comnena sometimes took him out to dinner. Once in the course of the meal Napoleon declaimed violently against the luxury of the young men of the military school and discussed the merits of Spartan training. He told him that he was composing a brief on the subject, which he was going to send to the Minister of War. The older man thought that, with his airs of superiority and intractable views, he must be unpopular with his school-fellows, and wondered if he would be lucky enough to escape being run through. M. Permon managed through the influence of his friends to get him leave at times, and at one period a sprained ankle kept Napoleon an inmate of the Permon's house for a week. The young man's shyness, hauteur and reserve prevented his becoming a friend of Albert Permon, who was a few years his senior. Joseph Buonaparte wrote to Demetrius Comnena, thanking him for his attentions to Marianna at school at

Saint-Cyr. One day Mme Permon and her brother visited Marianna at Saint-Cyr in the company of Napoleon.

When Marianna came into the parlour she appeared very sad, and at the first word addressed to her she burst into tears. Mme Permon embraced her and tried to comfort her. It was some time before the girl could tell the cause of her distress. At length she came out with her trouble. One of the girls (Mlle de Montluc) was to leave the school in a week, and the pupils of her class intended giving her a little entertainment on her departure. Everyone had contributed, but Marianna could not give anything, because her allowance of money was nearly exhausted; she had only ten francs left, and her next allowance was not due until six weeks time. Napoleon, on hearing this, made a move to put his hand in his pocket, but a moment's reflection caused him to pause, and he merely stamped angrily with his foot. Mme Permon gave Marianna the small sum required, and she immediately cheered up. In the carriage on the way back to Paris Napoleon gave vent to his anger at such establishments as Saint-Cyr and the military schools. Demetrius Comnena rebuked him, and he was silent for a while. But not for long; he came back to the subject. Comnena, whose temper was hasty, told him peremptorily to keep quiet.

'It ill becomes you who are educated at the King's bounty to speak like that.'

'I am not educated at the King's expense,' Napoleon replied, 'but at the expense of the State.'

'A fine distinction,' said Comnena. 'Is not the King the State? I will not stand by and hear you speak disrespectfully of your sovereign.'

'I will say nothing that is displeasing to you, Monsieur de Comnena,' replied Napoleon, 'only give me leave to add, that if I were the sovereign, and had the power to alter existing regulations, I should change them so that all should benefit from them.'

And later he was to do just this.

Some time afterwards, when he was commissioned as a sub-lieutenant in the artillery—he passed out before his time—, he came to the Permon's house to show off all the glory of his new uniform. One part of this struck Cecile as odd—his boots were so large that they appeared to flap round his spindly shanks. Cecile could not restrain her laughter, which upset Napoleon. At that early period, as much later, he could not relish a joke at his expense; his skin was always excessively thin. 'You are nothing but a child—a little *pensionnaire*,' he said to Cecile, who was then ten or eleven. 'And you are but a

Puss in Boots,' she retorted. This aroused a general laugh, and Napoleon
went off, his feelings very much mortified. But a few days later, to
show that he bore no malice, he arrived at the house with a toy that
he had had made—at this time he could ill afford it. This toy, which he
gave to Laure and she afterwards treasured, was of a cat in boots, in
the character of a footman running before the carriage of the Marquis
de Carabas. For Cecile he brought a very pretty edition of the tale of
Puss in Boots.

The meeting of the States-General was called for 5 May 1789.
Laure was too young to understand the significance of the moment
when the members of the three estates walked in formal procession
to the church of St Louis in Versailles to hear mass on the day before
the opening of the session. But she remembered vividly the excited
expectancy that was in the air of Paris. When, after the taking of the
Bastille on 14 July, the King went in person to the Hôtel de Ville, her
father told Laure how he was impressed by the King's demeanour, his
dignity and composure, which made a deep impression also on all
those who witnessed the ceremony. M. Permon had had business
dealings with M.Necker, and he felt himself under deep obligations
both to the King and to Mme Elizabeth—for what is not clear. He was
a royalist, but from his American experiences a constitutionalist. His
hopes, however, for reforms in accordance with many of the provincial
cahiers were speedily disillusioned. Violence soon appeared on the
streets. Laure's memory went back to certain fearful days. On 6
October she remembered seeing her mother, at three in the afternoon,
ordering the servants to close the drawing-room shutters which
looked on the quay. Her husband wished to go to Versailles, but she
wept and restraining him by the arm, entreated him not to leave them.
    M. Permon, seeing the way affairs were going, converted his
property into English stock, and taking Albert with him, set off for
London. In Paris the Sections were forming; on his return he was paid
a domiciliary visit by their representatives, and reasons were demanded
for his recent trip abroad. This appeared to him a gross infringement
on his rights as a citizen. In an access of rage, he seized a stick and
threatened to beat his interlocutor, who left the house saying that the
matter would be reported. Captain Buonaparte, when told of this
incident, went to the Section and lodged a complaint. 'If,' he said,
'M. Permon had fired a pistol at the man, he would only have been
defending his house against an insolent intruder, and no one could

have blamed him.' But legality was already a thing of the past.

The feast of St Lawrence, 10 August, was Laure's saint's day and a party had been planned for her. She was never to forget that day. Her room was gay and festive with flowers and gifts. Outside the streets were filled with restless crowds, patrols passed. Suddenly the house shook with the thunder of artillery; there was fighting below them in the street; shouts and cries of alarm were followed by the sound of musketry. Through the shutters could be heard the groans of the wounded. About noon her brother entered with one of his companions-in-arms, who was wrapped in a greatcoat. He was on the run, and had eaten nothing for forty hours. His family were under great obligations to the Queen. Having killed a man in a struggle, he was being closely pursued by his adversaries. The young man was hidden in Laure's room, and she received detailed instructions as to the answers she was to give in case she was interrogated. The cautious prudence she had then to observe was a lesson she took to heart, a lesson that was later to save those close to her. Watchfulness and extreme prudence, a word could give one away. Even children's games could reveal the political sympathies of their parents, and might lead to the guillotine.

In the afternoon M. Permon went out, and his wife and children anxiously awaited for hours his return. Albert went down frequently to the entrance to look for him. After several fruitless visits he ventured as far as the quay, and it was there he heard of the deposition of the King. But there was no sign of his father. Bodies of men, and one woman, lay on the cobblestones, as if quietly sleeping in stains of blood. The sound of gunfire was diminishing, but every now and then shots were to be heard. Night was coming on, and M. Permon had not returned. Albert went down again to look for him. He saw a man quickly turn the corner of their hôtel and pause. He immediately recognized his father, who advanced cautiously, looking anxiously behind him. On seeing Albert he called to him, bade him keep the door open, saying that he was just going back to the Mint to fetch someone. He returned, supporting a man who was scarcely able to walk. He led him, leaning on his arm, to a bedroom. There the wounded man took off the large military cloak that enveloped him. He was a friend of the family, M. de Bevy. Pale and faint, he was bleeding from several wounds. Tranquillity was not restored during the whole night, but the Permon's house, owing to its position on the quay, was safe from the attentions of the mob which roamed the streets till morning. Next day Albert went to the house of M. de

Condorcet, who lived in the *entresol* of the Mint, and through his good offices M. de Bevy was got away.

M. Permon had no fears of his own safety, but the following day a friendly butcher, a lieutenant in the National Guard, sent to inform him that he had been denounced for having harboured enemies of the people. At first M. Permon paid little head to the warning, but an hour later he received positive information that he was about to be arrested. The person who brought this news undertook to procure passports for a city in the South of France for M. and Mme Permon, but for them only. Mme Permon was distracted at having to leave the children behind in Paris. There was, however, no time to be lost. It was immediately determined that Albert should find lodgings and that the girls should be placed in a boarding school. By nightfall Cecile and Laure were installed in a boarding school, in the Faubourg Saint-Antoine, run by the Mlles Chevalier, and lodgings found for Albert nearby.

Although the two girls were miserable, their life was cheered by visits from Albert, who brought them news of the parents in Toulouse, where they were temporarily staying. In her *Memoirs* Laure recalls this melancholy period: 'Our only intervals of happiness were when my brother came to see us, which he did as often as he could. One day, when he came to pay us a visit, he saw as he came along groups of men and women whose sanguinary drunkenness was horrible. Many were naked to the waist, and their arms and breasts were covered in blood. They bore tattered garments on their pikes and swords. Their faces were inflamed, and their eyes haggard; in short, their appearance was hideous. These groups became more frequent and more numerous. My brother, in his uneasiness about us, determined to come to us at all risks, and drove rapidly along the boulevard until he arrived opposite the house of Beaumarchais. There he was stopped by a dense mob, composed of half-naked creatures besmeared with blood, and who had the appearance of demons incarnate. They shouted, sang and danced. It was the saturnalia of hell. On seeing Albert's cabriolet, they screamed, "Let it be taken to him! Let it be taken to him! He's an aristocrat!" In a moment the cabriolet was surrounded by the crowd and from out of the middle of it an object seemed to arise and approach. My brother's poor sight did not enable him at first to see the long auburn tresses clotted with blood, and a face which was still beautiful. The object came nearer and nearer, and was thrust in his face. My poor brother uttered a cry. He had recognized the head of Mme de

Lamballe.' This unfortunate woman had been married to Louis
Bourbon, Prince of Lamballe, descended from Louis XIV's illegitimate
son, the Count of Toulouse, but the marriage only lasted a year, the
Prince dying in 1768. Attached to the household of Marie-Antoinette,
the Princess of Lamballe became her closest friend. She visited England
in 1791 to appeal for help for the royal family, and she could have
stayed abroad, but out of loyalty, after making her will, she returned
to Paris. She shared Marie-Antoinette's captivity in the Temple, but,
removed to La Force, she was brought from there to the Abbey to
appear before the two representatives of the people, Hebert and
L'Hullier. Her trial was summary. 'Question: "Who are you?"
Answer: "Maria Louisa, Princess of Savoy." Q. "Had you any knowledge of the plots of the court on 10 August?" A. "I do not know that
there were any plots on 10 August; but this I know, that I had no
knowledge of them." Q. "Will you swear to liberty, equality, and a
detestation of the King, the Queen, and royalty?" A. "I will readily
swear to the first two, but I cannot swear to the last, as I have no such
sentiment in my heart." (Someone near her whispered, "If you do not
swear, you are a dead woman.") "That will do," and the 'trial' was
over. She was led out into the cloister, which was littered with
butchered bodies. There she was felled with a pike, her head and her
breasts cut off, and the body hacked to pieces. A wag took a piece of
her pubic hair to fashion himself a moustache.

The two girls, escorted by Albert, went to join their parents in
Toulouse. The family lodged in the house of M. de Montauriol,
president of the Parlement of Toulouse. Cecile was sent to the convent
of Les Dames de la Croix. M. Permon was taken ill and became too
unwell to answer a summons to appear before the local section, so
that Albert went in his stead. After having with some difficulty
persuaded them that Citizen Permon *the older* was too ill to attend,
Albert himself was asked why he was not with the army and then
denounced as a coward and an aristocrat. In spite of his protesting that
his father was seriously ill, his mother and sisters needing protection,
and that his defective eyesight rendered him unfit for service, he was
nearly arrested on the spot. They were politically suspect. Friends
pointed out to them their danger. Mme Permon took it on herself to
write at once to Antoine Salicetti, one of the Corsican deputies to the
Convention, whom she knew. He was in Paris awaiting the trial of the
King. His letter in reply reached them quickly. Salicetti would vouch
for M. Permon's political reliability to the Toulouse authorities, to

whom he sent a letter of recommendation, and he offered the post of
personal secretary to Albert, if he came immediately to Paris. His offer
was joyfully accepted. It was generous of Salicetti, since having met
Permon in his wife's drawing room, he knew his political opinions.
All he required of Mme Permon, he said, was her promise that they
would not emigrate. Mme Permon was herself suffering from a chest
complaint, so that when her husband was better she went off, taking
Laure with her, to drink the waters at Cauterets in the Pyrenees. Life
in these extraordinary times could still have its amenities for those who
could afford them.

It was while the Permons were in Toulouse that Cecile, aged then
sixteen, left her convent. Although her features were irregular, she
had youth and charm; a good figure was set off by ash-blonde hair.
One evening M. de Regnier, the military commandant, brought a
young officer, a M. de Geouffre, to dinner at the Permons. Afterwards
there was music and it was noticed that Cecile and M. de Geouffre, who
sang duets together, found much pleasure in each other's company.
Soon the young man—he was twenty-four and came from a good
family with an estate at Brives-la-Gaillard in the Limousin—presented
himself as a suitor to Cecile. Mme Permon was against the marriage,
but persuaded of the excellence of the match by M.de Regnier and
listening to Cecile's tearful entreaties, she gave way. Within a month
Cecile was Mme de Geouffre and installed in the Hôtel Spinola, the
headquarters of the military division to whose command her husband
had just been appointed. However, M. de Geouffre did not remain in
the army of the Republic, but following the wishes of his wife, he
resigned his commission, and the young couple retired to his estate at
Objat, near Brives-la-Gaillard.

In the meanwhile, in Corsica, where the *vendetta* was the law of the
land, the Buonaparte family, as supporters of the French interest, had
been proscribed by the adherents of General Pasquale Paoli. Paoli, the
friend of Dr Johnson and Boswell, had English sympathies. In June
1793 the Buonapartes fled the country, after running dangers that
brought out all the latent courage of Signora Laetizia; and she and her
children were living in poverty in Marseilles. In the South of France
there was civil war between royalists and republicans. In August 1793
the royalists in Toulon opened their gates to the English and the
Spanish troops, and the Royal Navy anchored in the port; they were
then in turn besieged by the republican forces. It was at the siege of

Toulon that Captain Buonaparte first came into the public eye; on the capture of the town in December he was appointed general, at the age of twenty-four. There were few skilled officers trained under the *ancien régime* remaining in the services, many having emigrated, and promotion, owing much to personal bravery, superior talents, and political reliability, could be rapid. It was in the course of the siege of Toulon that Napoleon Buonaparte met Andoche Junot, who was a volunteer from Burgundy in one of the famous Côte d'Or regiments, which later produced so many general officers. One day, being present in the French battery known as the Sans-Culottes, Buonaparte, who had recently been put in charge of the siege artillery, called for someone who could write a good hand to take down despatches at his dictation. Sergeant Junot came forward. To his comrades he was known as 'The Tempest' from his reckless bravery. As Buonaparte was dictating, a ball from an English ship landed in the battery and covered those present with earth and dust. Unperturbed Junot went on with his writing, merely remarking that they needed some sand to dry the ink. On 22 December 1793 Buonaparte was made general of brigade for his services, and shortly after he appointed Junot as his aide-de-camp. The two became inseparable friends. Not long afterwards Buonaparte was put into prison on suspicion, which may have been on account of his friendship with the younger Robespierre. In those days suspicion was enough to lead one to the scaffold. Realising Buonaparte's danger, Junot wanted to rescue him, even by force.

From prison Buonaparte wrote to Junot:

'I see a strong proof of your friendship, my dear Junot, in the proposition you make to me, and I trust that you feel convinced that the friendly sentiments that I have long entertained for you remain unabated. Men may be unjust towards me, my dear Junot, but it is enough for me to know that I am innocent. My conscience is the tribunal before which I try my conduct. That conscience is calm when I question it. Do not, therefore, stir in this business. Adieu, my dear Junot. Yours,

Buonaparte.'

Signora Laetizia never forgot Junot's loyalty to her son on this occasion. For a reason never adequately explained Buonaparte held Antoine Salicetti as in some way responsible for his imprisonment, and there was henceforth bad blood between the two men. Both were Corsicans, in whom vengeance is always close to the surface of the mind. Back in Paris, and unemployed, since he refused to take a command in La Vendée, Buonaparte spent much time in the company of Junot. The latter's father wrote to him reproaching him for leaving his Burgundian regiment, and asking what he found so attractive in attaching himself to General Buonaparte. Who was he anyway? Nobody knew him in Burgundy. Junot replied, 'You ask me who is this General Buonaparte. . . As far as I can judge he is one of those men of whom nature is sparing, and whom she throws into the world but once a century.' Each month Junot received a minimal remittance from his parents, who were farmers in a small way at Bussy-le-Grand in Burgundy; this he shared with his general, as he did any winnings that he gained at the tables. The receipt of this monthly money was known to the young men as 'the arrival of the galleons'. Junot was in love with Buonaparte's beautiful younger sister Pauline. One warm summer's evening the two men were strolling in the Jardin des Plantes. They were in a ruminative mood and discussed the future and their plans. Junot had received that day a letter from his father, setting out what he could expect on the latter's death, and opening his heart to his friend, he spoke of his love for 'Paulette', and asked if he could get his father to write to Signora Laetizia. Buonaparte replied that Junot's father was hale and hearty and might last long. 'In the meantime,' he said, 'you have nothing, Paulette has nothing—what is the total? Nothing.' The matter went no further.

With 9 Thermidor (27 July) 1794, and the execution of Robespierre, his brother, Couthon, St Just, Hanriot and others, the Reign of Terror virtually came to an end. People felt a weight lifted from them, but relaxation was not achieved all at once; one could never be sure that fresh terrorists would not seize power. Communication at a distance was carried on by ingenious means. One such was to send written messages in packets of *pâté de foie gras*, game, cakes, pastries, chocolates or baskets of fruit and other gastronomic delicacies. Or in boxes of dresses or millinery. Mme Permon once went a fortnight without telling her husband where a new hat came from, lest he picked it to pieces to extract the message. It was usual to accompany the parcel with a letter, saying, 'In compliance with your request, I send you such and such a thing.' By similar means the Permons heard from a friend in Paris, the lawyer Brunetière, that it would be safe to return from Toulouse to a more tranquil city; so in the late summer of 1794 they returned and took a suite of apartments on the second floor, overlooking a garden, of the Hôtel de la Tranquillité in the rue des Filles-Saint-Thomas. Albert returned to Paris with Salicetti, but left his service to go into business on his own account in Holland.

In Paris Mme Permon met old friends—though many were missing —friends like the Comte de Périgord, who had escaped the guillotine through the loyalty and resourcefulness of his valet Beaulieu. The latter believed in the wisdom of letting sleeping dogs lie. By means of bribes he had his master periodically moved from one prison to another. M. de Périgord wrote letter after impatient letter to the Committee of Public Safety and he was wrathful when he received not a single reply. His faithful valet destroyed all the Count's letters, knowing that the authorities more often than not dealt with such letters by guillotining the sender, whose presence had by this means been brought to their notice. M. de Périgord was a great favourite with Laure, whom he spoiled with gifts of expensive toys. Whenever the noise of his club-foot sounded on the stairs—like his nephew he was lame—she would run to greet him. Mme Permon's salon was the meeting place of the Corsicans in Paris—Salicetti, Moltedo, the Abbé Arrighi, Aréna, Chiappi, and above all the Buonapartes. And it became increasingly the resort of returning *emigrés*, who were known collectively as the Faubourg Saint-Germain.

Mme Permon was never happier than when surrounded by friends and acquaintances. Still ravishingly pretty, her social sense was gregarious; she was mercurial, essentially superficial and frivolous— she admitted to having read only one book in her life, *Telemachus*. Her deeper side only came out when her own family was concerned. She was, however, expert in holding her small society together, directing the conversation, turning men from the incessant political talk, planning musical recitals, providing tea and generally seeing that everyone felt at ease. Napoleon afterwards remarked that no one could rival Mme Permon in the art of 'holding a salon'—*tenir un salon*. Laure drew a picture of how Napoleon appeared at this period: 'I may say that it was then I first knew Buonaparte. Previously I had only a confused recollection of him. When he came to see us after our return to Paris his appearance made an impression upon me which I shall never forget. At that period of his life Buonaparte was decidedly ugly; he afterwards underwent a total change. I do not speak of the elusive charm which his glory spread around him, but I mean to say that a gradual physical change took place in him in the space of seven years. His emaciated thinness was converted into a fullness of face, and his complexion, which had been yellow and apparently unhealthy became clear and comparatively fresh; his features, which were angular and sharp, became round and filled out. As to his smile, it was always agreeable. The mode of dressing his hair, which has such a droll appearance as we see it in the prints of the passage of the bridge at Arcola, was then comparatively simple; for young men of fashion (the *muscadins*), whom he used to rail at so loudly at the time, wore their hair very long. But he was very careless of his personal appearance; and his hair, which was ill combed and ill powdered, gave him a slovenly look. His little hands, too, underwent a great metamorphosis: when I first saw him they were thin, long, and dark; but he was subsequently vain of their beauty, and with reason. In short, when I recollect Napoleon entering the courtyard of the Hôtel de la Tranquillité in 1793 [it was 1794] with a shabby round hat drawn over his forehead, and his ill-powdered hair hanging over the collar of his grey greatcoat, which afterwards became as celebrated as the white plume of Henri IV, without gloves, because he used to say they were a useless luxury, with boots ill made and ill blackened, with his thinness and his sallow complexion; in fine, when I recollect him at that time, and think what he was afterwards, I do not see the same man in the two pictures.'

Those *muscadins* were Buonaparte's particular aversion—'royalist coxcombs', 'all worthless Frenchmen', he termed them. They sported grey greatcoats, but with black collars, and green cravats. Their hair, instead of being worn in the stern republican style *à la Titus*, which was the prevailing fashion of the day, was powdered, plaited, and turned up with a comb, and hung on each side of the face in two long curls called dogs-ears (*oreilles de chien*). As these young fops were frequently attacked, they carried about with them heavy sticks, almost cudgels, which they employed as defensive, and often offensive, weapons. They affected a drawl and an inability to pronounce their r's—they spoke *pa-oles pa-fumées*. They were the precursors of the *incroyables* of a few years later.

Salicetti was a frequent, though a hardly welcome, visitor to Mme Permon's. When he and Buonaparte were present, the conversation, despite their hostess's displeasure, would turn to politics, and frequently would become bitter. Mme Permon could not bear the monotonous and irritating sound of Salicetti's boots, which creaked as he walked up and down in her drawing room, a habit of his. One evening before the disturbances of 1 Prairial (18 May) 1795 Mme

Permon gave a small party at which both Salicetti and Buonaparte, with a company largely consisting of Corsicans, were present. Politics were forbidden. 'Is it not enough,' said the hostess, 'for us to be roused out of our sleep by your tocsins and your kettle-drums, to say nothing of the harmonious choruses of your market-women? Let us have no politics.' But it was difficult to abide by the rule. The theatres produced nothing worth while and literature and the arts were dead. Conversational topics were lacking. Buonaparte tried to relieve the *ennui* by telling interesting anecdotes, which he did very well; his French was grammatically defective, but he always had an original and striking turn of phrase.

M. Permon was absent from Paris on business in Bordeaux, from where news was received that he was ill. Fears for him added to the family's disquiet. Conditions could hardly have been worse in Paris. There was little work, and bread was short. The queues often went away empty-handed. Angry crowds of women gathered in the streets and market places, calling for bread and a return to the constitution of '93. On 12 Germinal (1 April) 1795 the market women forced their way into the hall where the Convention was sitting and drove the representatives from the building. 'And what did the Mountain do during the disturbance?' someone asked in Mme Permon's drawing room. 'It sided with the mob,' another replied. Paris was indeed in the grip of anarchy. Amid extraordinary scenes, the Terrorists, under attack from all sides in the Convention, fought to save themselves, but they were defeated. Billaud-Varennes, Collot-d'Herbois and Barrère were ordered to be deported to Cayenne and six deputies of the Mountain were sent to the fortress of Ham. But although the Terrorists were momentarily silenced, the Convention had lost all authority with the people. Cries continued for a return to the constitution of '93. On the morning of 20 May the tocsin sounded to arms, and there followed another day of violence, rioting and bloodshed. The Faubourg Saint-Antoine, where misery was everywhere, was under arms. The better-off members of society feared a general pillage, and hid their valuables, while shopkeepers shuttered their shops against looters. There was fighting in the streets. The deputy Ferrand was brutally murdered, and his body cut to pieces. His head, carried by the mob to the Convention, was thrust in the face of Boissy d'Anglas, who was seated in the president's chair. Without losing his presence of mind, he saluted his dead colleague. On Buonaparte's advice

Barras was restrained from shelling the Faubourg Saint-Antoine, which he had strongly advocated.

During these days of confusion and chaos Buonaparte frequently called on the Permons, often to snatch a hurried meal and to rush out again. One day he enquired if they had recently seen Salicetti. He was implicated, he said, with Romme in the affair of Soubrani and Bourbotte. Buonaparte continually inveighed against Salicetti, whom he blamed for his imprisonment and the disgrace which still appeared to have frustrated his hopes of some employment worthy of his claims. Then it was heard that the Convention had ordered the arrest of Soubrani, Romme, Bourbotte and others. Salicetti's name was not on the list. On the following day, 21 May 1795, Mme Permon expected guests for dinner. It was six o'clock, and the first guest had arrived, when Mariette, the maid, came to her mistress and told her that someone wanted urgently to speak to her. The girl added, 'I know who it is, Madame—you may come.' Laure went with her mother. It was Salicetti. He was of a ghastly pallor; his lips were bloodless, and his eyes flashed fire.

'I am proscribed,' he said in a breathless undertone; 'that means condemned to death. Mme Permon, I trust I am not deceiving myself in relying on your generosity. You can save me now. I know I do not have to recall to you that I was once instrumental in saving your husband and son.'

Without saying a word, Mme Permon took him by the arm and shepherded him into the next room, which was Laure's bedroom. The girl followed her. Mme Permon told Salicetti that her foremost concern was for the safety of her children and that she could only put him up for a few hours. But he pressed her to let him stay for some few days, until he was able to get away. Reminding Salicetti that there were those among her friends who positively disliked him—Buonaparte, for instance—Mme Permon finally agreed that he could stay. 'My son will discharge his debt, and it is up to me to discharge my husband's,' she said.

As she left the room, Salicetti drew Laure back, saying, 'I have spoken in front of you, because I trust your discretion. I don't need to warn you of the consequences of an indiscretion.' At dinner that night —a gay one despite their personal and political anxiety—Salicetti's arrest was the subject of conversation; no one felt strongly for him. When the guests had left, Mme Permon told Albert of Salicetti's presence in the house.

After some deliberation, it was decided to follow Salicetti's suggestion and to communicate with Mme Grétry, the proprietress of the hotel. She proved only too willing to assist. They must first change their apartment, she advised, for one in which there was a hiding place that had saved four people during the reign of terror. This was done. Salicetti seemed to have ample funds at his disposal. Mme Permon was to maintain that she had received a letter from her husband in which he expressed his intention of coming back to Paris from Bordeaux. Hence the larger apartment. Some time later she was to give out that she had had a further letter countermanding the first and asking her to join him in Bordeaux.

Next morning at eleven o'clock General Buonaparte arrived at the hotel, with a bunch of violets for Mme Permon, so unusual a thing that they smiled at the unexpected piece of gallantry. His first comment was that Salicetti would now know from personal experience how it felt to be under warrant of arrest. He told Mme Permon that he knew of her debt of gratitude to Salicetti and that he was aware that she was now concealing him in her house. He then launched into a bitter denunciation of him. Cutting Buonaparte short, Mme Permon assured him he was not in her apartment, though she admitted that he had been the day before.

Buonaparte left; and it was high time, for Mme Permon was agitated beyond words. After a minute or two she asked Laure to bolt her bedroom door and to open that of Salicetti's retreat.

Laure had never liked Salicetti; to the young girl his appearance, manners and views were all repellant. His pale, jaundiced complexion, his dark glaring eyes, his lips which turned white when agitated by any powerful emotion, all alike repelled her. The scene that now met her eyes became indelibly fixed on her mind. 'When I opened the door after Buonaparte's departure the sight of Salicetti produced in me a feeling of horror that I shall never forget. He sat on a small chair at the bedside, his head leaning on his hand, and a small basin over which he was leaning, was full. He was seized with a haemorrhage, and blood was streaming from his mouth and nose. His face was frightfully pallid, and his whole appearance so affected me that it haunted my dreams for long to come. My mother ran to him; he had nearly fainted. She took his hand, which was quite cold.' With Mariette, they attended to him, and he came to himself. His seizure had been brought on by overhearing Buonaparte and her mothers' conversation.

While the police searched for Salicetti, the arrangements for the trial
of the other accused went on. Romme, a distinguished mathematician,
Goujon, a man remarkable for his personal probity and his honest
republican sentiments, Soubrani, Duquesnoi, Duroi and Bourbotte
were all in custody. It shocked public opinion to see such men in the
dock. Salicetti alone was distrusted and disliked by moderate men.
M. Permon, hearing of Salicetti's proscription, had written to his wife
to do anything she could on his behalf. When M. Emilhaud, a trusted
friend of the family, who had brought M. Permon's letter from
Bordeaux, was with a Spanish general named Miranda in the flat,
Laure, coming into the room, was instantly struck with the latter's
resemblance to Salicetti. On her mentioning this to her mother and
Albert, there occurred to Mme Permon an idea. A council was
immediately held with Salicetti and Mme Grétry, and it was decided
that Mme Permon should advertise for a valet, who so resembled
Salicetti that they could procure for him a passport. This was done,
the passport proceedings at the Section correctly carried out, Mme
Grétry acting as surety for her lodger's good faith; and the poor
valet, who thought he had secured a good, steady job, was sacked
with two month's wages.

Meanwhile the trial of the accused came on before a special court
martial held in the rue Neuve-des-Petits-Champs. Several of them
had been guests in the Permon's house, and Albert, partly at Salicetti's
request, was present at the court proceedings. One day he arrived
home in a state of extreme agitation; he had been witness of a terrible
scene. When sentence was passed on the accused men, they had
accepted it calmly, even serenely. On descending the grand staircase,
lined with spectators, Romme had looked about him, as if wishing to
recognize someone in the crowd. Albert was standing just near him,
wishing to say a friendly word as he passed. Suddenly Romme stopped
and said, 'No matter, with a firm hand this will do. Vive la liberté!'
and taking from his pocket a large penknife or small dagger, he plunged
it into his heart; then withdrawing it, he passed it to Goujon, who,
after stabbing himself, handed it in turn to Duquesnoi. The three
slumped on the steps without uttering a sound. The weapon, passed
by the trembling hand of Duquesnoi to Soubrani, he did likewise, as
did the others; but they were not so lucky as the first three. Grievously
wounded as they were, they were conducted forthwith to the place of
execution and, all bleeding, they were forced to ascend the scaffold,
where they were guillotined. Albert's frockcoat was splattered with

Romme's blood, the blood of a man, who only a few weeks earlier had sat in the chair in which he was sitting, as he told Mme Permon and Laure the gruesome story. Salicetti later heard it without turning a hair or showing any concern for his unfortunate colleagues. Afterwards he made Albert repeat several times details of the tragedy. Laure looked on him with unconcealed disgust, and henceforth even to see him sickened her.

For eight days previous to their departure Mme Permon gave out that her husband was expecting them at Bordeaux.

Buonaparte came to say good-bye, telling Mme Permon she was doing well to depart. On her surprise at this remark, he hinted that before they reached Longjumeaux, she would know the reason for his saying this.

They set out, Salicetti seating himself on the box of the berlin; their fears were very real; it meant death for Salicetti if they were apprehended—and possibly for Mme Permon and her husband. However, in leaving Paris they had no difficulties in the formalities at the city barrier. The postillions, being promised a tip if they kept up a good speed, quickly brought them to the Croix de Berny, when they stopped. They were about to restart, when the first postillion from the Paris post came up to the berlin and enquired for the Citoyenne Permon. Mme Permon thought that the man must be mistaken, but he insisted. Then Buonaparte's words crossed her mind. She took the letter and offered him an *assignat* for five francs, but he refused, saying that he had already been paid by *the young man*. She did not recognize the handwriting; afterwards they learned it was Junot's. The letter read:

'I never like to be thought a dupe. I should seem to be one in your eyes if I did not tell you that I knew Salicetti's place of concealment more than twenty days ago. You may recollect, Madame Permon, what I said to you on 1 Prairial. I was almost morally certain of the fact; now I know it positively.

'You see then, Salicetti, that I might have returned the ill you did me. In doing so I should only have avenged myself; but you injured me when I had not offended you. Which of us stands in the preferable point of view at this moment? I might have taken my revenge; but I did not. Perhaps you will say that your benefactress was your safeguard. That consideration, I confess, was powerful. But alone, unarmed, and an outlaw, your life would have been sacred to me.

Go, seek in peace an asylum where you may learn to cherish better sentiments for your country. So far as your name is concerned my mouth is closed. Repent, and appreciate my motives.

'Madame Permon, my best wishes are with you and your child. You are feeble and defenceless beings. May Providence and a friend's prayers protect you. Be cautious, and do not stay in the large towns through which you may have to pass.

'Adieu.'

The letter had no signature. Mme Permon was only too well aware that she was dealing with Corsicans. She showed the letter to Salicetti at breakfast, who read it through a number of times, and then exclaimed, 'I am lost! I am lost! What a fool I was to trust to a woman's prudence.' Mme Permon was as amazed as she was indignant, and Salicetti, realizing that he had overstepped even the bounds which he allowed himself, apologized profusely. He then said that he had overheard them express some doubts about Mariette. 'Never mind that,' said Mme Permon, 'you should rather admire Buonaparte's generosity.'

'Generosity,' Salicetti repeated with a tone of contempt. 'What would you have had him do? Betray me?'

Mme Permon looked at him. 'I don't know what I would have had *him* do; but I do know this, that I could wish to see *you* grateful.'

In passing it should be added that it was Mariette who betrayed him. Buonaparte's servant was her lover. From them what was a suspicion in Buonaparte's mind became a certainty.

After Tours, Salicetti travelled with them in the berlin. The towns and villages through which they passed resounded with imprecations against the Convention. When at length they reached Bordeaux, a note at the Hôtel Fumele, where they were expected, informed them that M. Permon had been called away to the country and that M. Emil-haud would attend them. They learned from him that no ship was then sailing for Italy, where Salicetti wished to go. Ships were leaving for the United States, St Domingo and England, but Salicetti was adamant for Italy, either for Genoa or Venice. The following day Laudois, M. Permon's valet, brought them the news that the latter had heard that a ship could be found at Narbonne or Cette bound for Genoa. He had made an arrangement for the carriage to be taken on board and berths booked on a sailing boat, which would go up the Garonne as far as Toulouse and thence by canal to Carcassonne. From there they would only have to travel a few leagues in the berlin to reach Narbonne or Cette. It was stressed that it would be safer for Salicetti to proceed in this way, with which view he was in full agreement.

As they sailed slowly up the Garonne, the young Laure enjoyed greatly the beauty of the landscape under the serene summer sky, the rolling countryside, the green woods, the riverside towns, with the high brown-tiled roofs, many of them mediaeval in their gabled appearance—Marmande, Agen, Tonneins, Langon, La Réole. Salicetti one evening came on deck and joined Mme Permon and Laure as they watched the moving scene and breathed in the limpid air. Laure retired to the cabin she shared with her mother, which was immediately below the spot where Salicetti and Mme Permon were sitting. She could overhear their conversation. She heard the talk turn on her and Salicetti speak praising her looks and amiability. Then she was aghast to hear him suggest to Mme Permon that she would be a good match for his nephew and was relieved to hear her mother extricate herself from the proposal, pleading Laure's youth and that M.Permon alone had the disposing of his daughters in marriage. When Mme Permon came down to the cabin, she embraced her mother. The latter thought that Salicetti had been thinking not of a wife for his nephew but for himself. The very thought revolted the girl. They arrived at Carcassonne, and from there proceeded to Narbonne, where they found no vessel leaving for Italy. They went on to Cette, and there they were relieved to find a ship, by coincidence named the *Convention*, due to sail that evening for Genoa. On taking leave of Mme Permon, Salicetti, after thanking her warmly, expressed a change of mind about Buonaparte and asked her to thank him. Salicetti reached Genoa safely. Many years after he became the feared and hated chief of police in Naples at the time of King Joachim Murat. The Neapolitans placed a bomb beneath his house, and in the explosion he narrowly escaped with his life.

That night mother and daughter slept at Mèze, and the next day they went on to Montpellier, which they found had suffered severely in the Revolutionary crisis. From there they journeyed to Tarascon and Beaucaire, where the fair, which had been interrupted by the Revolution, was starting again. Everywhere they saw the results of the troubles through which the country had passed or heard stories of atrocities then committed. At Tarascon men, women and children had been thrown from the top of the castle. In a cavity formed by the river at Beaucaire they saw the mutilated bodies of two women which

had been washed up there. They were happy to be back in Bordeaux
where M. Permon had had thoughts of setting up an establishment,
until quieter times would allow them to return to Paris. When they
joined M. Permon in the Hôtel Fumele, they were shocked to see the
ravages brought about by his illness. Ill-wishers sometimes spoke of
the 'aristocrats' disease', but in truth he was suffering in mind and
body. Since the execution of Louis XVI he had seen that no good
would come to a state which was out of the hands of reasonable men.
His anxiety and despair had affected him physically. Mme Permon
could not wait to get him back to Paris and into the hands of competent
physicians. In the meantime he was winding up his business affairs in
Bordeaux. On the first day of September 1795 the Permons left
Bordeaux for Paris, where they had secured a good apartment in the
Hôtel de l'Autruche. Arriving in the capital on the fourth of that
month, they were more concerned than ever over the condition of
M. Permon, which appeared critical. He had barely survived the journey.
M. Duchannois was summoned, and he called for a consultation. A
malignant fever declared itself, on top of his already weakened condition. Rest and absolute quiet were essential. Buonaparte, informed of
their arrival by Albert, came immediately to visit them. He was much
affected by the state of M. Permon, who in spite of the pain he was in,
insisted on seeing him.

Buonaparte called almost every day and frequently dined and spent
the evening with them. He gave them news of political affairs in Paris.
Something was *du train*, he said—the expressions used by the Parisians
to signify a political change or *coup d'état*. The people, incessantly told
by the Convention that they were the masters, were taking matters
into their own hands, the Sections were arming. 'Matters are going
from bad to worse,' said Buonaparte, 'the counter-revolution will
shortly break out, and that will only lead to fresh disasters.' One
evening, the condition of M. Permon took a turn for the worse, and
Mme Permon burst into tears. It was ten o'clock. No servant in the
hotel would go out after nine. Buonaparte said nothing. He ran
downstairs and went to fetch M.Duchannois, and despite his protests,
brought him back. It was raining in torrents, and they were both wet
through. In the daytime Buonaparte was much occupied, and they
saw little of him. But he called, or sent to enquire, each day. Then
came the 13 Vendémiaire. Buonaparte was looked on as the saviour of
the Convention; by his vigorous action he had anticipated the counter-
revolution. On the 17th M. Permon died.

TWO

The First Consul

ALBERT PERMON had set about finding them a house, for the accommodation in the Hôtel d'Autruche was inconvenient, and the place was associated with painful recollections. He found just what they wanted, an hôtel, or rather a small house, in the fashionable Chaussée d'Antin, once owned by M. de Varnachan, a farmer-general of taxes. The small appearance of the house, which was in reality quite commodious, was a recommendation at a time when one tried to avoid any outward show, which could be misconstrued. It was a form of distraction for Mme Permon to furnish her house; she ordered carpets from Leghorn, and achieved a style of décor which her daughter described as oriental combined with French good taste. Mme Permon's own taste was for the age of Louis XV; she had little liking for the newly fashionable mahogany and rosewood. She aimed at both comfort and elegance. When Albert had gone through his father's papers, he found that the family fortune had evaporated; the assets deposited in England were irrecoverable. They had some money in the Funds and some ready cash to go on with, but thenceforth they were to rely on Albert's earnings to keep the household going. Albert revealed the state of affairs to Laure, and both agreed to keep their true position from their mother, who had never been consulted by her late husband on financial matters. All bills had been paid by him personally. Mme Permon's style of living required money, and it is not at all clear from Laure's accounts in her *Memoirs* how they managed to live as they did, with their two servants, their dresses, jewels, flowers and constant entertaining. Laure inherited her mother's extravagances and feckless disregard for anything so commonplace as financial economy.

A great change had taken place in Buonaparte's mode and conduct of life since 13 Vendémiaire. The old carelessness in matters of dress was a thing of the past; the dirty boots, whose smell, when he dried them before the drawing-room fire, so offended Mme Permon that

he took to having the maid clean them before he entered her room—
all this was changed. He went out now in a handsome carriage and he
set himself up in a respectable house in the rue des Capucines. He was
an important personage. His habit of calling in frequently on the
Permons, however, was unchanged. Mme Permon was in deep
mourning and seldom went out. This seclusion had a serious effect on
her health, for society was essential to her very nature, and it preyed
more and more on her naturally delicate health. Seeing this, M.Duchan-
nois advised her to take a box at the theatre, which she did at the
Feydeau, and there she passed several hours every evening. She was
frequently accompanied by General Buonaparte, who shared her
preference for Italian music and style of singing to the French, and
indeed such popular singers as Mme Scio and Gaveau-Bouche (so
called to distinguish him from Gavaudan) were little calculated to give
him a liking for it.

One day Buonaparte had a singular conversation with Mme
Permon. He found her alone, and announced that he had a serious
proposal to put to her. This was that the two families should be united
by marriage. First, Albert Permon should marry Pauline Buonaparte.

'Permon has some fortune,' he said—not knowing the true state of
the family's financial affairs. 'My sister has nothing, but I am now in a
position to help them both. You know what a pretty girl Paulette is.
My mother is your old friend. Just say that you agree, and the matter
is settled.'

Mme Permon had some experience of the Corsican custom of
arranging marriages. She replied that Albert was his own master, that
she would not influence him one way or the other, that it was up to
him to decide so serious a matter. On hearing this, Buonaparte said
that he had a further proposal to make. This was a second match
between Laure and Louis or Jerome Buonaparte.

'Come, Napoleon,' said Mme Permon, laughing, 'Laurette is older
than Jerome. You are playing the high priest today; you are marrying
everyone, even children.'

Buonaparte laughed, but with some embarrassment. He admitted
that when he had got up that morning a marriage-breeze had blown
on him; and, as if to prove it, he took Mme Permon's hand and kissed
it. 'And to cement the union between the two families,' he said, 'I
make so bold as to offer you my hand, if you will accept me—just as
soon as decency will permit it.'

Controlling her laughter, Mme Permon replied, 'My dear Napoleon, let us talk seriously. You fancy you know my age. The truth is, you know nothing about it. And I shall not tell you. That is my own secret. But I am old enough to be your mother. Do spare me this kind of joke; it distresses me, coming from you.'

Buonaparte assured her, not once but several times, that he was serious, that he had given the matter mature thought, and that he spoke in earnest. A woman's age, he said, was indifferent to him, so long as she did not appear beyond thirty.

Mme Permon replied that, as far as it concerned herself, she had no reason to think further, that she would speak of Buonaparte's proposal to Albert, and would give him his reply on the following Tuesday—it was then Saturday.

Some days before this remarkable conversation, she had spoken to General Buonaparte at a dinner party she had given, seeking his help on behalf of a Corsican cousin of hers, a Stephanopoulos, who was hoping for a commission in the Convention Guards. Buonaparte had promised a speedy and favourable reply. But it now seemed to Mme Permon, after what had taken place between them, that he did not seem so well disposed as earlier.

On Monday morning General Buonaparte called to see them, accompanied by a numerous staff. There now occurred a painful and absurd scene that had long-lasting consequences. After the usual civilities in her salon, Mme Permon asked Buonaparte if the commission was ready. He replied that it was not, but that it was promised him for *tomorrow*. This unfortunate word provoked Mme Permon's anger.

'What does this mean?' she asked. 'Are you merely fobbing me off, or do you intend getting it for me? If so, it would have been better simply to refuse me from the start. You want a good shake up to waken you from the dream into which the grandeurs of your Republic have lulled you.'

The conversation in the room, which had been general, stopped, and an embarrassed silence followed. The mild Chauvet, who was a friend of them both, attempted to intervene, addressing two or three soothing words to Mme Permon, but she was in too much of a passion to listen.

Buonaparte went to kiss her hand, saying, 'Tomorrow I hope to find you calmer, and consequently more reasonable,' but she snatched it away, dealing him as she did so a blow on the eye, which must have given him some pain.

He advanced and whispered to her, 'We are making fools of ourselves in front of these people.' But she drew herself up and folded her
arms. Buonaparte looked at her for a moment, but she showed no
sign of relenting and so he left the room, followed by his staff.

'For God's sake, Mme Permon,' said Chauvet, 'don't part like this.
Call him back.'

But for whatever reason—whether it was *amour propre* or whether
she thought she was genuinely in the right—she would not allow
herself to be persuaded. An attaché returned to say that the General
wished to speak with M. Chauvet. 'Go, my dear Chauvet,' said Mme
Permon, giving him her hand, 'Go, and don't condemn me. I am not
to blame.'

Only a short time after this rupture, which friends on both sides
tried in vain to mend, they heard from his uncle Fesch and Chauvet
that General Buonaparte was going to marry Josephine de Beauharnais,
and that he had been appointed commander-in-chief of the Army of
Italy. They saw him only once more, and that but for a moment,
before his departure.

At the end of January 1796 they heard that Cecile de Geouffre had
given birth to a son, who was christened Adolphe. The boy was born
on the 23rd and the letter announcing the event arrived on the 27th.
On the evening of 1 February, while Laure and her mother were
sitting with Albert, who was in his room in bed with a cold, a letter
was delivered to them. It was from Geouffre, with the afflicting news
that Cecile had just died from puerperal fever. This sad event, coming
on the recent death of her husband, was too much for Mme Permon's
fragile health; she became very ill, and it was some months before she
could pick up again the threads of her life. Albert and Laure had
revealed to her the true state of their income. Their friend Admiral
Magon proposed to Albert that he take up a post which he, through his
contacts, had found for him in business trading with India. But to
accept this, it meant entering into an agreement which bound him to
remain for fifteen years in India. He felt that he could not leave his
mother and sister for so long and in so distant a country. Some little
time afterwards he was offered an administrative appointment with the
army in Italy, which he accepted. They suspected Buonaparte's hand
in this very advantageous turn of events. On Albert's departure for
Italy, Laure and her mother set out for the Pyrenees, to take the waters,
as they had some years previously, at Cauterets.

While General Buonaparte had been in Paris he had been occupied with other matters than quarrelling with Mme Permon and matrimonial concerns. At the office of the Topographical Bureau he had drawn up plans for operations against France's main enemy Austria. In the south the Austro-Sardinian allies in the foothills of the Alps watched the Army of Italy, lodged precariously along the Riviera towards Savona, undernourished, ill-equipped and with a poor morale, despite the victory of Loano in November 1795. Buonaparte's plan was to drive a wedge between the Sardinians and the Austrians, judging (correctly) that if he dealt the allies a smart blow in the foothills, the former would fall back to defend Turin and the latter to ensure the safety of Lombardy. But first, on joining the army, he had to raise the spirit of the sullen, ill-disciplined and starved troops. He addressed his men in the first of those stirring addresses that were to become the rousing calls to victory throughout Europe. 'Soldiers,' he told them, 'you are famished and nearly naked. The government owes you much, but can do nothing for you. Your patience, your courage, do you honour, but give you no glory, no advantage. I will lead you into the most fertile plains of the world. There you will find great towns, rich provinces. There you will find honour, glory, riches. Soldiers of Italy, will you be wanting in courage!' Though the generals subordinate to him looked askance at this young commander of only twenty-six, appointed, they thought, by political jobbery, he quickly won their confidence, and with theirs that of his men. Many of these lacked vital equipment, even boots. The cavalry was almost entirely deficient, those horses it had being ill-fed and unserviceable. Making good some of his material deficiencies—he sold a captured privateer for £5000 and borrowed £2500 from Genoa—he reported to a sceptical Directory on 28 March 1796 that 'the worst is over.' Then he led his men on Montenotte at the beginning of April. He struck first at the Sardinians. Montenotte, Millesimo, Dego, San Michele, Mondovi—these resounding victories led to the armistice of Cherasco on 27 April, before Beaulieu, the Austrian commander, could move a single battalion to his ally's assistance. With the Sardinians thus disposed of, Buonaparte turned on Beaulieu. His object was to drive the Austrians out of Lombardy and to advance into the Tyrol, thus rendering invaluable support to the French armies engaged on the Rhine.

Milan was his first main objective. By a series of forced marches that dazzled his opponents, he out-manoeuvred Beaulieu. The French

crossed the Po at Piacenza and the Austrians retired, to face about with
a strong rearguard at Lodi. On 10 May Buonaparte came up and seized
the town, the Austrians withdrawing across the river and guarding
the bridge with 9000 men and 14 guns. When the French troops
faltered in the middle of the bridge, Masséna and Buonaparte himself
rushed forward, the courage of the troops instantly revived, and the
bridge was secured. This battle marked a turning-point in Buonaparte's life. 'Vendémiaire and even Montenotte did not make me
think myself a superior being. It was after Lodi that the idea came to
me. . . That first kindled the spark of boundless ambition.' Milan was
occupied, and revolts among the Italians ruthlessly suppressed. The
Directory, fearful of the too successful and too ambitious young
general, ordered him to turn over the command of Upper Italy to
Kellerman, and to carry the war into Central Italy, there to preach the
Republic and the overthrow of princes. His immediate threat to
resign his command caused the Directory to have second thoughts.
They gave way. Beaulieu had withdrawn to Mantua, which he
prepared for a siege. With reinforcements from Austria, Wurmser,
who had replaced Beaulieu, continued the campaign, but everywhere
he was out-generalled. Lonato, Castiglione, Bassano, Caldiero,
Arcola, Rivoli—the bulletins of Buonaparte's victories filled the
Parisians with delight at the successes of the young general who was
acclaimed the nation's idol. The Directory could do nothing against
such popular applause. On his own authority, on 18 April 1797
Buonaparte signed the armistice of Leoben, that became the basis for
the eventual peace of Campo Formio, by which Austrian Lombardy
passed to France. Never in modern times had the world seen such a
splendid series of victories.

In the summer of 1797 Bonaparte (he had changed the spelling of
his name during the Italian campaign) set himself up in vice-regal
pomp in a mansion at Montebello, near Milan. There he supervised the
creation of the Cisalpine Republic, with an organization and administration based on that of republican France, and carried on diplomatic
activities virtually independent of the Directory. He fed and clothed
his soldiers by requisitions on the Italian towns and countryside,
levied huge sums on their cities, which he sent home to the almost
bankrupt government, as well as sending masterpieces of painting and
sculpture, which went to adorn the French galleries, particularly the
Louvre. Murat conveyed the first consignment of captured regimental
flags to the Directory. With the second batch he sent his aide de

camp, Junot, who escorted out to Italy Josephine, Bonaparte's wife. On the long journey Josephine set her cap at the handsome young colonel of hussars, who to avoid an entanglement with his general's wife flirted with Josephine's charming travelling companion. At Montebello Josephine caused Bonaparte uneasiness by her relations with a young man named Charles, who was very nearly shot at the commander-in-chief's order, before being sent home and dismissed the service. Bonaparte brought to Italy his mother, Signora Laetizia, and his two sisters Marianna (now rechristened Elisa) and Pauline. Elisa had recently married a dull Corsican named Felix Bacciochi. Napoleon Bonaparte, who, despite his elder brother Joseph, now assumed the status of head of the family, had not approved of Elisa's marriage, but his feelings in the matter were soothed by Signora Laetizia, to whom any differences in the family were painful. The beautiful Pauline, who had had a tempestuous affair in Marseilles with a much older man, Stanislas Fréron, a very dubious politician, which was ended on the instructions of Napoleon, was now married to a husband of his choice, the young staff officer General Leclerc. It was at Montebello that the opening shots were fired in what became a fight to the death between Napoleon's family and that of the Beauharnais.

Napoleon was kept posted in Italy with political news at home by his brothers, Joseph and the younger Lucien. The latter was a young man with opinions of his own, an ardent republican. In the South of France, where he was employed as a military storekeeper at Saint-Maximin, he styled himself Brutus and renamed the village Marathon. Falling in love with his innkeeper's daughter, Christine Boyer, without asking his family's permission, he married her. He was now in Paris with his wife. He was therefore well aware of the divisions within the Directory and the possibility of a counter-revolution of moderates in conjunction with the royalists of the Clichy circle. Since 13 Vendémiaire the five Directors had ruled France, despotically, inefficiently and, what was notorious, corruptly. In the elections of April 1797 the moderates and royalists had made gains in both the Council of Ancients and that of the Five Hundred. In the Directory the 'Jacobins' Barras, Rewbell and Larevellière-Lépeaux were opposed by the moderates Carnot and Barthélemy. Chiefly through the instigation of the royalist club of Clichy, General Pichegru, a known constitutional monarchist, was elected president of the Council of Five Hundred. Bonaparte deciding to act against 'royalist intrigues' and in favour of the 'Jacobin' directors, sent General Augureau, a rough and demagogic republican, to Paris. The result was 18 Fructidor (4 September) 1797, when Augureau, with 2000 soldiers, cleared the Tuileries, where the Councils were sitting. Barthélemy was arrested in bed; Carnot, tipped off in time, escaped to Switzerland. The 'Second Emigration' ensued, when the laws against *émigrés* and nonjuring priests were re-enacted; the elections in forty-nine departments were cancelled, the censorship of the press was strengthened, and many were sent into exile or death in the prisons of Cayenne. The Directory owed its existence to General Bonaparte, who returned to France in December as the conquering hero and the man of the moment. And of the future. M. de Talleyrand, casting a critical eye over the political scene, had written a congratulatory letter to Bonaparte in Italy; he now sought him out on his return.

In her *Memoirs* Laure recalls the period: 'After 4 September our society presented a most singular aspect. Among the returned emigrants there were a great number of old acquaintances of my mother's, who, still full of apprehensions were glad to find a drawing room where, while they could talk with tolerable freedom, they met several noted characters of the day, old friends, young acquaintances, all upon the same footing, and talking in the same voice, because the mistress of the house held her sceptre with a firm hand, and would not suffer discussions to degenerate into quarrels. This was a meritorious mode of procedure at that time, when people made themselves hoarse with bawling whenever politics were mentioned. At a former period people cured you of your sore throat by cutting it for you. They had now, however, got tired of this remedy, by far too heroic, as it is said, in modern medicine. We were no longer summoned before the revolutionary tribunal because we had an income of fifty thousand livres, because, to confess the truth, nobody had such an income, at least in appearance. The *Moniteur* indeed was no longer daily dishonoured by sanguinary lists; but there were still left the Temple, the plain of Grenelle, and the deportations; though the horizon had cleared these were still heard, as at the conclusion of violent storms, those isolated claps of thunder which almost always follow the tempest.

'Notwithstanding all this, people recovered their gaiety: they went to dine at taverns, they would dance at public gardens, or take an ice at a coffee-house. Verry's, the balls at the Richelieu, Tivoli and Marbeuf rooms, as well as at the Pavillon de Hanovre and Frascati, were in fact no more than what I have said; but this did not prevent good company from flocking thither and seeking amusement. Amidst this dissipated life, and those pleasures which were sought as diversions from the remembrance of so many past sorrows and so many apprehensions of the future, a curious meeting of opposite parties took place. It began in my mother's house, and, strange to tell, it was the Bonaparte family that first found itself face to face with the *ancien régime*.'

The revived Faubourg Saint-Germain looked down their noses at the more absurd caperings of those fired with revolutionary ardours and ideals, some comic enough. In Paris several hundred men still affected the Greek and Roman costume first given vogue by the pupils of the painter David. It was still possible to find under the entrances of the Louvre men gravely discussing affairs of state clothed in white togas with red borders, for all the world as if they were under the porticoes of the Stoa. The *muscadins*, many of them young men of good families, were giving way to the *incroyables*, whose dress even excelled the former's in ridiculousness. They wore a frock coat tightly pinched in at the waist, baggy trousers, an enormous flowing muslin cravat, and on their long pomaded and curled hair was perched a tiny hat.

In Mme Permon's salon all worlds met, but the majority came from the Faubourg Saint-Germain, since their hostess shared their political and social opinions. M. d'Aigle, M. de Noailles, M. de Rastignac, M. de Caulincourt (the father), M. d'Hautefort, Mme de Caseaux, Mme de Lostanges, Mme de Chalais, Mme de Contades, M. de Périgord, Mme de Brissac, Mme de Vergennes, M.Alexandre Delaborde, Mme de Maille, Mme de Fontanges, M. Albert d'Orsay, and many more, if not all intimate friends, belonged to the ordinary company to be found in Mme Permon's drawing room. Of the new society the Bonaparte family, from when it settled in Paris, were the most prominent and assiduous in their attendance.

Joseph, the real head of the family, with his plain but good-natured wife, a Mlle Julie Clary, the daughter of a rich Marseillais merchant, was settled in his pretty house in rue du Rocher. Since Fructidor he had been nominated deputy of the Liamone, in Corsica, to the Council of Five Hundred. To his house came from Italy Signora Laetizia, with the three youngest children, Louis, then aged eighteen, Caroline, who was fifteen, and the youngest Jerome, aged twelve—a little younger than Laure. Caroline, a charming graceful girl, was put to the fashionable school run by Mme Campan at Saint-Germain, not to finish her education, since it had never really begun, for all the younger children had, from their roving existence, little chance of proper education.

Jerome was sent to school at Juilly. Lucien and his wife, back in Paris from a journey to Germany, were installed in Grande rue Verte in the Faubourg Saint-Honoré. In the same street resided Elisa, Mme Bacciochi, with her nonentity of a husband. Elisa cultivated the arts and literary men. Pauline, Mme Leclerc, who arrived from Italy soon after, took a house in rue de la Ville-l'Evêque. Not a day passed on which the Permons did not see members of the Bonaparte family at the Chaussée d'Antin or at one of their houses. Mme Permon was particularly fond of Joseph and Lucien and of Pauline, whose childish whims she indulged—in fact, she hopelessly spoiled her. Napoleon, whose remembrance of his quarrel with Mme Permon was green, only called about twice between his arrival from Italy in December 1797 and his setting out for Egypt in the summer of 1798.

Laure's education had not been neglected. During her father's lifetime he himself had supervised it, reading and discussing with her much history, particularly Plutarch, whom she greatly admired for his accounts of republican patriotism, and the works of Jean-Jacques Rousseau, a favourite of his. Of languages she spoke and read Italian and had a speaking acquaintance with Greek. She read the classical authors, presumably in French, since she apparently did not know the ancient tongues. She claimed later that it should not be thought unusual for women to know Greek and Latin, but it is unlikely that she had more than a passing knowledge of the latter. Tutors were engaged for her in music and drawing, and she attended dancing lessons from the then most fashionable teacher, M. Despreaux. Although Mme Permon was of the Greek Church, she brought up Laure in the Roman Catholic faith, and about this time she went to religious instruction and took, with two friends, her first communion. At the time of General Bonaparte's triumphant return from Italy she went, although she was but thirteen, to her first ball, given in his honour by M. de Talleyrand. She describes it in her *Memoirs:*

'One of the most magnificent entertainments, and above all one of the most elegant in its magnificence, was that given by M. de Talleyrand at the office of Foreign Affairs. He always displayed admirable skill in the arrangements of the entertainments which he gave; indeed, when a man possesses good sense he shows it in everything he does. He then resided at the Hôtel Gallifet, rue du Bac, and, though the rooms were too small for the company assembled there that evening, the *fête* was admirable. All the most elegant and distinguished people then in Paris were there. My mother was absolutely bent on going.

She was not quite well; but when she was dressed and had put on a little rouge she looked enchanting; and I can affirm that I saw that night few women who surpassed her in beauty. We were both dressed alike, in a robe of white crepe trimmed with two broad silver ribbons, and on the head a garland of oak-leaves with silver acorns. My mother had diamonds and I pearls. That was the only difference between our dresses.

'In the course of the evening my mother was walking through the rooms, arm in arm with M. de Caulaincourt on one side and me on the other, when the General advanced a few steps and spoke to her. My mother was, in my opinion, rather too dry: her ill-humour was not yet quite dispelled, but in her excellent heart there was nothing like rancour. It was the reverse with the General. Be this as it may, he appeared to look at my mother with admiration. Indeed, that evening in particular she was truly captivating. The General spoke in a low tone for some seconds to the Turkish ambassador, whom he held by the arm. The Turk uttered an exclamation, and fixed upon my mother his large eyes, and then made a sort of obeisance. "I told him that you were of Greek extraction," said Bonaparte to my mother, saluting her by way of adieu. Then holding out his hand, he pressed hers in a friendly manner, and left us after a short conversation, which nevertheless drew that attention of the company, though it lasted but a few minutes.'

General Bonaparte, whom the Directory feared but could not overlook, was first appointed to command the Army of England, gathered at Boulogne, but his mind was further afield. He dreamed of some vast expedition to the Orient. Having rivalled Caesar's actions in the West, he now sought to emulate Alexander's conquests in the East. Taking with him a number of *savants* from the Institute of France, he set sail from Toulon on 19 May 1798 and, eluding the Royal Navy, effected a landing near Alexandria. Despite Nelson's resounding defeat over the French fleet at Aboukir Bay, Bonaparte rapidly defeated the Mamelukes and gained possession of Egypt. Serious differences arising between the commander-in-chief and his generals over matters of policy, Junot, promoted general at the age of twenty-seven, loyally supported his commander. Junot's attitude to Bonaparte was one little short of adoration—he could do no wrong; he was a God. Junot was not a man who could bear to be without female company; he procured himself an Abyssinian slave-girl, named Araxarane, by whom he had a child, who was called Othello. Nor was his general less resourceful, but in a way that is little to his credit. An officer volunteer from the South of France by the name of Fourès had married a beautiful girl, who insisted on accompanying her husband to Egypt. One day, when out riding on a donkey, Pauline Fourès was remarked by the commander-in-chief. Soon after she received an invitation to attend a function in an officer's mess. The husband was surprised that he was not included in the invitation, but he let his wife go. In the middle of the party the door suddenly opened and General Bonaparte appeared. He looked straight at the young woman, said nothing, and left. A few days later Lieutenant Fourès was, without further warning, ordered by Berthier to prepare himself to take despatches back to France. He was saddened in that he had to leave Pauline behind him in Egypt. The unfortunate man was intercepted by the English, who found that the despatches were trifling and put the Frenchman ashore near Alexandria. Arrived back at the camp, he was unable to find his wife. She had been set up in comfortable quarters by the commander-in-chief, whose mistress she already was. Poor 'Bellilote' genuinely loved Bonaparte, and ultimately followed him back to France, but he refused to see her again, although he provided for her. The abandoned husband found no redress.

Among the generals most hostile to their commander was General Lanusse, whose outspoken criticism of Bonaparte was heard by Junot and very much resented. Although they maintained amicable appearances, the two men were deeply estranged. Murat, wishing to reconcile them, invited them to dinner. The meal passed off agreeably enough, and afterwards they sat down to a game of *bouillotte*. During the game the conversation turning on some future military operation, Lanusse allowed himself a sarcastic smile, which exasperated the hot-headed Junot. Misinterpreting the silence around him, Lanusse then spoke of the state of the army in most unflattering terms. In the middle of his observations he asked Junot to lend him ten louis, but Junot, who had a heap of gold in front of him, refused, and in the heated exchange of words that followed called Lanusse a traitor. This bitter quarrel could only be settled there and then by a duel, which took place in Murat's garden, sloping down to the Nile. Junot was known to be the best pistol shot in the army, but he chose swords. Although a good swordsman, nimble, brave and usually coolheaded, his anger got the better of him and he slashed wildly at Lanusse's head, cutting his hat in two and wounding his temple. Lanusse, with a backhanded cut, laid open Junot's abdomen, inflicting on him a wound more than eight inches in length. The nature of the wound was most dangerous in a country where inflamation of the intestines was to be feared. They removed him with difficulty, and he was carefully looked after by the army surgeons.

Bonaparte, who had strictly proscribed duels, was furious when he learned of the occurrence next morning and showed his displeasure by not visiting Junot until he was convalescent. Hearing later, however, the reasons for the quarrel, and Junot's defence of his name, he was touched by his loyalty. When Bonaparte secretly left Egypt, Junot was at Suez, where he received an affectionate letter from his commander:

'Bonaparte, General-in-Chief, Member of the Institute, to the General of Brigade Junot.

'I am leaving Egypt, my dear Junot, and you are too far from the place of embarcation for me to take you with me. I shall leave orders with Kléber to let you set out in the course of October. Be assured that, in whatever place and whatever situation I may be, I will give you positive proofs of the affectionate friendship which I have vowed to you. Health and friendship,

Bonaparte.'

When Junot eventually set out, his ship was taken by the patrolling English men-of-war, and he himself sent prisoner to the Middle East. There he became friendly with his gaoler, Sir Sidney Smith, who effected his release by an exchange with twelve English prisoners. By the time he returned to France much had happened in that country.

When Bonaparte set foot in France at Fréjus on 9 October 1799, the country was ripe for some governmental change. He had been kept well informed by Joseph and Lucien. Public feeling felt outraged by the disasters in Italy, and although Masséna's successes had secured Switzerland, yet it was felt that Austria again threatened the frontiers of France. At home the reputation of the Directory was at the lowest ebb; the inefficiency was only too apparent and the corruption quite blatant. Nevertheless, what change was to take place was not at all certain. What was certain was the overwhelming support Bonaparte had among all sections of the country. This was shown to him by his triumphal progress from Fréjus to Paris. With his brothers and Talleyrand and Fouché he felt his way forward with extreme caution. He

first came to an understanding with Sieyès. Much of the success of 18
and 19 Brumaire (8 and 9 November) 1799 is owed to the political
resourcefulness and firmness in action of Lucien Bonaparte.

On his arrival in Paris Bonaparte found his house empty. Josephine,
hearing of his landing had hurried south with Louis to Lyons to meet
him, but they had taken different routes. The Bonaparte family had
kept Napoleon well acquainted with Josephine's resumed affair with
M. Charles at Malmaison. When she arrived back in the rue Chantereine,
she found her bedroom door locked against her. She spent a night
weeping on a back stairway, begging to be allowed to see her husband.
It was her two young children, Eugène and Hortense, who finally
broke down Bonaparte's resolve. There was a tearful reconciliation,
and when Lucien arrived at seven the following morning, he was
ushered into the bedroom to find Bonaparte in bed with Josephine at
his side.

On 18 Brumaire the Council of Ancients decreed that both Councils
should move from the Tuileries to the palace of Saint-Cloud for the
sitting of the following day, on the ground that Jacobinical plots made
Paris insecure, it even being feared for the deputies' safety. The
command of all the troops in the Paris region was given to General
Bonaparte. In her *Memoirs* Laure recalls those anxious two days,
when everything seemed poised in the balance. Her brother-in-law
Geouffre was with Lucien to whom he acted as lieutenant, and on
the morning of the 18th he visited Napoleon on his brother's behalf.
He noticed that Bonaparte had two loaded pistols by him. Mme
Permon and Laure kept other members of the family company on that
fateful day. 'We went to see Mme Laetizia Bonaparte, who lived with
Joseph. She appeared calm though far from being easy, for her extreme
paleness and the convulsive movement she evinced whenever an
unexpected noise met her ear gave her features a ghastly air. In those
moments she appeared to me truly like the mother of the Gracchi.
And her situation added force to the idea; she had perhaps more at
stake than the celebrated Roman matron. She had three sons under the
stroke of fate, one of whom would probably receive the blow even if
the others escaped. This she strongly felt. My mother and I remained
with her a part of that tantalizing day, and only quitted her on the
restoration of her confidence by Lucien's different messages, who
frequently sent Mariani, his *valet de chambre*, to calm her disquiet as
well as that of his wife. . . Leaving, then, these ladies in comparative
ease, we proceeded to Mme Leclerc, who was but little frightened,

because indeed she never reflected upon anything, but who nevertheless raised the loudest clamour of any. Every quarter of an hour she wrote to Moreau. . . On our departure she made us promise to revisit her early on the morrow. We had scarcely left her when we met my brother-in-law coming to tell us the news. He quitted us to rejoin Lucien, whom he did not wish to leave during these perilous hours, for even now tranquillity was only apparent, and might be delusive to the Bonaparte family. . .

'But the 9th was to develop the whole plan of the conspiracy (for we must make use of that expression) which was only announced by the events of the 8th. . . A fact sufficiently singular is the entire ignorance in which all that portion of the Bonaparte family who had no share in the action were placed. Everything had been arranged so quietly in Paris; Fouché had so well taken his measures to prevent the escape of any intelligence that Bonaparte's mother and sister were obliged to obtain information of what was passing in the manner I have described.

'The events of the evening had proceeded so quietly that the uneasiness of Mme Laetizia Bonaparte was entirely dissipated. It was thought the Councils, after having sanctioned the relegation of three Directors, and voted the dispensation with regard to his age, would proceed to the nomination of Bonaparte, and that everything would thus be settled. Albert thought that M. de Talleyrand would be one of the peacemaking Directors, and of this I was glad, because his niece was a friend of mine. . .

'That very day [the 9th] I had occasion to mark the maternal tenderness of Mme Laetizia. We had no company for dinner, and she conversed for hours with my mother with greater freedom than she had done since her arrival from Corsica. . . While this conversation was going on Mme Leclerc was seated on her favourite divan, admiring herself in a glass which was opposite her, and at length having arranged the folds of her cashmere shawl she reminded her mother of all the sufferings they had endured during their flight from Ajaccio. . .

'On the evening of the 9th we went to the Theatre Feydeau, which at that period was the most pleasant in Paris. Martin, Mme Saint-Aubin, Mlle Philis, Juliet, and Chenard performed there. I forget what was the first piece represented that evening but *L'Auteur dans son ménage* was the second piece. When we arrived Mme Bonaparte appeared to be in a state of mind both restless and unquiet. She said nothing but often she glanced at the door of the box, and we saw, my

mother and I, that she expected to see Albert or my brother-in-law
enter, but the evening went on and no one appeared. The curtain rose,
and the latter piece was proceeding very quietly, when all of a sudden
the actors stopped and *l'auteur dans son ménage* himself advanced to the
footlights. He bowed to the audience, although he was in a dressing-
gown of white dimity, and exclaimed in a very loud voice: "Citizens,
General Bonaparte has been nearly assassinated at Saint Cloud by
traitors to this country." On hearing those words, Mme Leclerc
uttered so piercing a shriek that immediately the attention of all the
company was attracted to our box, in spite of the agitation which the
news had universally excited. Mme Leclerc still continued crying;
and her mother, who was doubtless as much affected as she could be
at the intelligence, endeavoured to quieten her, though she herself
could hardly hold the glass of water the box-keeper handed us, so
great was her agitation. . . It was necessary to leave. It was only half-
past nine. Mme Bonaparte had sent away her carriage, and my mother
had equally ordered hers only for the end of the performance. But by a
lucky chance, our servant was found in the corridor and told us that
our carriage was below. My mother proposed to her friends to drive
them home, for the state of Mme Laetizia above all became alarming:
"I am going to take you home," my mother said to her, "and then I
will take back Paulette." "No, no," said Mme Bonaparte, "let us go
to the rue Chantereine, to my daughter-in-law's. It is there that we
will have certain news." And the poor mother trembled so that she
could hardly walk. However, she was calm in appearance and did not
cry. We all got into our carriage and in a few moments we were in rue
Chantereine. The courtyard, the avenue, all were filled with horses,
carriages, people on foot who jostled and shouted. There was a
hubbub to deafen one. "I should like to have some news from Lucien
and Joseph," said my mother to Mme Bonaparte when they got out
of the carriage. "As I don't know your daughter-in-law, I can't come
in." "What does it matter," cried Mme Bonaparte, "in a moment like
this. And a friend like you." My mother would not agree to go up. At
that moment we saw my brother-in-law get down, arriving from
Saint-Cloud. He informed us of the events. . .'

He told them how Bonaparte, entering the Council of Five Hundred,
had been met by furious shouts of 'Outlaw him'; how the moment
had been saved by the presence of mind of Lucien; how Bonaparte had
addressed the soldiers and ordered them to rescue Lucien and clear
the chambers. Now all was over; Bonaparte, Sieyès and Ducos were

appointed provisional Consuls; sixty-one Jacobins were expelled from the Council; and a legislative commission to review the constitution was appointed, which was to report back, when the sitting resumed on 19 February 1800. It was soon seen that a firm hand was in control. Bonaparte was named First Consul, with the widest powers, assisted in subordinate roles by Cambacérès and Lebrun. How readily the new constitution, which was Bonaparte's work, was welcomed is shown by the plebiscite in January 1800, when 3,001,107 votes were cast in its support, and only 1562 votes against it. When the First Consul moved into the Tuileries in hired cabs with their numbers painted over— there were no state carriages—it may be said that a new period was inaugurated in France, a glorious one, that of the Consulate. The fifteen-year-old Laure was enthusiastic in her feelings for the man who in so short a space of time was regenerating France.

Shortly before 18 Brumaire Mme Permon and Laure were the guests for a stay of six weeks at Lucien Bonaparte's country house at Le Plessis Chamant, near the Forest of Senlis. All the older members of the Bonaparte family were acquiring country properties in addition to their town houses—Joseph at Mortefontaine and Pauline Leclerc at Montgobert. Josephine was already in possession of Malmaison, and was at work to make the gardens and hothouses the most magnificent in France. Joseph entertained with much taste and good feeling at Mortefontaine, where his guests rode, boated on the lakes, played billiards and spent the evenings in reading aloud, listening to music and telling ghost stories. The Permons continued to see much of the Bonapartes in Paris and in the country. Napoleon, however, living in consular splendour in the Tuileries, never visited Mme Permon, nor did she visit the First Consul in his official residence.

On 21 June 1800 Mme Permon and Laure had driven out in the carriage to the pretty village of Saint Mandé, where they had lunched and dined. The place was solitary, and no visitor but they had come from Paris, so that returning in the cool of the evening it was not until they had reached the barrier on the outskirts of the city that they became aware of the excitement of the crowds on the news of the victory of Marengo. The news was greeted with a delirium of joy by the populace. Bonfires blazed on the quarters of the city through which they drove, and around the fires the people, wild with enthusiasm, danced to the shouts of *Vive la République! Vive le Premier Consul! Vive l'Armée!* embracing and congratulating each other as on an occasion of personal or family festivity. They drove home by a roundabout route to enjoy the spontaneous feelings of the people in this fresh triumph of Bonaparte. Marengo placed the seal on the First Consul's popularity with the people of France. On the very day of the battle, 14 June, General Junot set foot on shore in the South of France, home after his captivity.

As soon as Junot arrived in Paris, after visiting his parents in Burgundy, he hastened to greet his general, who was at Malmaison. Junot's loyalty to Bonaparte was, if possible, heightened by his dazzling successes. At this interview the First Consul told him that he intended to appoint him principal aide-de-camp and Commandant of Paris, a most responsible post, with command over the troops of the capital and surrounding military districts. But, he told him, he must add ten years to his age—he was twenty-eight—and he must straightway find himself a wife, a rich one. Junot was then lodging at the Hôtel Méo, a good place at the period, comparable to what was afterwards the Meurice. He first had to find himself a residence befitting his new and exalted position. Instead of choosing one of the many fine houses to let in the fashionable Faubourgs of Saint-Germain or Saint-Honoré or in the Chaussée d'Autin, he fixed on an hôtel in the gloomy rue de Verneuil, and in the dullest and dirtiest part of it. The truth is that Junot, loyal to his place of origin, favoured above all Burgundians, and it was a Burgundian who found him his house, a Burgundian who furnished it for him, and it was a Burgundian whom he put in charge of his new establishment.

On the important question of finding himself a rich wife Junot consulted two of his women acquaintances, Mme d'Orsay and Mme Hamelin, both of whom suggested to him the name of Mlle Permon. But, protested Junot, she was only a child. Although she reassured him on this point, saying that Laure was now sixteen (she was in reality still fifteen), Mme Hamelin thought that Mme Permon had already an eye on a suitable match for her. Laure herself recounted the story in her *Memoirs:* 'Thus the summer of 1800 elapsed. The end of September arrived. A great change had taken place meanwhile in our family. The two marriages which my mother had proposed for me were broken off; one for pecuniary reasons, the other because I had thrown myself at her feet, entreating her, by her love for me, not to make me a sacrifice and my life miserable. My mother was perfectly amiable, and she loved me; she therefore broke off a marriage which, in other respects, was suitable enough, but to which I had so thorough an antipathy that I should have ratified a doom of misery to myself and my husband in saying *Yes*. I was delighted with this change in my lot. All my friends, whether from attachment to me, or whether from that sentiment that makes a young girl always unwilling that her companion should marry before her—all my friends rejoiced in seeing me at liberty for the following winter.'

One evening—21 September—a group of about a dozen friends were assembled in Mme Permon's drawing room, when the *valet de chambre* announced General Junot. These ladies of the Faubourg Saint-Germain looked frigidly on the presence in their midst of a republican general, and it was Mme Permon herself who went forward and greeted the young man warmly. Drawing up a chair she seated him at her side and entered into a most friendly conversation with him. Seeing their hostess's reception of the General, the ladies looked with interest at this specimen of the new society. Junot was tall, strongly built, with a cheerful open expression on his browned face, furrowed by several sabre scars, and with a mop of auburn hair. He was a very presentable man, and his uniform of colonel of hussars set off his figure well. After a little while, Albert, who had been spending the evening with Mme Leclerc, came in, and his presence emboldened Junot to propose to Mme Permon that she should, on the following day, go to the Hôtel de Salm, on the Quai de Voltaire, to witness the military procession which was to escort the remains of Marshal Turenne from the Jardin des Plantes, where it had been deposited since the spoliation of Saint-Denis, to its resting place in the Invalides. Junot, as Commandant of Paris, was in command of the troops at the ceremony. After some hesitation, Mme Permon, who was not in good health, was finally persuaded to agree to be present.

The following day Laure and her mother went to the Hôtel de Salm, where they were conducted to armchairs, with pillows and a footstool for Mme Permon, placed in a window-bay. Mme Permon was pleasantly gratified by Junot's kindly attentions. They looked out on crowds lining the quay to watch the spectacle. When Junot passed at the head of the troops, he turned to look up at the window and formally saluted. Someone in the crowd was heard to remark, 'No doubt it is the widow of Marshal Turenne'.

For the next ten days Junot regularly visited the house every evening, apparently devoting all his attentions to Mme Permon, for he never once addressed a remark to Laure, who naturally assumed that he was paying his court to her mother. But among the society they frequented

Junot's visits were differently interpreted; nevertheless, once, when Laure de Caseaux spoke to her about it, she was indignant with her young friend. One day about noon Laure was in her room, having a lesson from her drawing master, M. Viglians, when Junot called and asked if he might be admitted. Albert was in the drawing room with his mother. With military brusqueness Junot came straight to the point. He was glad Albert was present, he said, since he had come to ask them for Laure's hand in marriage. Mme Permon showed her pleasure in hearing his request; she was just telling Albert, she informed him, that there was no one in Paris whom she would prefer as her son-in-law. But there were difficulties. Laure was very young; she herself was far from well and Laure might not like leaving her; finally, and it was a serious matter, Laure had no, or very little, dowry. Junot would be wise to give himself time to think over it. He replied that he had given the matter very serious thought. Turning to Albert, he asked him if he had his permission to marry his sister. Albert answered that the day when he could call him brother would be the happiest in his life. 'And I,' said Mme Permon, extending her arms to him, 'am happy beyond description in calling you my son.' They embraced each other. Then Junot said that he had another favour to ask—that he might be able to put the same question personally to Laure. Mme Permon thought the thing absurd; it had never been heard of; but Junot persisted, and Albert went off to fetch Laure. The poor girl, suddenly presented with Junot's demand, could find nothing to say. She stood rooted to the spot, blushing deep red, for several minutes, then, turning on her heel, she rushed from the room and did not stop running until she found herself in the attic. There Albert found her and, calming her tears, conducted her to her own bedroom. Junot thought that Laure's extraordinary behaviour betokened a refusal, and he was overjoyed when he heard Albert say that Laure sent him a message that she would be 'proud to bear his name.'

It was Mme Permon who first came back to the realities of the situation. Had Junot approached the First Consul, to ask his permission? He might not agree to Junot's marriage with Mme Permon's daughter. What would he do if the First Consul should refuse his permission? Junot replied that he would marry without it; it was no concern of the First Consul's. Nevertheless, he agreed to go straight to the Tuileries and seek an interview with Bonaparte.

When he arrived at the Tuileries, he saw Duroc, who was on duty. The latter said that the First Consul was free, and he would announce

Junot. Contrary to what the Permons had expected, Bonaparte was not adverse to the marriage. But how could Junot, he asked, choose to have Mme Permon as mother-in-law. Junot replied that he was not marrying his mother-in-law. Bonaparte next asked him how he thought he was going to provide for a wife, and a family, on his army pay and his salary as Commandant of Paris. Junot answered that he looked to him, the First Consul, his general, to help him in that matter. Bonaparte was as good as his word, which he had given Junot when he left him in Egypt. He made him a gift of 100,000 francs for the bride's portion, and a further 40,000 francs for her wedding-clothes. As Junot, after thanking him warmly, was taking his leave, Bonaparte pressed his hand with affection, remarking as he got to the door, 'I wish you happiness. But, oh, you will have a terrible mother-in-law!'

A portrait of the young Laure Permon as she appeared at the time of her marriage comes from the pen of General Thiébault: 'It is impossible to imagine anything prettier, more alive, more amiable, more striking than was this young lady, dressed with an elegance, a freshness which accorded so perfectly with all that nature had bestowed of coquetry, of luxury in forming her. She was charming, and although I was a thousand miles from anything that might be termed love, or simply desire, such she has remained for me, the most graceful of apparitions.' Laure was small, beautifully formed, with a white satin skin and raven black hair. Her eyes too were jet black, and her little mouth, when she smiled, revealed her perfect teeth.

Junot wanted the marriage to take place without delay, and 30 October was decided on, as being the earliest date by which arrangements could be made. Each day between the engagement and the wedding he called with a bunch of flowers from Mme Bernard the famous *bouquetière* to the Opera. On 27 October Junot's family arrived from Bussy-le-Grand. Two days later Albert Permon accompanied Junot to the Tuileries, where the marriage contract was signed in the presence of the First Consul. Laure's gratitude to her brother was unbounded, when she learned that he was giving her, from his own savings, 60,000 francs towards her dowry. To this sum was added 50,000 francs from M. Lequien de Bois-Cressy, an old friend of her father, who was to marry shortly after Mme Permon. This was from a mortgage on his estate in Brittany. Laure and her mother had taken it for granted that she would be married at the church of St Louis in rue Thiroux, which was nearly opposite their house. Great was their surprise then, when they heard that Junot, on the orders of Bonaparte, was not willing, as Commandant of Paris, to be married in public in a church. The First Consul was already feeling his way towards the Concordat with the Roman Church, and did not want at this juncture to prejudice his policy by too openly offending the susceptibilities of many atheistic republicans. It was Junot's wish that the civil ceremony should be performed in the town hall in rue de Jouy by an old friend of his, M. Duquesnoy, who was the mayor of the Seventh Arrondissement, the Quartier Saint-Antoine. Laure was adamant; she would call off the marriage if it were not to have the sanction of the church. The difficulty was solved by proposing to have two ceremonies, the civil one to be followed by the religious, to be held after the midnight mass.

Laure took pride in the part she played in re-establishing an old French marriage custom, which had fallen into abeyance during the civil turmoil brought about by the Revolution. In this she had been anticipated by Caroline Bonaparte, who had married Joachim Murat some months previously. This was the furnishing of the *trousseau* and the *corbeille*, the first being provided by the bride's family and the second being the bridegroom's present to his bride. The money lavished on thus setting up a newly married woman could be very considerable. We have Laure's own account of her's.

'On entering the drawing room, though it was large, I found myself much in the situation of Noah's dove, without a place of rest for my foot. From an immense basket, or rather portmanteau, of rose-coloured *gros de Naples*, embroidered with black chenille, made in the shape of a sarcophagus bearing my cipher, an innumerable quantity of small packets, tied with pink or blue ribbons, strewed the room; these contained full-trimmed chemises with embroidered sleeves, pocket-handkerchiefs, petticoats, morning-gowns, dressing-gowns of Indian muslin, nightdresses, nightcaps, morning-caps of all colours and forms:—the whole of these articles were embroidered, and trimmed with Mechlin lace or English point. Another portmanteau of equal size, of green silk embroidered in orange chenille, contained my numerous dresses, all worthy in fashion and taste to compare with the articles all ready described. This was an hour of magic for a girl of sixteen.'

Junot had solicited the help of Mme Murat in selecting the articles which went to make up his *corbeille*. These had been bought by Mlle L'Olive, dressmaker to Mme Josephine Bonaparte. Laure describes it:

'At this time the custom of giving a basket or case for the articles of the *corbeille* was not yet exploded. Fifty or sixty livres were spent upon a kind of basket covered with rich silk or velvet. . . Mine was an immensely large vase, covered with green and white velvet, richly embroidered with gold. Its foot was of gilded bronze; its cover of embroidered velvet, surmounted by a pineapple of black velvet, transfixed by an arrow, from which were suspended on each side a crown, the one of olives, the other of laurel, both cut in bronzed gold.

'This *corbeille* contained cashmere shawls, vests of English point, gown trimmings of blond and Brussels point, dresses of white blond and black lace; pieces of Indian muslin and Turkish velvet which the General had brought from Egypt; ball dresses for a bride; my presentation dress, and Indian muslin dresses embroidered in silver lama. Besides all these there were flowers bought from Mme Roux in rue Saint-Anne; ribbons of all sizes and colours; bags (or as we now say, reticules), they were then all the fashion, one of these of English point; gloves, fans and scents. At each side of the *corbeille* was a sultan, or scented bag. The first contained all the implements of the toilet in gold enamelled black; the apparatus of the work-table—thimble, scissors, needle-case, bodkin, etc., all in gold set with fine pearls. The other bag contained the jewel case, and an opera-glass of mother-of-pearl and gold set with two rows of diamonds. The case contained settings for an entire set of ornaments without the stones; six ears of golden corn and a comb set with diamonds and pearls; a square medallion set with large pearls, containing a portrait of General Junot by Isabey, for the resemblance of which the artist's name will vouch, but of a size more fit to be affixed to the wall of a gallery than to be suspended from the neck; but this was the fashion of the day, and Mme Murat had one of her husband, also painted by Isabey, and larger than mine. The case contained also a number of superb topazes brought from Egypt, of an incredible size, Oriental corals of an extraordinary thickness, which I have since had engraved in relief in Florence by M.Hamelin, and several antique cameos; all of these were unset. The bridal purse of gold links, the clasp also enamelled green, contained too heavy a sum of money had it not consisted of bank-notes, except about fifty louis in pretty little sequins of Venice.'

Nor was Madame forgotten in Junot's prodigality. A small basket covered with white *gros de Naples* contained, besides a magnificent red cashmere shawl (which she had always wanted), a purse like Laure's, except that the enamel was deep blue and that inside was a topaz of perfect shape, the size of a small apricot; gloves, ribbons and two beautiful fans. Laure was deeply touched by this attention to her mother.

On the morning of her wedding day she rose at dawn, and escorted by Sister Rosalie, the nun who had accompanied her at her first communion, she went to the church of the Capuchins to ask the abbé to officiate at the marriage ceremony after his midnight mass. To her dismay the abbé refused, giving the reason that he did not see why the marriage should have to take place in such a hole-in-the-corner fashion, and besides, how was he to know that the republican general was not already married? Nor would Laure's, and Sister Rosalie's, pleading overcome his rigorous scruples. He refused also at first the purse that Laure offered, and only accepted it, not for himself but for the poor of his parish.

At nine o'clock she dressed for the civil ceremony. Her cap, which was made by Mlle Despaux, was of Brussels lace, crowned with a wreath of orange flowers; her veil of fine English point reached to her feet. At eleven punctually the general arrived, with the rest of his family. Junot was accompanied by two of his aides-de-camp, Captain Lallemand, who had been on his staff in Egypt, and M. Bardin, son of the well-known painter. When they were about to leave for the town hall four lusty *marchandes de la Halle* asked if they might come in to offer the compliments of the market people to the Commandant of Paris and his bride. They presented Laure with bouquets of the rarest out-of-season flowers, and each of them kissed her. Outside, when they set off for the rue de Jouy, the street was filled with onlookers, and as the carriage drove off there were rousing shouts of 'Long live the bride and groom!'

THREE

La Commandante de Paris

WHEN JUNOT expressed a wish to give a dinner for his companions-in-arms at his mother-in-law's house on the day after the marriage, Mme Permon was aghast, remarking that it was just like a journeyman carpenter offering his fellow workers a treat on his wedding day. On Junot's insisting, she wisely gave in. But she foresaw a difficulty. Would they come without having been introduced to her? Junot gravely assured her that they would. All she could find to do was to invite herself a leavening of the Faubourg Saint-Germain, and this she did, among them M. de Lavalette and the old family friend M. de Caulaincourt. Of his military friends Junot asked Duroc, Bessières, Rapp, Berthier, Lannes, Eugène Beauharnais and others. Laure had not met these; the only generals with whom she was acquainted were Moreau, Macdonald and Beuronville, whom she had previously met at Mme Leclerc's. Lucien Bonaparte, who had been appointed Minister of the Interior, was unable to be present, but of his sisters, Mme Murat, who was heavily pregnant, and Mme Leclerc, who as usual looked pretty as a picture, were there. Also Mme Bacciochi, who that morning had presided over a female literary society, for whom she had taken it into her head to design a literary dress, in which she arrived. Laure thought it a medley of Jewish, Roman, Middle Age and modern Greek dress—of everything, in short, except French good taste.

It was curious to observe how the Faubourg took these members of Consular society. On their side contempt, veiled under the appearance of extreme politeness, combined with an hauteur which showed that this politeness was out of deference to their hostess; and an occasional smile or whispered observation betrayed their opinions of their parvenu associates. For their part, self-reliant in the knowledge of their military prestige, these soldiers paid little heed to their social superiors. M. de Caulaincourt, noticing Colonel Rapp, whom he had known at the Tuileries, drew Laure aside and asked her if he had visited her mother. She replied that he had not. Then, he had left a card? No. It was not possible, he protested, that he should come and sit down in the house of a woman of good society without having first been introduced and paid his respects to her. While he was speaking to Laure, Rapp crept up behind him and shouted in his ear, 'What are you talking about, dear papa? Please move out of my way on a wedding day. The old must give way to the young.' So saying, he threw his arms around the old gentleman's waist, lifted him up and set him down at a little distance.

Looking at Rapp with an expression of dignified disapproval, M. de Caulaincourt said, 'Colonel, you and I are neither old enough nor young enough for such play,' then bowing coldly to him, he turned to Laure, 'Will you come and see what is passing in the next room?'

Laure was trying to placate the old man's injured feelings, when Junot came up, and she told him of Rapp's unfortunate behaviour. Immediately Junot went off to find him, and in a few minutes returned with a repentant Rapp. 'Junot tells me,' he said, addressing Laure and M. de Caulaincourt, 'that I have failed in my respect to you, in acting so very rudely in your presence. I might, nevertheless, refuse to apologise, because apologies are only necessary when one has done wrong intentionally, and certainly I did not intend to offend.' The strangeness of the excuse caused M. de Caulaincourt to relent, and smiling he held out his hand, 'You are a good fellow,' he said, 'and I shall be happy to be numbered among your friends.' Mme Permon was not so easy to mollify, when she heard of Rapp's conduct; she was so offended that she scarcely could bring herself to be polite to him afterwards.

A few days later Mme Junot was presented to the First Consul and Mme Bonaparte. Junot and she went on from the opera, leaving the ballet *Psyche* in the middle, so as not to be too late at the Tuileries, and arrived at the Pavilion of Flora at ten o'clock. As they were talking to Duroc and Rapp, the door of Mme Bonaparte's apartment opened and Eugène de Beauharnais came running down the steps to greet them. He had heard the noise of a carriage drawing up in the courtyard and thought it was they. When they entered Mme Bonaparte's drawing room, they found her sitting beside the fire engaged in her tapestry work. Unkind persons said that, hearing that Marie-Antoinette used to do this, she had taken up the work. Opposite her sat Hortense de Beauharnais, a charming-looking girl of seventeen, with a slim figure and beautiful fair hair. Between them was the First Consul, with his hands behind his back, standing in front of the fire. If Mme Bonaparte had been opposed to the marriage—she resented her husband's old acquaintance with the Permon family—and had some reason not to care for Junot after the Italian journey—her gracious behaviour on the evening did not betray it. Bonaparte was most considerate, speaking in a natural easy way. He told Laure that he hoped to see much of her, that he intended to draw around him a numerous family, consisting of his generals and their young wives. His voice took on a harsher ring when he told her not to expect to find there her fine acquaintances of the Faubourg Saint-Germain. He disliked them as much as they disliked him, but he did not fear their harming him. She could tell them this.

Mme Permon, in her desire to keep up old established customs, proposed to give a ball for Laure a fortnight after her wedding day. A family conference was held, to draw up the list of invitations. Junot wrote out the names of the ladies to be asked, beginning with that of Mme Bonaparte and Hortense de Beauharnais. There was some surprise when Mme Permon declared her intention of inviting the First Consul. Junot, delighted at the possibility of healing the breach between his mother-in-law and his general, told her to name the day and he would come to fetch her. 'Fetch me! To go where?' she asked. 'To the Tuileries,' replied Junot, 'to present your invitation to the First Consul and Mme Bonaparte.' But Mme Permon had no intention of doing this; she would write to him, and he ('like any gentleman') would call or leave his card before the ball. The young people doubted whether the First Consul had visiting cards, but they held their peace. She insisted, 'I don't see why he should not visit, and certainly I shall not go first.' Firm in her belief that she was doing the right thing, she wrote to Bonaparte. The following day Junot and Laure, with Albert, went to the Tuileries, destroying Mme Permon's letter on the way. They saw Mme Bonaparte—Hortense was not in—and she accepted for them both. They gave as an excuse for Mme Permon's not coming in person her ill health. They then went to see the First Consul. He, too, said he would be delighted to accept, and asked the date of the ball. 10 November, they told him.

'10 November,' he repeated, 'Let me see, that seems some particular day.' He turned over the leaves of a calendar. 'I thought so,' he said, that is the anniversary of 18 Brumaire, and it would not do to have a party on that day. The Faubourg Saint-Germain would hardly want to celebrate the day of the refounding of the Republic.'

At Bonaparte's request they changed the date to the 12th.

True to the way she did everything, Mme Permon intended that her ball should be one of the most agreeable to be given in Paris that season. Small though the house was for such an occasion, when the trees, plants and flowers were in the place her taste demanded, and innumerable lights shone among them of every colour, Laure thought the staircase, hall and rooms resembled an enchanted palace. Mme Bonaparte arrived about nine o'clock, with her son and daughter, and escorted by Colonel Rapp. Mme Permon received her in the hall and led her to an armchair to the right of the fireplace in the drawing room. In Laure's eyes her mother that evening was the prettiest woman in the room, after the First Consul's two sisters, Pauline Leclerc and Caroline Murat. She played the hostess to perfection, with a grace that was her particular charm. Laure described her mother's appearance: 'As she could not, or rather did not choose to, appear on the occasion of my marriage with her hair wholly uncovered, she had a toque of white crepe (made by Leroi, who then lived in the rue des Petits-Champs, and had already acquired some reputation), through the folds of which her fine black hair appeared, resembling velvet, intermingled with branches of jonquil, like those which trimmed her gown. The flowers were furnished by Mme Roux. She wore in her bosom a large bouquet of jonquils and natural violets, but exhibited neither necklace nor jewels of any kind except two very fine diamond drops in her ears. This attire was set off by a person whose elegance of figure and manner were at least her most striking ornament. I was proud of my mother'.

At a quarter to nine Junot went to the Tuileries to escort the First Consul, but found him so overwhelmed with work that he could not say when he would arrive; but come he certainly would, at however late an hour. The ball began at nine-thirty, Junot dancing with Hortense de Beauharnais, her brother Eugène with Laure and Hippolyte de Rastignac with her friend Laure de Caseaux. Mme Permon and her older friends had insisted that Laure should obey the custom of the former régime and dance the *minuet de la cour* and the *gavotte*. Her partner was to be M. de Trénis, who with M. Lafitte was considered the best dancer in Paris and was in great demand. At ten-thirty the First Consul had not yet come, although all his family, with the exception of Joseph, who was at the conference of Lunéville, had arrived early.

Mme Leclerc, who as always looked beautiful and elegant, commented on the poppies and wreath of corn ears worn by Mme Bonaparte. 'How a person of forty can wear garlands of flowers,' she said. Laure pointed out that her mother too was wearing flowers. 'But that is quite a different thing,' she said—'quite a different thing.'

A few minutes before eleven the sound of the hooves of the First Consul's horse-guards was heard, and several seconds later his carriage drew up at the entrance. Almost immediately he appeared at the door of the dining room with Albert Permon and Junot, and Mme Permon went to greet him with a gracious curtsey. 'Eh, Mme Permon, is that the way you greet an old friend?' and he held out his hand. Mme Permon gave him hers and they entered the ballroom together. The music had stopped. Several ladies remained seated when he came in to the room; he was at once aware of it, and passed directly into the bedroom. Despite the heat, he was wearing his familiar grey greatcoat, which he kept on. 'Do let the dancing continue,' he said; 'Young people must be amused, and dancing is their favourite pastime. And if you will, you and I shall dance the *Monaco*—the only one I know.' 'Come, I have not danced these thirty years,' replied Mme Permon.'

'I don't believe it,' said Bonaparte, looking at her with admiration, 'you could be your daughter's sister tonight.'

M. de Talleyrand was present and, after the First Consul had spoken to Laure and some others and made himself generally agreeable, he entered into conversation with him. This lasted without interruption for three-quarters of an hour.

Meanwhile, Mme Permon called on Laure for her minuet, and for a moment she thought that she was saved from an ordeal which she dreaded, since M. de Trénis had not yet arrived. Then she must dance it with M. Lafitte, Mme Permon declared. But he had no hat. Mme Permon quickly procured one for him. There was no getting out of it, and dance it she did. M. Lafitte was escorting her to a chair beside her friend Mlle de Merigny, when M. de Trénis appeared and was disconsolate when he learned that he had missed the dance, in which, in his opinion, he excelled. He sat down beside her, and confessed that he had seen the end of the minuet, and that he had never seen such a spectacle. Laure was alarmed; but it was not of her dancing that he complained—far from it—he had nothing but praise. 'That you should dance a minuet with that man—a good dancer, no doubt; but he is good only for a country dance. For a minuet, however, he never, never in his life, knew how to make the grand bow with the hat—he cannot make the grand bow.' The two young women laughed at this unexpected turn; but he was in all seriousness. 'That seems to surprise you. Not to know how to put on one's hat!—for that is the science—it is not hard to explain. Come, let me show you,' and he led the girls into Mme Permon's bedroom. There he poised himself in front of a pier-glass. Then humming the close of the minuet, he went through the motions of the salute with perfect gravity, placing on his head the three-cornered hat with all the dignity so important a matter demanded. While he was thus engaged, Junot came into the room, and behind him, unnoticed, the First Consul. The latter made a sign to Junot to engage M. de Trénis in conversation, which was easy if dancing were the subject. Junot asked M. de Trénis how he agreed with such an accomplished dancer as M. Lafitte. 'Why,' he replied, 'as well as two men of talent can be expected to agree, when so nearly upon an equality. But he is a good fellow, not at all envious of my success. It is true that his own may well make him indulgent. His dance is lively and it has power. He has the advantage over me in the first eight measures of Panurge's gavotte. But in the *jetés*! oh! there he has no chance: he has verve, but I have grace.'

The First Consul could scarcely believe a grown man could deliver himself of such drivel. 'It is prodigious,' he said at length, 'this man is infinitely more irrational than many who are locked up in madhouses.' He returned to his place beside M. de Talleyrand, and Laure could see by their looking in his direction that they were discussing M. de Trénis. Laure, thinking that her mother had rather neglected Bonaparte, went to find her. When she returned with her, she saw that Junot and M. de Villemanzy had replaced M. de Talleyrand at Bonaparte's side. When the latter saw Mme Permon, he came straight over to her.

'Well, Mme Permon, what have you to say to one of your old friends? It seems to me that you easily forget them.' He then referred to a recent occasion at the Opera, on the night of the Ceracchi and Aréna attempt on his life, when he had bowed to Mme Junot from the Consular box. 'But why would you not return my friendly salute? I took the first moment of recognising you to make it.'

Mme Permon alleged the weakness of her sight; but Bonaparte was not to be put off with excuses.

'What am I to think,' he said; 'are we no longer friends?'

She answered him in Italian, 'I am not able to forget, dear Napoleon, that you are the son of a friend, brother of my good Giuseppe, of dear Luciano, and of Pauletta.'

'So, then, if I hold a place in your regard, I owe it to my mother and my brothers and sister.'

The discussion was painful to Laure. The First Consul walked in silence to the fire. Mme Permon was seated on a sofa opposite him, her arms folded, and her foot shaking in a fashion that usually preluded a violent scene. At that moment Albert came in, and approaching the First Consul, offered him a water-ice. 'I assure you,' he said, 'that neither Mme Permon nor myself require ice. Indeed, I believe we are petrified. I know very well that absence stifled remembrance, but not to such a point as this.' He had touched on a tender point with Mme Permon.

'Truly,' she said, with a forced smile, 'one may be allowed to forget after an interval of some years. Do you want to persuade me that it was difficult to remember, after just a few days, something that may have affected a man's career?'

'Ah, so that is it.' Bonaparte was then silent, walking up and down, with his hands behind his back. Then his face resumed an expression of serenity, and he took one of Mme Permon's hands, as if to kiss it. He paused. 'It does seem that you do not correct any of your faults, Mme Permon,' and he pointed to her bitten finger-nails.

'No,' she replied, 'they and I have grown old together. Leave all in its place. It is you who are forbidden to remain as you are. You have still so many steps to climb before you reach the summit of your glory, that to wish you repose would be to wish harm to ourselves.'

'Do you really think as you speak?'

'You know my sincerity?' Mme Permon replied: 'I do not always say all I think; but I never say what I do not think. Have you forgotten my frankness?'

The First Consul took her hand and pressed it affectionately. At that moment the clock struck two. He asked for his carriage.

'You will not stay to supper?'

'I cannot possibly stay,' he said, regretfully, 'but I will come again.' Mme Permon smiled, and shook her head gently.

'Why do you smile? Do you doubt me, Mme Permon?'

Mme Permon said nothing. Bonaparte never came to her house again.

When on 30 Pluviose in the year VIII (19 February 1800) the First Consul, accompanied by the two subordinate Consuls, the Councillors of State and Senators, drove from the Luxembourg to the

Tuileries in the procession of shabby hackney carriages, a new era may be said to have begun for a Revolution-weary France. That evening he said to Josephine as they were about to retire, 'Come, little Creole, get into the bed of your masters.' During the course of the day he had taken the salute at a military review in the Place de la Tuileries and the Place de Carrousel, a parade which thenceforth he held every Quintidi (the tenth-day republican holiday), the regiments coming in turn to Paris from the garrisons all over France. With them paraded the Household Guards. In this way he centred the regenerated life of the country on the army and the capital, and roused the enthusiasm of Parisians at the spectacle of the nation's military splendour and power. The young Laure Junot, placed by her husband in the window of Duroc's rooms on the first floor of the Tuileries, was filled too with enthusiasm and was often moved to tears at the sight of this outward expression of the glory of France. The First Consul, mounted on his white horse Le Desiré, would take the salute and ride along the ranks; then he would dismount, and moving among his officers and men, would address questions to casually selected soldiers or, recognising familiar faces, would speak a few words with them. On these occasions he would be accompanied by his aides-de-camp of the day, the Minister of War, the general commanding the first division, the Commandant of Paris, and commissaries of the various branches of the army. He encouraged the men to speak to him without fear or restraint. Complaints were carefully noted (and quickly put right), praise was given where it was due; rebukes, if necessary, were administered—and they were few. The army thus became the centre of national life; and the adoration of the soldiers for their victorious general, who had their welfare so much at heart, and their martial readiness in view, became the rallying point for a new national consciousness. France seemed to live again, restored to her primacy among nations, in the person of the First Consul.

This solicitude for the army was extended by Bonaparte to the administration of the entire country. The prefects, carefully selected by him—and in his choice he showed his administrative discretion—brought order out of the chaos of post-Revolutionary France, an order whose effects were quickly felt. The bands of brigands (*chauffeurs, rôdeurs*), who had rendered unsafe the countryside and the roads, were brought to justice. Dubois, the prefect of police was zealous in rounding up the robbers of coaches, thieves, forgers and false coiners—these last being very numerous. With security restored, agriculture, industry and commerce revived, and the vast potential wealth of France, which for so long had lain untapped, was seen in the great increase in material goods and services. With the restoration of financial stability, the Funds rapidly rose. And from this revival of material prosperity there came a renewed spirit in society. This too was the conscious intention of the First Consul. He was lavish in his financial provision for his own family and for his generals, and encouraged them and their young wives to set up grand town houses and country estates, where they were to entertain and give the tone for the new Consular society. As a sign of the change, the exhibition of 1800 was brilliant, with the paintings of David, Gros, Guérin, Gérard and Girodet. The *émigrés* began to return, subtly encouraged by Fouché's tolerance. At this time Laure's uncle, Prince Demetrius Comnena, re-entered France without a passport and, at Junot's personal request to the First Consul, was allowed to stay. By the Congress of Lunéville peace was made with Austria and the treaty of Amiens ended the war with England. Russia became France's ally. And all this within so short a time from 18 Brumaire. To one so observant as Laure Junot it was clear that these brighter hopes for a regenerated social order owed everything to the inspiration and will, and to the practical genius, of Bonaparte. It was he who had provided the miracle. For him her admiration was unbounded.

Junot, as first aide-de-camp, and Laure became members of the intimate circle which the First Consul gathered about him at the Tuileries and Malmaison. On most evenings, after a dinner which was usually set for no fewer than thirty places, they would attend the theatre or the Opera, and from there would drive to the Tuileries, to join the select group of men and women who attended the First Consul in the private rooms of Mme Bonaparte. At this time there was no court, but Mme Bonaparte had been given 'four women in attendance', to keep a check on both her generosity and her indiscretions. One of these ladies was the remarkable Mme de Rémusat. The first time that Laure dined at the Tuileries she was as a bride placed on the First Consul's right, Mme Lannes being on his other side. Bonaparte explained to her, now, as he said, that she was part of his family staff, that she must see everything, hear everything and forget everything. He added that he knew that she would do this admirably, and he referred to the Salicetti affair. Laure possessed just those qualities that were required in the society in which she was placed after her marriage. For a young wife of sixteen she was well educated, but what is more she had an alert, open and prehensile mind. Listening on these evenings at the Tuileries to the conversation around her, when Bonaparte discussed any matter that might arise, with such men as Roederer, Talleyrand, Fouché, Portalis, Fontanes, the actor Talma, and men eminent in all walks of life, she learnt much. At times Bonaparte would address a remark to her, and her responses seemed to give him pleasure. It might thus be said that her education proper only began after her marriage. But in addition to this, she had learnt to observe and be silent during the darkest days of the Revolution; she took a delight in reading by an expression on a speaker's face, by what he said and did not say, by a gesture, the nature of his innermost thoughts. She had been trained in her mother's drawing room in the niceties and conventions of this fashionable world. As the wife of the Commandant of Paris, she met not only Junot's many military friends but anyone of distinction who might be in Paris. She dined out often, attended fêtes and balls, and entertained much herself. Freed from her mother's over-strong tutelage and basking in the love of her husband, she shone.

The First Consul heard of her success in society and personally sought her aid in carrying out his plan, what he termed his 'system of fusion', the bringing together of the Faubourg Saint-Germain with the new Consular society of military men and administrators, untutored and often uncivilised, that was growing up around them. Her function in the social life of the Consulate was, like her mother's before her, *tenir un salon*. And for this, young as she was, she was perfectly equipped. Unlike the dinners of Cambacérès, the Second Consul, where the food and wines were exquisite, but the conversation intolerably boring, the house of Mme Junot soon gained a reputation for the elegance of the furnishings and service and the intelligence and wit of the company to be habitually found there. Of this Laure was the centre, for Junot had not her particular qualities.

When Bonaparte, in appointing Junot commandant of Paris, had told him that he needed ten years added to his age, he was referring to a certain callowness, a want of discretion, and a stubborn impetuosity, that were part of his character. He was twenty-nine when he received this appointment and married Laure Permon. There remained something of the child in him. He had had some education, having studied law before volunteering for the Côte-d'Or regiment in 1790, and he prided himself on his literary taste. He could, indeed, write pleasant verses. He was addicted to the theatre, and acted well himself. Liking to do everything on the grand scale, he had pretensions to the role of the *grand seigneur*. One day M. de Montmorency was holding forth on the claims of nobility. 'The difference between us,' said Junot, 'is that you people had ancestors, whereas I myself am an ancestor.' Ready to spend the last drop of his blood, or to fling money about indiscriminately, or even to drink anyone under the table (he built up the finest cellar in Paris), he was moreover an incorrigible womaniser. In these times, when the army was regarded so highly, especially in its own eyes, it became customary for the soldier actively to despise the civilian—as M. de Rémusat found to his dismay among the military men who thronged the Tuileries. An officer, entering a café, would take a newspaper from the hands of a reader, quietly sipping his coffee; and a blow with the flat of a sword would be the reply if he protested; a soldier would remove a wife from her husband's arm; and it was thought only natural that an officer should go to the head of any queue. A civilian was expected to give way to one in uniform. Something of this way of thinking and acting had found its way into Junot's style of behaviour. He was one of that group of *casseurs d'assiettes*, like Generals Auguste Colbert, Lasalle and Fournier or M. de Clermont-Tonnerre, who would end a convivial dinner by sweeping off the table dishes, glasses, bottles, everything, and hurl them out of the window. One day at the *glacier* Garchy's in rue de la Loi, Junot, offended by the behaviour of some of the young waiters, used the billiard cue in his hand to give them corporal chastisement. Yet with all this tempestuousness of the rampant male he possessed an almost feminine sensitivity; an unkind word from his adored General Bonaparte could make him so ill that he had to take to his bed. A staunch republican by conviction, nevertheless, he followed Bonaparte's imperial career, benefiting by it, materially and socially, at every stage. He was a mass of contradictions, which his wife alone knew how to unravel. This she learnt early on in their marriage.

In the first days of the Consulate, when Bonaparte was established in the Tuileries, the intimate circle around the First Consul frequently stayed at Mme Bonaparte's estate of Malmaison. Saint-Cloud came later, and Fontainebleau only with the Empire. At Malmaison the park and the grounds and woods above the Seine were enchanting, and Mme Bonaparte was already laying out her colourful flower beds and building her immense hothouses that were to make her gardens unrivalled in France. Bonaparte loved Malmaison, and liked the company to feel at ease there, although he worked continually, rising at six each morning, and not appearing until the evening. On Wednesdays there was usually a more formal dinner, the guests driving out from Paris, and afterwards there were theatricals. The First Consul was a stern critic, and Laure for one was fearful of acting in his presence. Both at the Tuileries and at Malmaison the younger members of the consular circle rehearsed and put on plays, comedies for the most part —Les Héretiers, Les Etourdis, Les Rivaux d'eux-mêmes, Défiance et malice. Laure, who took part in all of them, considered that their performance of Le Barbier de Seville could not have been bettered by any professional company in Paris. The best actors were Bourrienne, Eugène de Beauharnais, Junot, and the painter Isabey. On warm summer evenings Bonaparte would order dinner to be served outside on the lawns beneath the trees. On some days hunts were arranged, and the youthful company would at times, when Bonaparte felt in the mood, play games like barre, which he vastly enjoyed, taking off his coat and running like a schoolboy over the grass. Most of the inhabitants at Malmaison were young and gay, and there was much laughter.

One day in the early years of her marriage, in the summer of 1802, Laure was staying at Malmaison. She was then seventeen. Junot, whose post of commandant of Paris required his presence in the city during the day, drove out in the evening for dinner and returned to town afterwards. Mme Bonaparte had gone to Plombières to take the waters, leaving her daughter, Hortense, recently married to Louis Bonaparte, to do the honours of the house. Mme Bessières was also one of the young guests whom the First Consul so liked to have about him. Laure did not remember seeing Bonaparte so amiable as during that fortnight; he was good-humoured and even gay, amusing himself with making her recite Italian verse and playing reversis and chess with her. He did not play the latter well, and in both he invariably cheated. In the daytime he arranged from time to time a hunting-party. Laure was happy, but she wanted to go home, to see her mother, who was unwell, and to supervise the settling-in at their house at Le Petit-Bièvre, a small estate which Junot had bought with some of the money of the First Consul's wedding present.

One morning she was in a deep sleep, when she was awakened by a noise in the room. Looking up, she saw the First Consul at her bedside. As she blinked, he laughed: 'Yes, it's me. Why so astonished?'

By way of reply, she pointed to the window which, because of the heat, she had left opened. Looking at her watch, she saw that it was not yet five o'clock.

'Really,' he said; 'no later than that? So much the better; we are going to have a little chat.' And drawing up an armchair, he sat down at the foot of the bed, crossed his legs, settling himself there, as he used to do five years before, in her mother's easy chair at the Hôtel de la Tranquillité. He held a thick bundle of letters, on which was written, in a large script, 'For the First Consul, for him personally'.

When Laure suggested that he had other more important things to attend to, that other competent persons could relieve him of going through his mail, he answered, 'By and by, yes; but not at present. I must answer everything. At the beginning of the return to order I must not be ignorant of anything that needs attention, especially of any complaint.'

She pointed to one large letter, the bad handwriting in which it was addressed suggesting that it came from someone not accustomed to writing letters. Why not leave that one to a secretary? Napoleon opened the letter and carefully read through its three pages. 'Well,' he said, 'this letter proves that I do right in seeing things with my own eyes. Here, read it.'

It was from a widow whose son had been killed in Egypt. Her husband, too, had died on service, and she had no pension. She had written more than ten letters to the Minister of War, the First Consul and his secretary, and had received nothing in reply.

'You now see why I should attend to everything myself,' said Bonaparte. He got up, fetched a pen from the table, and marked the letter, possibly for his secretary Bourrienne's attention. He resumed his reading. 'Ah, here is a trap,' he suddenly exclaimed, taking up several envelopes, all heavily scented and marked with the all-necessary words, 'For the First Consul personally'. Opening the last of them, he burst into laughter. 'It is a declaration of love,' he said, 'from a beautiful lady, who says she has loved me from the day she saw me present the treaty of Camp Formio to the Directory. All I have to do is to tell the sentry on the Bougival gate to let pass a lady dressed in white who will give the word "Napoleon".' He paused. 'Now when is this for? My word, it's for tonight!'

'My God,' said Laure, genuinely alarmed at the prospect, 'you're not going?'

Bonaparte looked straight at her, 'What does it matter to you if I do? What harm can it do me?'

Laure was astonished at the questions. What if the woman was in the pay of his enemies?

Bonaparte looked at her again, and laughed, 'I said it as a joke. Do you think me so simple as to fall for this sort of thing? I get such letters every day, suggesting assignations at the Luxembourg, at the Tuileries. And I do the same thing with them all,' and approaching the table, he addressed the letters to the Minister of Police.

A clock struck. 'God, it's six,' he said. Stepping up to her bed, he collected together his papers. Then, tweaking her foot beneath the bedclothes, and smiling in his good humour, he went away, singing in a voice which contrasted so unfavourably with his normal sonorous manner of speaking—

> *Non, non, z'il est impossible*
> *D'avoir un plus aimable enfant.*
> *Un plus aimable? Ah! si vraiment. . . .**

It was his favourite song.

About nine o'clock that evening Bonaparte came up to Laure in the drawing room and whispered in her ear, 'I am going to the Bougival gate.' Laure took her cue from his tone. 'I do not believe a word of it,' she said, smiling. He passed into the billiard room.

The following morning she was again awakened, this time by a knock on her maid's door, the room she occupied adjoining Laure's. The First Consul entered, as before with a sheaf of papers and a packet of letters. He again asked her pardon for waking her three hours too early. He drew up his chair, set to reading his mail, addressing her a word from time to time. Then, collecting up his papers, he pinched her foot beneath the bedclothes, and took his leave, singing as before in high good humour. When he had gone, Laure called her maid, who had not long been with her, and without going into explanations told her that she was not to open her outer door to the knock of anyone who should come so early in the morning. 'But, Madame, if it is the First Consul?' 'I will not be wakened so early by anyone, not even the First Consul. Do as I say.'

The next day, Sunday, resembled the others. Bonaparte joined the the party for a drive in the direction of Butard, accompanying Laure in the carriage. On their return, when they were at the pavilion in the park, Bonaparte announced that he planned a breakfast there for Laure in two day's time. They would have a little hunting party; it would do him good. 'Then the day after tomorrow, Tuesday, I give

---

*Oh! no, there surely never breathed
　A sweeter child; I could not wish
　To meet with one more charming. Ah! if truly. . . .

you all a rendezvous here at ten,' he said as he left them in the hall of the château.

That night, on reaching her room, Laure repeated the orders of the morning to her maid. She was in low spirits. She missed Junot, who had been kept for some days in Paris. At Malmaison she was kindly treated, she liked being there, but she wanted her own home, her mother and friends. She felt lonely and obscurely threatened. She burst into tears. At length, worn out with weeping, she fell asleep. Next morning she woke early, when the light scarcely penetrated the Venetian blinds. She fancied she heard a noise, but it was nothing. Getting out of bed, she went into her maid's room and tried the outer door. It was unlocked, with the key on the other side. She withdrew the key, and closing the door, locked it from inside and took the key. Then she returned to bed. She was angry with the maid; she was determined to put a stop to these early morning calls; already tongues must be wagging. Sleep did not come to her. Looking at her watch she saw that the hand pointed to six, when she heard the First Consul's footsteaps in the corridor. After a moment he knocked on the door, then knocked again louder. This wakened the maid, who told him that Laure had taken the key.

When the sound of his footsteps died away, Laure lay back with a feeling of relief. But when she thought over what had happened, tears came to her eyes. She looked on the First Consul as a brother, rather a father; she had known him since she was a child; he was the protector, the support of their family. Junot owed everything to him, and regarded him with feelings of the most tender affection. Yet why had she this mistrust which would deprive him of the pleasure, amid all his work and preoccupation, of a few moments in the company of a girl whom he had known since birth. But having taken her resolution she became more tranquil. Having told the maid to shut the door from her room, she had fallen again into a sound sleep, when the door was flung open and she saw the First Consul.

'Are you afraid of being assassinated, then?' he asked, with none of the previous good humour in his voice.

His tone roused in Laure a spirit of resistance. She told him, that having risen early, she had taken the key from the maid's door, wishing her room to be entered by her own door. Bonaparte's look of anger and suspicion prevented her telling him her resolution.

'Tomorrow is our hunting party at Butard,' he said; 'you haven't forgotten it since last night, have you? I shall come myself to wake you.

You are not among a horde of Tartars; there is no need to barricade yourself in. You see that all your precautions against your old friend have not prevented him from reaching you.'

He went away; this time not singing. Laure called her maid to ask her why she had not obeyed her orders. Bonaparte had opened the door with a master key, and she had not dared to stop him.

All day Laure was in a state of irresolution as to what she ought to do. She first thought of asking Hortense for a carriage to return to Paris, but second thoughts showed her that this would require explanations. With Mme Bessières it would be the same. There was no one in the house to whom she could turn. Duroc, with whom she was very friendly, was absent in Lorraine. She went up to her room, perplexed and downcast. Suddenly the door opened and in came Junot. She flung herself in his arms and again burst into tears. Junot asked her tenderly what was the matter. Laure gave out that it was his absence and her desire to return to Paris that had upset her. She could rejoin him when Mme Bonaparte returned, he told her. It would not be long. She did not press the matter, for she had already made up her mind.

Junot, like other serving officers whose duty was in Paris, was under orders not to remain away from his post for the night. The Paris visitors usually took their leave in the evening, when the household at Malmaison was about to retire for the night. The First Consul had left word that Junot was to stay for dinner. After dinner they talked— the *savant* Monge was present; and then they played billiards. Bonaparte and Laure had a game of chess. When it was time for Junot to leave, she asked him to accompany her to her room, in the pretext of giving him a letter for her mother. There she had little difficulty in persuading him to spend the night with her, and to return to Paris early in the morning without his general's knowing. Before going to bed, she double-locked the maid's door and shut her own, leaving the key on the outside.

Laure woke as the church clock at Reuil was striking five. It was a beautiful summer's morning. Junot was sleeping, but her fears of what was about to take place made all sleep impossible for her. She lay there, waiting. The Reuil clock had just struck five-thirty when she heard the First Consul's footsteps in the corridor. The door of her room was opened unceremoniously and Bonaparte came in.

'What, still asleep, Mme Junot, and on a hunting day! I told you that—' and he saw Junot's figure in the bed at Laure's side.

Junot, suddenly wakened, raised himself on his elbow, regarding his general more with astonishment than with fears for himself. 'Why, General, what are you doing in a lady's bedroom at this hour?' he asked, in a tone of perfect good humour.

'I came to wake Mme Junot for the chase, but'—and he looked pointedly at Laure—'I find her provided with an alarm earlier than myself. And I did not expect to find Parisian contraband here.'

'My General,' said Junot, 'if ever a fault deserved pardon, it is mine. If you had seen how this little siren worked for more than an hour last night to seduce me, you would forgive me.'

The First Consul smiled, but his smile was forced. 'I absolve you, then, entirely. It is Mme Junot who shall be punished. To show you that I am not angry, you too must come to the hunt. Have you a horse?' When Junot replied that he had come by carriage, Bonaparte said that his groom Jardin would provide him with one. 'Come, Mme Junot, he said, 'get up, show a leg.' And he left them. The naive Junot, when Bonaparte had gone, was full of his praises. 'What a man!'

When they came down to the party assembled in front of the château, they found the First Consul already seated in a small phaeton. 'Mme Junot,' he said, with a smile she did not like, 'will you honour me with your company?' She got in, and they set off, surrounded by members of the hunt on horseback. Until they were out of the park, Bonaparte was silent, watching the horsemen. Then he turned to Laure, 'You think yourself very clever, don't you?' When she did not reply, he repeated his question.

'I do not credit myself with extraordinary sense,' she replied, 'but I am not simple.'

'Simple, no; but you are a fool.'

'The explanation is easy, General. I love Junot; we are married. There is surely nothing wrong for a husband and wife to sleep together.'

'You know that he had his orders. And you knew, too, that my orders are to be obeyed.'

'They do not concern me. When the Consuls let us know their will as to the degree of intimacy that shall hold between a married couple, and the number of days and hours that shall be allowed for their interviews, then I shall think of submitting. Until then, I confess, General, my own good pleasure shall be my only law.'

Bonaparte's tone took on a note of asperity, not unmixed with curiosity, 'You have no reason, then, beyond your love for your husband for making him stay?'

'No, General.'

'You are lying.'

'General—'

'Yes, you have told a lie. I understand your motives. You distrust me. You should not.'

'And if I have acted from a different motive from the distrust you speak of—if I consider that your visit at such an hour to the bedroom of a young woman of my age might compromise me in the eyes of the other people staying in the house?'

Bonaparte's expression at this moment betrayed a rapid succession of feelings. 'If that is so,' he said at length, 'why did you not tell me of your uneasiness?'

'There I was perhaps wrong,' Laure replied. 'I should have considered that you knew me as a child, that our families have long known each other, that you once had some feeling for my mother'—at this, Bonaparte turned his head aside. 'Above all, I should have reminded you on the second or third of your visits that I am Junot's wife—Junot, who loves you perhaps more than he loves me. This morning, when I heard your step on the corridor, I confess I was afraid of your anger. But, looking at Junot's scars, received in part for your glory, I felt that you could never cause Junot suffering.'

'You are reading me almost a homily. Who talks of hurting Junot? Why did you not speak to me?'

'And how was I to do so? Yesterday morning you forced your way into my room in a way that was unworthy of you. By my actions I had shown you that your visits were unwelcome. Your humour then was not such to invite confidences. I was then left to my own resources, and perhaps my judgement has been wrong.'

'Is there none of your mother's advice in all this?'

'My mother, General, how could she have advised me?'

'You could have written.'

'General, I have not written to my mother. How could I have told her that I felt unsafe under your roof?'

'Mme Junot, you have known me long enough to know that the continuance of my friendship for you is not helped by the way you are now speaking. All that is wanting is that you should have let Junot know how you have acted.' And he looked fixedly at her.

'I shall not reply to that remark, General,' Laure said, not disguising her annoyance. 'If you allow me neither sense nor judgement, allow me at least the heart not to hurt a person I know, and you know also.'

'Again!' and he struck the side of the carriage with his fist, 'Again. Keep quiet!'

'No, General, I shall not. I shall say what I have to say. I ask you to believe that neither my mother, my husband, nor any of my friends has been told of what has passed between us. I impute no ill intentions to you, and it would be stupid of me to complain to your friendship because it might compromise me. But I thought proper to put a stop to it. No doubt my youth has led me into error—I see this, since I have displeased you. I am sorry for it—but that is all I can say.'

They had nearly arrived; the hounds, the horns and voices could be heard. The First Consul's sombre expression relaxed somewhat. 'And you give me your word of honour that Junot knows nothing of this foolish affair?' he said.

'Good heavens, General, how could you think such an idea, knowing Junot as you do? If I had told him, neither he nor I would have been here this morning. You know Junot well enough for that, don't you?'

Bonaparte made no answer, but played with his fingers on the side of the carriage. At last he turned towards Laure. 'You will not believe then, that I meant you no harm?'

'On the contrary, General, I am so convinced of it, that I can assure you my feeling for you, a feeling I have had since childhood, and my admiration for you are in no way lessened. And I give you my hand as a pledge of it,' and she held out her hand.

But Bonaparte, half smiling and gently shaking his head, refused to take it. She was hurt by his refusal.

'Well, we are in disagreement, then,' she said, 'because you think all the blame is on your side. Like a Corsican "you want to let the beard grow, and wear the dagger", because you have hurt me.'

For a moment he stared straight ahead, then, taking off his glove, he extended to her his small hand: 'Be assured of my friendship, Mme Junot. If you had wanted to, you could have strengthened it. But your early education is too strong for you. You have been taught to be unfriendly towards me; you do not like me—'

'I take the liberty of interrupting you, General, to ask you not to speak in this way. You hurt me—the more so that your arguments and your inferences are both untrue'.

The First Consul was looking at the hounds that the kennelmen were leading in pairs; then he turned towards Laure. 'You are going?' he asked.

'On our return from the hunt, General. It is nothing to do with what has happened. I had a letter from my mother this morning. She is unwell. Junot will take me back with him.'

'And when do you return here?'

'Whenever I am wanted, for my part, General. But you may dispose of my room. I shall never occupy it again.'

'As you will. You are right to go. You and I would not meet with much pleasure at present. Yes, you are right to go. Jardin, my horse!' And opening the door himself, he jumped down from the carriage. Mounting, he quickly rode away.

Laure visited Malmaison again some time after Mme Bonaparte's return from Plombières. The First Consul greeted her cordially enough, but she could see that he was still under the impression that she had been prompted in all she had done in the last days of her stay. She left it to time to soften the impress of the unpleasantness.

Laure Junot was already pregnant with her first child at the time of her stay at Malmaison in the summer of 1801; in the autumn she gave birth to a daughter, whom they called, after Mme Bonaparte, Josephine. In the same year the Concordat with Rome had opened again the churches. The First Consul and his wife were god-parents to the child, Josephine Junot being Bonaparte's first god-daughter. The ceremony, which took place at Saint-Cloud, was performed with imposing state by Cardinal Caprara, the Apostolic Nuncio. At the same time the son of General and Mme Lannes was christened Napoleon. The day following the baptism Mme Bonaparte sent Laure a christening gift of a necklace, consisting of several rows of fine pearls of the size of large currants, the clasp being composed of a single pearl of the purest whiteness. The First Consul's gift was equally princely; it was of the receipted purchase-contract of a magnificent hôtel in the Champs-Elysées. This was worth two hundred thousand francs. In addition to this, in order that the Junots should be able to live in a state suitable to the post of Commandant of Paris, Bonaparte gave Junot the sum of three hundred thousand francs, against the receipts that accrued from the gaming tables.

Shortly after Josephine's birth the health of Mme Permon (or rather Mme Bois-Cressy, since she had married her old admirer), which had always been delicate, gave cause for grave concern. Laure, who adored her mother and saw her almost every day, was shocked by her death, which occurred at the close of 1801. Great as was her love for her mother, she was young and loved life, and her position in Consular society soon demanded her presence, so that her period of mourning was not prolonged.

The signing of the Treaty of Amiens in March 1802 brought crowds of foreigners, particularly English and Russians, flocking to Paris, which seemed at that time to have gone a long way towards fulfilling the First Consul's desire of making it the capital of the civilised world. Such was the interest of Englishmen in the changes in France, Mme Junot tells us, that they would come to France only for a few hours, go to the parade and return to England. One of the English to come to Paris, to see for himself the regeneration of France, was Charles James Fox. Laure first met him at the Tuileries, but was disappointed in his appearance. She reported how 'Mr Fox's aspect did not at the first glance seem to justify his prodigious fame; his demeanour was even ordinary; and for the first time I saw him, dressed in a dark grey coat, and with his head somewhat inclined, he gave me the idea of a good Devonshire farmer—a man incapable of any pretension.' Her opinion of Fox was changed after he had dined at her house: 'But how rapidly were those opinions put to flight when the course of conversation brought out the energies of his mind. His countenance became animated with the first sentence of interest that passed his lips, and gradually brightened with increasing intelligence till it was absolutely fiery and sparkling. His voice, subdued at first, rose in modulation till it burst upon the ear in thunder; and the same man, who, but a few minutes before, had appeared the most commonplace of mortals, was now an object of intense admiration.'

Among others of the English whom she met were Lord and Lady Cholmondeley, Lord Yarmouth, the Duchess of Gordon and her daughter Lady Georgiana, Lord and Lady Conyngham, Colonel James Green (who became a friend of Junot), and Lady E. Foster, afterwards the Duchess of Devonshire. Of the Russians Laure Junot was acquainted with the Countess Divoff, Mme Dolgoroucki and Mme Demidoff, who became a close friend. The foreigners were astonished to find in this wife of the Commandant of Paris, the republican general, a beautiful young woman, with the grace and fine manners of the *ancien régime*, but with an intelligence, breadth of interest, and a knowledge of those places in Paris most likely to attract an educated foreigner, to which few of those ladies of that former society could aspire. For after her marriage Laure had set herself to fill the deficiencies in her education by visiting museums and galleries and conversing with artists, scientists, literary men and *savants*, which her excellent mind and attentive memory put to the best use. During her mother's illness she had to forgo these activities, but in the period of mourning she had resumed them. The First Consul, hearing of her extra-mural occupations and approving them, suggested to Laure that she should conduct distinguished foreigners around Paris, to show them those sights that made it the queen of cities. 'You are the wife of the Commandant of Paris', said Bonaparte; 'it would be an agreeable way of doing the honours of the city to show your friends that we are worth the trouble they take in visiting us.' These visits began with the Louvre, where they were shown around by the director M.Denon, who was then engaged in restoring, hanging and displaying the masterpieces of painting and sculpture ransacked from the galleries of Italy and the Low Countries by the victorious armies of the Republic. 'Saving them from barbarians' was Laure's way of describing this wholesale pillage. In the Gallery of Apollo, which had just been opened, they saw the drawings of such masters as Raphael, Michelangelo, Leonardo da Vinci, Correggio, Guercino, the Caracci, Perugino, Tintoretto and others. The painters David and Robert explained to the parties their views on the nature of this art. At the National Library they were conducted on a tour of the cabinet of medals and antiques by Laure's learned friend M. Millin; in the museum of armoury they were shown the exhibits, which included the armour of Joan of Arc and Charles the Bold, by the Superintendent, M.Regnier; and in the main section of the library M. Langles displayed the rare books and the precious manuscripts. Besides the museums and galleries, Laure took her guests to see the *camera obscura* of M.Charles, to visit the Gobelins manufactory, the steam engine at Chaillot which raised the Perrier waters, and the barriers of the city. And she conducted them further afield, to Jouy, Virginie and Versailles. Laure's English and Russian friends, who were joined by the Austrian ambassador M. von Cobentzel, were much impressed by the width of her interests and knowledge and by the intelligence and acuity with which she discussed questions with acknowledged experts in their own fields. They thought her quite remarkable, which indeed she was.

In the spring of 1802 the Senate by a *senatus consultum* prolonged the term of the First Consul's office by a further ten years. At this time the Junots decided that they should celebrate this event and show their gratitude to Bonaparte by inviting him and his wife to luncheon in their new house on the Champs-Elysées. The First Consul accepted the invitation on the understanding that he, Duroc and Junot should be the only men present in the company of some twenty-five of his generals' young wives. In the event Bonaparte and Duroc were unable to attend but Mme Bonaparte and her daughter Mme Louis Bonaparte, Mme Bacciochi and Mme Murat came, as did the other young wives of Junots brothers-in-arms. In her description of these women Laure gives that little touch of malice which with the years would become characteristic of her: 'Some were very agreeable, and all in the beauty of freshness and youth; so that no spectacle could be prettier than that our table exhibited, when surrounded on this occasion by from twenty-five to thirty young and cheerful faces, of which not more than one or two could be called ordinary. Mme Bonaparte was an astonishing woman, and must have formerly been extremely pretty, for though no longer in the first bloom of youth, her personal charms were still striking. Had she but possessed teeth, I do not say ugly or pretty, but only teeth, she would have certainly outvied nearly all the ladies of the Consular Court.' After lunch Mme Bonaparte suggested to Laure a drive in the Bois de Boulogne, which they took accompanied by General Suchet and his brother. In the course of this outing Mme Bonaparte said that she was commissioned by Bonaparte (as she always called him) to make the Junots a present of a hundred thousand francs for furnishing their house. 'It is ready,' she added; 'Estève has orders to hold it at your disposal. For it is of no use, Bonaparte says, to give them a house unless it be made habitable.'

When the furnishing was completed, they gave a grand ball as a house-warming, and on this occasion the First Consul was present. He insisted that Junot should act as cicerone and show him over the house, which he visited from cellars to attics. Bonaparte stayed until one o'clock, which was a late hour for him, and for this honour they were appropriately grateful. The expenses of this style of living were prodigious, but, relying on the generosity of the First Consul, neither Junot nor Laure counted the cost, and money just slipped through their fingers. If Junot aped the *grand signeur*, Laure's expenditure was little less than his. Her upbringing did not assist in teaching her the principles of ordinary economy; like her mother, she did not bother her head where the money came from, so long as her style of living was un-affected.

On Laure's fête-day, 10 August, Junot gave a party for her at Petit-Bièvre. Taking advantage of the beautiful summer weather, dinner was laid for seventy guests outside on the lawns, the tables grouped at the foot of an immense plane tree, where branches and leaves provided a pleasant shade. The flower beds were bright with flowers; in their cages birds sang; later lanterns and devices gave the air of a fête. There was music. In the evening they danced on the lawns. Afterwards Ruggieri put on a magnificent display of fireworks, and the guests admired on a pavilion, where Laure kept her turtle doves, a banner lit by torches on which Junot had had written a gallant quatrain, composed by himself:

> *Quand ma Laure vient visiter*
> *Ses amoureuses tourterelles,*
> *C'est pour leur apprendre d'aimer*
> *L'art charmant qu'elle sait mieux qu'elles.**

It all had the air of the eighteenth century, of a fête given by the Duchess of Maine at nearby Sceaux, rather than the entertainment of a general of the Republic for his wife—a general who, little more than ten years before, had left his father's humble house in Burgundy to volunteer as a private soldier in the regiment of the Côte-d'Or. To the jealous eyes of the Faubourg Saint-Germain it would suggest the extravagance in poor taste of *nouveaux riches*.

The life of the Junots at Petit-Bièvre, however, was not all gaiety. An event took place there about this time that brought sadness to Laure, and a foretaste of the future. The château of Bièvre had been recently taken by an Englishwoman, Lady Clavering, who had with her a young French former *émigré*, the Comte de Las Cases. The lady was attracted by her neighbour, this dashing young general, dressed in his splendid uniform of colonel of hussars. She invited the Junots to her house. In a short space of time Junot's intimacy with her ripened into an affair, his first infidelity since his marriage. When Laure learned of it, she wept and remonstrated with her husband. Junot pleaded that his lapse was no serious matter, that she was wrong to weep over it, that he loved her, and her alone. It ended by her forgiving him.

The gratitude of Frenchmen to Bonaparte for securing peace abroad and for the restoration of order at home had been marked by

---

*When my Laure comes to visit her amorous turtle doves, it is to teach them to love the charming art that she knows better than they.

prolonging his First Consulship. But this did not satisfy many, and now, urged on by Cambacérès in the Council of State, the question was put to the people in a plebescite whether Napoleon Bonaparte should be made Consul for life. The result was an overwhelming affirmative, 3,568,885 votes being cast in favour, and only 8374 against. Thus was the monarchy restored, for not only retaining his powers for life, Napoleon (he now adopted this form) had the right to name his successor. Despite Junot's sincere attachment to his General, he was equally sincerely a republican at heart. One day, before the plebescite, when Junot and his wife were dining with the First Consul at Saint-Cloud, Laure noticed that her husband's usually open countenance was overcast on his returning to Mme Bonaparte's drawing room after a half-hour's interview with Bonaparte. In the carriage on their way back to Paris he seemed thoughtful and sad, and at first he declined to answer her questioning as to the reasons for his abstraction. At length he told her of his conversation with the First Consul. The latter had asked him what the opinion in Paris and the country was in respect of the life Consulship. Junot answered the truth—that opinion was favourable, but he said it in a way that aroused Bonaparte's suspicions. 'You tell me this,' he said, 'as if it had been just the reverse. Approved by all France, am I to find censors only in my dearest friends?' These words, and others which followed, cut Junot to the quick. He had to take to his bed.

Some days afterwards the Junots were invited to luncheon at Saint-Cloud, and to bring with them little Josephine. Laure went alone, and Bonaparte enquiring why Junot was absent, she frankly told him the cause of his illness. Bonaparte listened and looked at her for some moments without speaking. Then, kissing Josephine's dimpled arm, giving her a smart tap on the cheek, pulling her nose and embracing her, all in a minute—he left the room abruptly. That evening Laure was relating to Junot the day's events, sitting at his bedside, when to their surprise in walked the First Consul, unannounced. After some conversation, he asked Junot to show him around those parts of the house that were already furnished. Junot got up, and did what he was asked. When they had returned to his room, Bonaparte said, 'I hope this little journey around your domains has radically cured you?' Before leaving, he invited Junot to lunch with him at Saint-Cloud on the following day. Junot was quite recovered by the morning, went to Saint-Cloud, and returned enchanted.

Some time after these events, the uneasy peace that had existed between England and France was broken and hostilities began between the two countries. Lord Whitworth, the English Ambassador, left Paris on 15 March 1803. One morning, at five o'clock, when day had scarcely dawned, an order came for Junot to attend Napoleon at Malmaison without delay. On his arrival he found the First Consul in one of those states of agitation that could be terrible for those present. He gave Junot the order that all the English in Paris were to be arrested, without exception, by seven that evening. The Temple, Montaigu, Laforce, the Abbaye—there were prisons enough. Never for a moment overstepping the bounds of deference, Junot pointed out the unwisdom of so precipitate a measure. But Napoleon would brook no criticism of his policies or delay in carrying out his commands.

'Lannes and you take strange liberties,' he said, with anger. 'Even Duroc considers himself licensed to preach to me. But by heavens, gentlemen, I will let you see that I can put my cap on the wrong way. Lannes has found it out already, and I suspect is not much pleased with eating oranges at Lisbon. For yourself, Junot, do not trust too much to my friendship. The day when I doubt yours will destroy mine.'

The dialogue was prolonged, but all that Junot could obtain by way of mitigation was that the English should not be imprisoned, but, treated as prisoners of war, their movements should be restricted to the city or town in which they found themselves.

Junot had enemies at court, above all Fouché and Savary; and the result of their reports of some scenes of his violence in Paris, including possibly an exaggerated account of the incident in the *glacier* Garchy's in rue de la Loi, taken together with what Napoleon saw as his less than total subjection to his will, had serious consequences for him. It may be that Napoleon, knowing his republican sentiments, wanted him out of the way while he was maturing in his mind the momentous steps he was about to take. At the end of 1803 he was relieved of his post as Commandant of Paris, which was given to Murat, and he was sent to Arras to take over the command of the training there of the reunited grenadiers. This was an important command, but after the splendid position he had held in Paris, it could only be seen as a disgrace. In February 1804 Laure, with Josephine, joined him in Arras, where they occupied the house once owned by the Prince of Condé. There Junot set about his training programme, bringing about some innovations, which received the warm approval of Napoleon. He made alterations to the soldiers' dress and equipment, and had them cut their hair, leaving off the custom of powdering it and wearing it in a queue. These reforms were later adopted throughout the army. Laure set up house, entertained, and constantly regretted Paris.

In Arras they heard of royalist plots against the life of the First Consul, then of the arrest of Georges Cadoudal, General Pichegru and others. The police, aware of what was going on, allowed the conspirators to come to Paris, and there arrested them. On 16 February General Moreau, the hero of Hohenlinden, was taken into custody, suspected of complicity in the plot. The police were mystified as to the identity of a stranger who had meetings with the conspirators in Paris; he was thought to be tall, young, and was said to be treated with marked deference by the others, all remaining standing in his presence. Suspicion fell on the young Duc d'Enghien, the only son of the Prince of Condé, who had served with his father and grandfather in the army of the *émigrés*, and was then living in retirement in Ettenheim in Baden, near the Rhine. Spies reported that he was sometimes absent from Ettenheim for periods of six days—time, it was thought, to travel to Paris, spend forty-eight hours in the city, and then return to Ettenheim. Orders were given for his arest. Disregarding the neutrality of his place of residence, a strong body of gendarmes crossed the Rhine, surrounded the house at Ettenheim, and seizing the Duc d'Enghien, conveyed him to Paris, to the Château of Vincennes. Under orders from Murat, as Commandant of Paris, and Savary, a court of colonels was hastily set up. Despite the fact that Napoleon had by that time evidence that the mysterious stranger was not the Duke, and despite the appeal for clemency of both Josephine and Mme de Rémusat, Napoleon was determined to make a terrible example. The original charge was speedily changed to one of bearing arms against France in the late war and preparing to join the new coalition against his country. He was found guilty, and an appeal for a personal interview with Napoleon was refused by Savary. The sentence was death. Allowing but a short time for him to prepare himself, the Duc d'Enghien was escorted out into the moat of the castle, where a firing party was drawn up, and a grave already dug. It was night, and a cold rain was falling. With the Duke was his dog, that had accompanied him from Ettenheim. At the sound of the volley the dog was terrified, then, seeing his master fall, he rushed up to him and licked the blood on his face. Finding there was no response, he let out a long howl.

Public opinion in Europe was shocked by this political murder. Napoleon later tried to exculpate himself, placing the blame for the Duc d'Enghien's death on Savary and Talleyrand, but at St Helena and in his will he acknowledged his personal responsibility, and said that if the choice had been given him again, he would have acted as he had. One wonders, if Junot had been Commandant of Paris, whether he could have dissuaded the First Consul from this senseless crime. He said afterwards to Laure that it was fortunate for his good name that he was at Arras.

It was felt in official circles that the most effective way to deal with conspiracies was to ensure the principle of heredity in the head of state. The Senate took the first step in beseeching Napoleon 'to complete his work by rendering it, like his glory, immortal'. Addresses coming in from all sides in a similar strain, Napoleon invited the Senate 'to make known to him its thoughts completely'. A *senatus consultum* granted to Napoleon the title of Emperor, the succession, in case he had no heirs, devolving in turn on the descendants of Joseph and Louis—Lucien and Jerome were debarred from the succession, having made marriages displeasing to the autocrat. A plebescite confirmed the nation's over-whelming approval of this change in the constitution. On 18 May 1804 it was decreed, with a curious twist of terminology, that 'The govern-ment of the Republic is confided to an emperor, who takes the title Emperor of the French.' The situation was well summed up by the *mot* of Georges Cadoudal, the brave Breton peasant, who was guillo-tined on 24 June for his share in the plot: 'We meant to give France a king and we have given her an emperor'. Napoleon's own way of putting it was that he had found the crown of France on the ground, and that he had picked it up with the point of his sword.

In the summer the Emperor came to Arras to review Junot's grena-diers. Junot had recently been created Grand Officer of the Legion of Honour, and almost immediately after he was given the Grand Cross. During almost the entire seven hours of manoeuvres Napoleon was on foot. Mounting his horse, he was about to take the salute, when he caught sight of Laure, who was on the arm of M.Maret. He sent Colonel Lafond to ask her to come nearer, so that she could see better. After the review he came up to her and asked how she liked Arras and whether she did not wish to return to Paris. Laure attributed the slight *gaucherie* of her replies to the novelty of pronouncing the words "Sire" and "Your Majesty". After the review Junot and his officers dined with the Emperor, where during the course of the dinner he complimented Junot on his work at Arras. By his friendliness it appeared that Junot was entirely reinstated in his good graces. 'Junot,' he said before departing, 'mention in tomorrow's order of the day that I am satisfied, extremely satisfied, with my brave grenadiers of Arras.'

In November orders came for Junot to relinquish his command, and to return to Paris with his family to be present at the imperial coronation.

FOUR

The Ambassadress

WHEN IN November 1804 Laure arrived back in Paris from Arras, she found their house in the Champs-Elysées invaded by Junot's family, who had come to witness the coronation. Paris was filled to capacity, the streets thronged by eager and lively crowds. In Notre-Dame the seats which had been allotted to the public were all taken, and a family of Laure's acquaintance from Artois were obliged to pay three hundred francs for a second-floor window on the route by which the procession was to pass from the Tuileries to the cathedral. Sightseers visited the work-rooms of Dallemagne, the embroiderer, to inspect the Emperor's train, where the crimson velvet, furnished by Lavacher, was being embroidered in gold and silver. They went on to Foncier's, the goldsmiths and jewellers, to inspect the crowns of the Emperor and Empress, and the Emperor's sword, the hilt of which was adorned with the famous diamond known as the Regent. Everyone repaired to the cathedral to see the magnificent decorations, the walls being hung with priceless tapestries, and to view the thrones for the Pope and Emperor and Empress, which had been placed at the farther end, before the high altar. The Emperor had gone to Fontainebleau to meet the Pope and to escort him to Paris, where he was lodged in the Tuileries in the Pavilion of Flora. The approaching ceremony had given an impetus to trade—tailors, couturiers, jewellers, florists, hotels, restaurants, touts and pimps all did a flourishing business.

Before daybreak on 2 December Paris was awake and in motion; hundreds of people had stayed up all night to obtain good places. It was a cold, wet morning. Many of the ladies, who were to be present in Notre-Dame, had got up to have their hair dressed at two o'clock in the morning, and then sat patiently in their chairs until it was time to complete their dressing. All had to be in their places by nine o'clock, when the imperial procession moved off from the Tuileries. Laure, accompanied by Mme Marmont, set out from the house at half-past

seven, leaving Junot, who was to carry one of the honours of Charlemagne, dressing himself in his robes. The behind-the-scene preparations
in the Tuileries were described by Mme de Rémusat, who was a lady-in-
waiting to Josephine: 'Before setting out for Notre-Dame, we were
admitted to the apartment of the Empress. Our attire was very
brilliant, but it paled before the magnificence of the dresses of the
Imperial family. The Empress especially, sparkling with diamonds,
and wearing her hair in countless curls, a style of the time of Louis XVI,
did not look more than twenty-five. She wore a white satin gown, and
a court mantle of the same material, both profusely embroidered in
mingled gold and silver. Her jewellery consisted of a diadem, a
necklace, earrings, and a girdle of diamonds of immense value, and all
this gorgeous attire was worn with her customary easy grace. Her
sisters-in-law were also adorned with a vast quantity of jewels. The
Emperor inspected each of us in turn, smiling at this luxury, which
was, like all the rest, a sudden creation of his sovereign will. His own
apparel was brilliant. He was to assume the Imperial robes at Notre-
Dame, but for the present he wore a French coat of red velvet, embroidered in gold, a white sash, a short cloak sewn with bees, a plumed
hat turned up in front with a diamond buckle, and the collar of the
Legion of Honour in diamonds. This superb dress became him well.
The whole court wore velvet cloaks embroidered in gold. It must be
acknowledged that we paraded ourselves a little for our common
amusement; but the spectacle was really beautiful.'

The setting for the actual ceremony had been arranged with the
advice of the painter David. Compared with the dullness of the day,
inside the cathedral was a blaze of light and a riot of colour. Napoleon
and Josephine, for the coronation, were to be surrounded by their
court, the foreign sovereigns and the high dignitaries of state. Laure
Junot, as the wife of the Emperor's principal aide-de-camp, was
therefore in a position to see everything clearly. 'The waving plumes
which adorned the hats of the Senators, Counsellors of State, and
Tribunes; the splendid uniforms of the military; the clergy in all their
ecclesiastical pomp; and the multitude of young and beautiful women,
glittering in jewels, and arrayed in that style of grace and elegance
which is seen only in Paris;—altogether presented a picture which has
perhaps rarely been equalled, and certainly never excelled.' The Pope
arrived first, and as he advanced with great dignity to take his place
on the throne by the high altar, the choir sang the anthem *Tu es
Petrus*. The old man had long to wait in the cold before the firing of

cannon announced the departure of the imperial procession from the
Tuileries. There was cheering as the Emperor proceeded in his gilded
state coach, but it seemed to be in recognition of the splendid spectacle
presented rather than from spontaneous, heartfelt affection. (Joseph
Turquan relates that before the procession arrived an old member of
the National Convention, who had lost a leg at Hondschoote, was
passing along the quays lined by troops in a cabriolet, when he said
to his son, 'They are crowning an emperor'. Philarète Chasles was
never to forget with what bitterness and disdain his father uttered
those words.) On reaching Notre-Dame, Napoleon went into the
archbishop's palace to put on his robes of state, before entering the
cathedral. On his head he wore a simple laurel wreath. The ceremony
was long, and Laure from her place, which was within ten paces of
the Emperor, noticed that on several occasions he stifled a yawn. At
one moment he caught her eye, and she realised that he had seen her.
She wondered what was passing through his head at that moment. At
the point in the service, when the Pope said, 'Diffuse, O Lord, by my
hands, the treasures of Thy grace and benediction on Thy servant,
Napoleon, whom, in spite of our personal unworthiness, we this day
annoint Emperor in Thy name,' Laure thought that the Emperor
listened to the prayer 'with an air of pious devotion'. But his devotion
did not prevent him from showing in what light he held the Pope.
As is well known, Napoleon did not allow the Pope to crown him,
but taking the crown of Charlemagne from the altar, he lifted it up
and placed it on his own head. When it came the time to crown
Josephine, there was a slight contretemps. The Emperor's sisters had at
first refused to carry the train of the Empress, and had only complied
on the angry order of Napoleon. When Josephine had to walk from
the altar to the throne, the Princesses, who bore her train with an
evident ill-grace, so little supported it as to cause her almost to stumble.
The Emperor perceived it, and with a few sharp words brought them
back to their duty. At the conclusion of this part of the ceremony a
magnificent *Vivat* was sung by the full choir. Prayers followed. The
service seemed interminable. It was between two and three before the
imperial cortège left Notre-Dame, and the early winter's dusk had set
in before it finally reached the Tuileries.

Even before the coronation the formation of the imperial court
engrossed the attention of the Faubourg Saint-Germain, whose
members vied with each other in seeking those places which in their

eyes were their rightful and natural prerogative. Not only was there the court of the Empress Josephine, but there were also those of the Imperial Princes and Princesses. Later still there was to be that of Signora Laetizia, Madame Mère; but she had absented herself from the ceremony in Notre Dame, remaining in Rome with Lucien, who because of his marriage, was out of favour with the Emperor. Nevertheless, on the latter's order his mother is shown in David's official painting of the coronation ceremony.

A few days after the coronation Laure saw the Emperor at a ball given by M. de Talleyrand. Coming up to her in one of the small rooms off the ballroom, he asked, 'Why did you wear a black dress at the coronation? Was it in mourning? Tell me why did you choose that sombre, I may almost say sinister colour?'

'Your Majesty did not observe that the front of my dress was richly embroidered with gold, and that I wore my diamonds. Many others were wearing dark dresses. I am not a court lady, and therefore obliged to wear court dress.'

'Is that remark meant to convey an indirect reproach?' the Emperor asked. 'Are you like certain other women who sulk because they have not been appointed *dames du palais?* I don't like sulkiness and ill humour.'

'Sire, I have shown no ill humour, for I feel none. Junot has told me that when a husband is one of the military household, his wife cannot be a *dame du palais*.'

'Junot told you, did he? And how did he happen to mention it? Were you complaining? Are you affected with ambition? I hate ambitious women. But now tell me, were you not put out at not being appointed *dame du palais?* Answer me candidly—if a woman can be candid.'

'I will, Sire. But your Majesty won't believe me.'

'Come, come, let me have an answer.'

'Then I am not put out.'

'How? Why?'

'Because I am not one of those who easily wear the yoke; and your Majesty will probably frame the protocol for regulating the Court of the Empress on the model of a military code.'

'Not unlikely.' He smiled. 'However, I am satisfied. You have given me a good answer, and I shall not forget it.' Then, after a pause, he said, 'Poor Junot; did you observe how his feelings were moved at the coronation? He is a faithful friend. Who could have foreseen, when we were both at Toulon ten years ago, that we should live to see such a day as 2 December?'

'Perhaps Junot, Sire.' Laure's answer surprised the Emperor. He looked at her with an expression which could have been one of admiration, before he left her and moved on.

A few days later Junot returned home from the Tuileries to announce that the Emperor had proposed that he should conduct an embassy to Lisbon. He was disturbed at the prospect. Remembering Napoleon's remarks about Lannes and the oranges, he was not at all happy in the appointment. There were rumours of war in Eastern Europe, where there were fresh laurels to be won; he did not feel that he was cut out for a diplomat; all in all, as he said, he did not wish to go to take a siesta in Lisbon. Laure, who in reality dreaded the idea of leaving Paris, nevertheless tried to persuade her husband that the opportunity was an excellent one to show what he was capable of. Junot, in his dilemma, sought the advice of the Arch-chancellor, Cambacérès, who advised him to accept it, adding, 'My dear General, you must obey His Majesty.' And that is what finally Junot did, being charged with an additional secret and important mission to the Court of Madrid. The aim of French diplomacy at this period was to strengthen their alliance with Spain and to wean the Portuguese from the support of their ally England.

Before they left Paris, Laure had a private audience with Napoleon. He impressed on her the importance of her role as ambassadress, a point that had been considered in making the appointment. It must be her endeavour, he told her, to give the Spaniards and Portuguese a just idea of the manners of the imperial court. She was to be scrupulous in her behaviour to the émigrés, whom she would find at the courts she was to visit, and she was to be particularly careful not to ridicule the customs of the country, or of the court. He advised her to be circumspect, while appearing to be frank and open. 'When I say circumspect,' he said, 'I mean you must not gossip. The Queen of Spain will ask you questions about the Empress and the Princesses; you must be prudent in your answers. The interior of my family may be displayed to every eye, yet I do not wish that the portraits of my sisters should be sketched by a bad painter.' 'Your Majesty,' Laure replied, 'must be aware that I have no intention of doing anything that will be displeasing to you.' 'I know it. . . I know it. But you are satirical. You like to tell a good story. That is one thing that you must avoid.' He completed his instructions by telling her to entertain, to make her house in Lisbon as attractive as her one in Paris, when she was Mme la Commandante.

In Junot's audience he asked that should war break out the Emperor would recall him. The memory of his missing the battle of Marengo still rankled. The Emperor promised to do this. The Junots set out from Paris on Shrove Tuesday 1805. They took with them Josephine; their second daughter, Constance, being a baby and too young to travel, was left in Paris in the charge of a competent nurse. When they passed the barriers, Laure's heart was heavy, but as they rolled along the tree-lined roads her thoughts became more cheerful; she was twenty and she was an ambassadress of France. Junot was the first ambassador that Napoleon had sent abroad since the coronation, and orders were given that he be received as befitted his rank and ambassadorial status. In every town through which they passed they were saluted with the firing of cannon or musketry, and received with adulatory addresses from the mayors and prefects. On their arrival at Bayonne, Junot found orders that demanded his immediate setting out on horseback for Madrid, leaving Laure to proceed more sedately with the carriage, escorted by M. de Rayneval and de Cherval. To relieve the monotony of the journey and to stretch her limbs, Laure from time to time got out of the carriage and walked by the roadside, picking the wild flowers she found there. Her companions were surprised to see her carefully preserve these specimens, each flower being pressed and labelled with its Latin botanical name. During the halts she took out her sketch book.

They reached Madrid on 10 March, and were met by Junot in company with the French ambassador General Beurnonville. The question of a house for them had presented difficulties. The size of Junot's own staff precluded their staying at the French embassy, and the *posadas* in Madrid at that period were scarcely habitable. The difficulty had been overcome in Paris by the offer of one of their friends, Alfonso Pignatelli, of his house in the Calle del Clavel, although he warned them that it was only a small bachelor establishment. To her pleased surprise Laure found it delightful, in appearance like an English house, with excellent furniture, a fine collection of pictures and French bronzes and porcelain. Immediately on her arrival in Madrid she was visited by several of the court ladies, who showed her every kindness and attention—the Duchesse of Ossuna and her two daughters, the Marquise de Santa Cruz and the Marquise de Camarasa; the Marquise d'Arizza, formerly the Duchess of Berwick,

and the Marquise de Santiago. It was arranged that she was to be
presented *en confidencia*—that is, without the formality of full court dress.

The Court was at Aranjuez, and there she went on 23 March to be
presented to King Charles IV and Queen Maria Luisa on the following
day. After the barren chalk plains of New Castile, Laure was charmed
with Aranjuez, with its luxuriant fertility—everywhere verdure,
flowers and trees laden with fruit. The Tagus surrounded the royal
palace and formed a pretty, artificial cascade in front of the terrace
beneath the windows. The water was so close that the King could
enjoy fishing from the terrace. For her presentation she wore a dress
such as she might wear at the Tuileries, and a diamond tiara. The long
white gloves which she had put on were removed, much to her
resentment, at the door of the royal apartments by the *camerara-mayor*,
it being forbidden by etiquette to wear gloves in the presence of their
Majesties. The Queen questioned her closely about the Empress
Josephine—how she dressed, did she wear rouge, did she wear artificial
flowers. During her audience, which was a long one, she noticed a
man of about thirty-five who lounged on a sofa at the other end of the
room, idly playing with a curtain tassel that was within his reach. It
was the royal favourite, Manuel Godoy, the Prince of Peace.

In her *Memoirs* Laure tells an anecdote of Godoy, at a time when he
was superseded as the Queen's lover by a young man in the guards
named Mayo. The Prince of Peace was indignant at Mayo's success,
but the latter was in possession, and as it was difficult to eject him, he
took his revenge in other ways. 'One day, when he was on a balcony
looking into the courtyard at La Granja (San Ildefonso) with the King
and Queen, a carriage drove up drawn by four horses, with servants
and outriders in splendid liveries—in short, the equipage was fit for a
prince. "Hallo," said the King, "who have we here? Why, it is Mayo,"
and with great astonishment the King looked alternately at Maria
Luisa and the *privado*. "I have observed for some time," he added,
"that Mayo lives in great style. The other day I saw him in the Prado
with an equipage more splendid than yours, Manuelito. What does
this mean?" "Oh, nothing extraordinary," replied the Prince of
Peace, casting a glance at the Queen, who, firm as she was, trembled
lest Manuel Godoy should be jealous; but he was no such fool, he had
more sense. "The thing is easily explained," he said to the King, "a
foolish old woman is smitten with him, and gives him as much money
as he wants." "Indeed," said the King, "and who is this old woman;
is it the Marchioness of Santiago?" The Prince thought this sufficient

punishment, and changed the conversation. This was not a difficult matter with poor Charles IV. It was only necessary to say that a dog was running past and the thing was accomplished.'

Laure could not help contrasting the purposelessness of the lives of the Spanish monarchs with the creative activity that went on around Napoleon. Every day the King hunted and every evening there was a concert in his private apartment: the King himself played the violin and took part, whether it was in a quartet by Haydn or a piece by Boccherini. Leading performers were brought in to play with the King. Olivieri, the first violin of the Lisbon Opera, was one day present, when there was some confusion over the playing of a *tutti* passage. Olivieri ventured to point out to the king that the fault was his, he had gone on without pausing for the three bars' rest in his score. The simple-minded monarch appeared astonished, and then laying down his bow, said in Italian by way of excuse, '*I re non aspettano mai*'—Kings never wait for anyone.

On the same afternoon as her presentation to the King and Queen Laure was presented to the Prince and Princess of the Asturias. She was most interested to meet the latter—who was a daughter of the Queen of Naples and an attractive and intelligent young woman—by reason of the unfortunate position of the young couple, who as heirs to the throne were treated as if they did not exist by Godoy. Laure was enchanted with her reception. Etiquette prescribed that she should call on the *camerara-mayor*, and this visit she carried out a few days later. While Junot was engaged with the Prince of Peace in the negotiations to do with his mission, Laure saw all that Madrid had to offer of interest to a curious visitor. Every evening they dined with General Beuronville at the embassy. Junot having fulfilled his task of securing Spain's loyalty as an ally, they left Madrid on 29 March 1805.

As they crossed from Spain into Portugal the salute of guns, which was fired in their honour at Badajoz, the birthplace of the Prince of Peace, was answered by welcoming salvoes from the Portuguese frontier town of Elvas. On Holy Thursday, at four in the afternoon, they reached Aldea Galega, a little town on the Tagus opposite Lisbon, where a charming villa had been put at their disposal by their banker, a French merchant in Lisbon, who was introduced to them by M.Serrurier, the French Consul. After the severe, often desolate, countryside of Spain, Laure was delighted with her first glimpses of Portugal, so fresh and smiling, so green, so blue from the Lusitanian sky, which was reflected in the sparkling waters of the Tagus. The next morning they walked on the banks of the Tagus, admiring the splendid panorama of river and Lisbon built on its hills, and awaiting the arrival of the Queen's *escaleres*, the state barges. The *escaleres* arriving, Laure was struck with the neat appearance of the rowers, who were all dressed in white, with black velvet caps ornamented in front with the arms of Portugal in silver. Laure stepped aboard the Prince Regent's barge, accompanied by Junot, M. de Rayneval, first secretary of the embassy, M. Lageard de Cherval and Colonel Laborde, Junot's principal aide-de-camp. Her daughter Josephine, her nurse, and other members of their staff followed in the succeeding barges. The crossing between Aldea Galega and Lisbon took nearly two hours, as the crews had orders to show the visitors different aspects of the city from the water. They landed between Belem and the quay of Sodres, to be greeted by a Portuguese grandee, the Count de Castro Marino, who was to introduce Junot to the Prince Regent. The latter was head of state in place of the mad Queen. Junot and Laure were much amused by the absurdities of Portuguese court etiquette, and she had a bet with him that he would not get through the day without laughing. Three carriages were drawn up; Junot and the count entered the first; M. de Rayneval and M. de Laborde were requested to ride in the third; the second proceeded empty. Laure, whom etiquette required to step ashore five minutes after the ambassador, followed with the remaining staff in carriages drawn each by six horses, but taking a different route from that taken by the ambassador. She arrived first, which pleased her, as she was curious to see Junot alight from his carriage at their hôtel.

One of the ceremonies at the court of Portugal was that the ambassador, immediately on arrival in Lisbon, should offer a collation to the person who was to introduce him at court. Laure stationed herself near a door, where she could observe the dining room. She described the scene in her *Memoirs*: 'Their excellencies gravely ascended the grand staircase of the hôtel, bowing to each other at every door, the Count de Castro Marino keeping on the left of the ambassador with scrupulous care. In this manner they ascended from one flight of stairs to the other, bowing and bowing until they reached the reception room. Here they each made a most profound bow, looking for all the world like two Chinese mandarins. After a little pause the *maître d'hôtel* entered to announce to their excellencies that the collation was served. Then the two poor victims, tortured as they had already been bowing, made each three or four more bows, and at length adjourned to the dining room. Here I was waiting for them. To my astonishment

I soon discovered that the wretch of a Portuguese, far from being a *victim*, as I had imagined, went through the ceremony with evident complacency. He preserved his gravity so decorously that Junot conceived himself bound to return it with interest, and there they sat as if challenging one another which would longest refrain from smiling. At length, at the expiration of six minutes, which I counted precisely by the clock, the Count de Castro Marino rose, and Junot followed his example. They then resumed their bows, and having made about a dozen, the Portuguese grandee took his leave, and set off in his large carriage, which, I may observe, resembled one of the carriages of Louis XIV's time, after the model of which it was actually built. Junot accompanied his guest downstairs with the same formalities he had observed on coming up, and having bowed the Count into his heavy rumbling machine, bade him farewell. Two or three long strides up the stairs brought him back into the drawing room, where he found me mortified at having lost my bet and not a little astonished to find that a *young* man could go through the ceremony I have just described without even a smile. After a hearty laugh we sat down to partake of the collation, which was excellent.' This had been provided for Junot by the Spanish embassy.

General Lannes, Junot's predecessor, had taken a spacious and beautiful house, one of the finest in Lisbon, situated at the Fountain de Loretto, near the Opera House and not far from the Tagus. This was now the Junots' Lisbon residence; they afterwards took a villa in the beautiful and luxuriant countryside at Cintra. When they had settled in, Junot requested M. d'Araujo, the Minister of Foreign Affairs, whom they had known and liked in Paris, to fix the day of presenting his credentials to the Prince Regent. This took place at Queluz at the conclusion of the Easter festival. Laure was proud of her husband when he set off in his magnificent full-dress uniform of colonel-general of hussars, which he had had made at a cost of fifteen thousand francs at the time of the Emperor's coronation. The dolman was white, with red facings, the breeches blue, the pelisse also blue, richly embroidered with gold. The sleeves of the dolman and pelisse were adorned with nine gold chevrons, beautifully embroidered in an oak-leaf pattern. The pelisse was bordered with magnificent blue fox-fur. In his shako he wore a heron plume, the gift of the Empress Josephine. This outfit so caught the imagination of the Prince Regent that the following day his *valet de chambre* arrived to ask if the French ambassador would be good enough to lend his hussar uniform as a pattern for His Royal

Highness's tailor, to make one like it for the Prince and one for the Infant Don Pedro.

Laure's turn came to be presented to the Princess of Brazil, the only visit that etiquette demanded of an ambassadress. She had ordered her court dress, whose skirt was held out by hoops, in Paris, but as the time came to wear it her heart sank. She felt she looked ridiculous, and begged Junot to let her wear something else, but he was vigorously following what etiquette required, and insisted on her going in her court dress. With the help of the Countess Lebzeltern, the wife of the Austrian ambassador, she made some adjustments to her hoops so that she could walk normally. It needed Junot's assistance, however, to get Laure into her carriage, so wide were her hoops and so high were the six large feathers in her *toque*. It was in a state of purgatory, she said, that she travelled the two leagues from Lisbon to Queluz.

The portrait of the Princess of Brazil, the daughter of Queen Maria Luisa of Spain, and married to the Regent, the son of the mad Queen Donna Maria I, as drawn by Laure in her *Memoirs* is a little masterpiece of malicious observation: 'Picture to yourself a woman four feet ten inches high at the very most, and crooked, or at least both her sides were not alike; her bust, arms and legs being in perfect unison with her deformed shape. Still, all this might have passed off in a royal personage had her face been even endurable; but, good heavens, what a face it was! . . . She had two bloodshot eyes, which never looked one way, though she could not absolutely be accused of squinting. . . Then her skin! there was nothing human in it; it might be called a *vegetable* skin. Her nose descended on her blue livid lips, which when opened displayed the most extraordinary set of teeth that God ever created. Teeth, I suppose, they must be called, though they were in reality nothing but huge pieces of bone stuck in her large mouth, and rising and falling like the reeds of a reed-pipe. This face was surmounted by a cranium covered with coarse, dry, frizzy hair, which at first sight appeared to be of no colour. I suppose it was black; for, looking at me, the Princess exclaimed: "She is like us. She is dark-complexioned. She has hair and eyes like Pepita." "Heaven preserve me," I inwardly remarked, while I involuntarily turned my eyes towards a mirror, as if to assure myself that what she said was not true. Pepita was the Queen of Etruria. The dress of the Princess of Brazil was in discordant unison, if I may so express myself, with her person. She would have been natural, at least, in a dress of dark-coloured silk, made perfectly plain. However, she had thought proper to array herself in a dress of Indian muslin, embroidered with gold and silver lama. This dress, which was wretchedly ill made, very imperfectly covered an enormous bosom, and a chest all awry, while diamond brooches ornamented the sleeves, whose extreme shortness displayed a pair of arms which would have been much better concealed. Her frizzy dingy hair was plaited, and decorated with pearls and diamonds of admirable beauty. The body of her dress, too, was edged with a row of pearls of inestimable value. Her ear-drops were perfectly unique: I never saw anything like them. They consisted of two diamond pears, perfectly round, of the purest water, and about an inch in length. The exquisite beauty of these jewels, combined with the extreme ugliness of the person who wore them, produced an indescribably strange effect, and made the Princess look like a being scarcely belonging to our species.'

Etiquette prescribed that, following her presentation to the Princess of Brazil, she call upon the *camareira-mor*. This she did, and she was then launched on the society of Lisbon, such as she found it. Of the diplomats in Lisbon the position of the English ambassador, Lord Robert Fitzgerald, was unique, owing to the old alliance between England and Portugal. For the Austrian ambassador, Count von Lebzeltern, and his charming Spanish wife, Laure quickly gained a firm friendship. She found the diplomatic dinners unbearably dull. After her presentation she herself kept open house. She received company every day, and three times a week she gave a grand dinner party. Her balls became something that was remembered by Lisbon society; in a word, the French embassy became the centre of what social and intellectual life was to be found in Lisbon. She carried out the Emperor's orders to the letter. Besides the Countess von Lebzeltern, Laure became most intimate with two Frenchwomen, both *émigrées*, married to Portuguese. One of them was the Duchesse de Cadaval, the sister of the Duc de Luxembourg; the other was Mme de Brancamp de Sobral, daughter of Count Louis de Narbonne, her mother's friend. Mme de Cadaval was still beautiful, although Laure detected in her smile a tinge of grief. She was married to an impossible husband. When she married him, she found his fortune dissipated by debts, mostly from gambling. She courageously adopted the most stringent economies and finding one day that he owed 50,000 francs to their cook, she paid it. Her husband was furious with her, saying the man was little better than a thief. Next day she found the Duke somewhat appeased, and enquiries provided her with the reason for this change of temper. The previous evening he had sat down with his cook to a game of faro and had won back all the money.

The Junots rented a *quinta* at Cintra, where the house stood in a garden entirely planted with orange and lemon trees. It was delightfully fresh in the hot summer months. For neighbours they had the Duke and Duchess de Cadaval and the Lebzelterns, the latter occupying part of the old royal palace of Cintra. It was there that Junot received letters from Paris that announced the formation of the third coalition of England, Austria and Russia against France. He therefore wrote to the Emperor Napoleon and sent off his letter by extraordinary courier. It was at this time that Laure heard of her appointment as one of the ladies-in-waiting to Signora Laetizia, now known as Madame Mère. While they were at Cintra Laure was taken ill with what was thought to be a nervous affection of the stomach, and she was advised by the medical men to take the tepid spring waters at Caldas da Raynha. She had little faith in the cure, but she went there, and after a week she was able to walk in the royal *quinta*, and within a fortnight she ate a partridge for dinner. While she was at Caldas da Raynha, Junot came for a very brief visit to say good-bye. True to his word, Napoleon had sent for him to join him in Germany. Junot immediately returned to Lisbon, and mounting a post-horse, rode to Bayonne. There he transferred to a *calèche*, and losing no time, set off for Paris, where he stayed only twenty-four hours, before leaving in a post-chaise for Germany, driving with all speed. He arrived on the field of Austerlitz on the morning of the day of the battle, 2 December 1805, when he served as aide-de-camp to the Emperor.

Returning from Caldas da Raynha to Lisbon, Laure reached the Tagus, where one of the royal *escaleres* was waiting to transport her down the river to the capital. The weather, which had been exceedingly fine, a typical Lusitanian autumn, became suddenly overcast. A dead calm preceded a violent storm, the wind splitting the sail, and the rowers only with difficulty maintaining their head against the force of the wind. They were in great danger of capsizing. The master ordered the men to make for Saccavin, the nearest village on the bank. They were thrown up on shore within two hundred paces of the landing place, and Laure was carried to dry land by the sailors. She then despatched an express for her carriage and later that evening she was seated in her little yellow drawing room in her hôtel in Lisbon, with Josephine on her knee. It was 21 October, and the storm was that which dispersed the ships after the battle of Trafalgar. Some days later intelligence was received in Lisbon of the outcome of the battle. Laure was wakened one morning by the firing of guns; this was from the British and Portuguese shipping in the Tagus, celebrating the victory. It was only later that she learned of the death of her old family friend Rear-Admiral Magon, who had blown up his ship, *L'Achille*, rather than surrender.

Laure discovered that her illness was in fact pregnancy, and she hastened the preparations for her departure, to return to France. A letter from M. de Talleyrand, at the Foreign Office, however, caused her to alter her plans. She was ordered on a secret mission to Madrid. She requested an audience of the Princess of Brazil, to take her leave, and was agreeably surprised when the Princess offered her the Cross of St Elizabeth. This she politely refused, although she wished very strongly to possess it, since the order was a beautiful one; she gave as her reason the fact that, since the Empress wore no orders herself, none of the court ladies might do so. As she was on the point of leaving Lisbon, Captain Baudin, the commander of a French frigate, which had put in to Lisbon to refit, after an action with English ships off Portugal, gave an entertainment on board in her honour. A fine band played on the quarterdeck, while the officers and their guests lunched under awnings. A succession of toasts was drunk: to the Pope, whose nuncio Monsignore Galeppi was one of the party, then to the Emperor Napoleon, the King of Spain, the Queen of Portugal, the Prince and Princess of Brazil, and lastly the King of Holland. The toasts were accompanied by salvoes of the ship's guns. Monsignore was, Laure thought, a little stunned by the firing. He drank off three glasses of Madeira for the Pope's health, and then varied his wines for the others: port for the Emperor's, Carcavello for the King of Spain's, Oyeras for the Prince of Brazil's, and so on, until by the time he got to Laure's, he was quite drunk, and, to the embarrassment of his chaplain, began to sing in a husky, tipsy voice. Laure, who never touched wine, kept to water.

On her departure from Lisbon, Laure drove straight to Madrid, where she took up residence, as she had earlier, in Alphonso Pignatelli's pretty little house. Strange reports were circulating about the serious illness of the young Princess of the Asturias. Knowing the emnity of the Prince of Peace to the Princess, people talked among themselves of the possibility of poison. Laure never divulged the nature of her secret mission for Talleyrand in Madrid. She wrote in her *Memoirs*, 'I was desired to do something which unfortunately I was unable to effect.' Her protracted stay in the capital was attributed by some to her love of pleasure, but no doubt she kept Talleyrand informed of what was being said in Spanish society at the time of the Princess's death. She frequently visited the Comtesse d'Ega, the wife of the Portuguese ambassador, where she enjoyed the very agreeable musical evenings. The Duchesse d'Ossuna gave a charming fête in her honour at the Alameda, her country house outside Madrid. Laure received a letter from Junot, who was in Vienna, telling her that he was being sent by the Emperor on a mission to Italy, and that it was the latter's wish that she return to Paris to enter on her duty in the service of Madame Mère. She therefore left Madrid at the beginning of February 1806, and arrived in Paris on Shrove Tuesday, exactly a year to the day since she had set out on the Portuguese embassy.

On the following day Laure wrote to Mme de Fontanges, lady of honour to Madame Mère, asking when Her Imperial Highness would be willing to receive her. On Sunday 25 February she went to the Hôtel Brienne, rue Saint-Dominique, where Madame Mère had moved from the house of her half-brother Cardinal Fesch on coming into her new imperial title. When on her arrival Mme de Fontanges presented her by name, the old lady came forward from the fire in front of which she was standing, and said: 'You need not introduce Mme Junot to me. She is a child of mine, and I love her as much as my own daughter. I hope everything will be done to make her situation in the household of an old woman agreeable for her, for it is a serious affair for so young a person.' It was agreed that she should come into waiting on the following Sunday. The next morning M. Rollier, steward of the household of Madame, arrived, bringing with him her entire year's salary of 6,000 francs.

Characteristic is Laure's description of one of her associates as lady-in-waiting: 'The four lady's companions were Mme Soult, Mme de Fleurieu, wife of the minister of marine under Louis XVI; Mme de Saint Pern and myself. There was but one among us all who might be said to be completely in her place. Mme de Fleurieu seemed born to be the companion of an elderly princess, for she never seemed to have been young herself. She had never been handsome, nor even pretty, and she possessed all the characteristics of a plain and virtuous woman. I have seldom seen any person so directly the reverse of pleasing as Mme de Fleurieu; dancing with as melancholy air as if she was begging at St Roche, and holding her petticoat to the extent of her two arms, offering a good representation of an espalier tree. Having no pretension to grace, she aspired to be considered a *bel esprit*. She had, however, two serious faults: the one was the mania, or rather the monomania of etiquette; a pretension which had dazzled the Emperor, who never imagined that anyone could persist in talking for ever upon a particular subject without being perfectly well versed in it. Her second great fault was that of being an eternal talker; a spout of lukewarm water, always open and always running; the recollection of it is terrible even at this distance of time. To sum up, hoever, I should say with Brantôme: *She was a very respectable and very virtuous lady.'*

Another person who, though not a lady-in-waiting, was much in Madame Mère's company was Mme de Brissac, wife of one of the gentlemen of her household. Mme de Brissac was rather deaf. Before her presentation to the Emperor, fearing that in her trepidation she might not catch what he said, she enquired what questions he was likely to ask. She was told that he habitually enquired what department a person came from, how old they were, and how many children they had. The day of her presentation came and Mme de Brissac made her three curtsies before the Emperor, who, having laid down no law to himself to ask precisely the same questions to all the extraordinary faces that appeared before him, said to her: 'Is your husband brother to the Duc de Brissac who was killed on 2 September; and did he not inherit his estates?' 'Seine and Oise, Sire,' she replied, which was not far off the mark, since he did have estates there. The Emperor, somewhat surprised, went on: 'I believe you have no children?' 'Fifty-two, Sire.' By this time Napoleon had gathered that she was hard of hearing and passed on.

At public receptions Napoleon would frequently come up to someone present and curtly, abruptly ask who he was. One day the famous actor Grètry was present at the Tuileries, and the Emperor approached him. 'What do *you* call yourself?' 'Grètry, Sire.' A few weeks later he was again there, and Napoleon came up to him. 'And you, Sir, who are you?' 'Sire, still Grètry.' The Emperor henceforth remembered him.

Napoleon, in furtherance of his policy for the reorganisation of Europe, was making members of his family sovereign princes. The Princess Eliza was the first to be raised to this dignity; he conferred on her the Republic of Lucca, which he created into a Principality. When Princess Caroline was made Grand Duchess of Berg, Princess Pauline sought from her brother a state which she could call her own. She was created Duchess of Guastalla. Laure Junot commented on this: 'It was no great thing to be sure, but even a molehill seemed too much for her to govern. If there had been kingdoms in the air, as in the time of the sylphs, she might have been enveloped in a pink and blue cloud, nicely scented, and sent to reign in those fortunate regions where the sceptre of government is a sprig of flowers.' Joseph Bonaparte was dragged from his quiet pursuits at Mortefontaine and sent to reign in Naples in place of the deposed Bourbons, and Louis was raised to the throne of Holland. The Princesses were far from satisfied with their lot, and complained bitterly to the Emperor. There was a chorus of resentment and grievances. One day their continual complaints were too much for him, and he expostulated, 'Really, Mesdames, to hear your pretensions, one would think we held the crown from our father, the late King!'

In Parma, where Junot had been sent, he ruled like a petty sovereign; in fact Napoleon was compelled to rebuke him for his severity—'you treat a prefect as if he were a corporal in your garrison.' Laure became acquainted, through malicious tongues, with his open infidelities. Junot, to find out how long he was to remain in Italy, wrote to Laure, asking her to seek an audience of the Emperor, and request if she might join him in Parma with the children. Napoleon, who did not like to have his policy or plans questioned, enquired of Laure if Junot had appointed her his ambassadress, and if so, were her letters of credence perfectly regular. However, it was settled that she should go out to Parma in May, when her children, who were ill, were fit to travel.

One day Laure accompanied Madame Mère to Saint-Cloud to visit the Princess Pauline, who occupied the ground-floor of the palace. The Emperor, coming into the drawing room, addressed her, 'Well, Mme Junot, so you are not gone yet?'

'Sire, I am waiting until my daughters are completely recovered, and then I shall immediately set out.'

'Napoleon,' said his mother, 'you ought to leave me my ladies. Here is Mme Junot who is just back from Portugal and has been absent from her duties, and you now go sending her to Italy.'

'It is not I who send her. It is she who wants to go. Ask her yourself.' He smiled. When Laure did not answer, he went on, 'Why don't you say that it is you who are determined to go to Parma?'

'But, Sire, I can't say what is not true. I have not the slightest desire to go there.'

'A good wife should always follow her husband. It is the law of the Gospel.'

'Sire, Your Majesty will permit me to say that the Gospel has nothing to do with the case. I am not a good wife in this particular. And, besides, perhaps I would be *de trop*.'

'Ah, you have been listening to gossip. Why do you listen to these people? Besides, the hen should be silent in the presence of the cock. What is it to you, if Junot amuses himself in Parma? Wives must not torment husbands, or they may make them worse.' This last he said, looking at the Empress, who appeared as if she had not heard him. Laure did not reply.

'Well, then you are upset over a trifle,' the Emperor went on. 'A trifle which you wives make a great concern of when you know it, and is of no consequence when you do not. Now, shall I tell you what you should say on these occasions? Do you wish to know?'

'I listen, Sire.'

'Just nothing! But if, like the rest of your sex you can't keep silent, if you must speak, then let it be to approve.'

'Indeed,' said Madame Mère.

'Shocking,' said the Princess Pauline. 'I should like to see a husband of mine expect me to approve such proceedings.'

The Empress said nothing, but Laure noticed tears in her eyes. If Josephine had caused Napoleon jealousy in the past, he amply made up for it. He expected to sleep with, and often did, any woman who caught his fancy. Mme Récamier, who refused to be persuaded by Fouché's entreaties that she become Napoleon's 'special friend', found herself joining Mme de Staël in exile. The Emperor took a perverse pleasure in speaking to wives of their husband's infidelities. He was both crude and a bully. Mme de Rémusat, who as lady-in-waiting to the Empress, had witnessed many scenes between husband and wife, reports Napoleon's speech on such occasions. 'It is your place,' he said, addressing Josephine, 'to submit to all my fancies, and you ought to think it quite natural that I should allow myself amusements of this kind. I have a right to answer all your complaints by an eternal I. I am a person apart; I will not be dictated to by anyone.' And again, 'I am not an ordinary man, and the laws of morals and of customs were never made for me.' It was on this assumption that he acted.

Laure had completed her preparations for her Italian journey, and was about to set out in two days time, when one evening General Bertrans, the aide-de-camp to the Emperor, was announced. He brought her Napoleon's command that she abandon her journey to Parma, and he expressed his own opinion that this change boded no harm. Later she heard it whispered that Junot was to be re-appointed

Governor of Paris. Rumours were also rife that war was about to break out with Prussia. The Emperor, in appointing Junot to this important position, would have considered not so much his administration qualifications as his proved loyalty to his own person. When Napoleon departed for the East, the arch-chancellor Cambacérès would be left at the head of the government, and all orders would reach Junot through him. At the moment nothing of this was official. One evening Laure was visiting a friend, when a message was brought that Junot had unexpectedly arrived. As it was a fine evening she had sent away her carriage; she was walking home in the rue de Choiseul, when she met Junot who, not finding her in the Champs-Elysées and knowing where she was visiting, had driven to meet her. He confessed that his orders contained no reason for his recall, and he did not know what his next appointment was to be. The following day, when he went to the Tuileries, he was received by the Emperor with every mark of kindness and cordiality, but no word was said of his future. Prince Louis Bonaparte, who had been Governor of Paris, had just been recognised King of Holland. It was Princess Caroline who confirmed Junot in the impression that the post was to be his, and he confided to Laure that, of all the favours the Emperor could grant him, to be Governor of Paris would be the highest point of his ambition. Still the Emperor was silent. At length the mystery of his recall and future was explained. On 19 July 1806 Junot was nominated Governor of Paris. A few days later the Emperor showed his confidence in him by appointing him to the command of the First Military Division.

Napoleon had at this time overreached himself diplomatically; war clouds gathered, when the fourth coalition was formed against him; Prussia mobilized. On 25 September 1806 Junot was invited to dine at Saint-Cloud. The Emperor was to set out for Germany that night. He appeared to be moved by the grief Junot showed at not being able to accompany him, and the old friendship that Junot had found in him, when he had been his companion in his walks in the Jardin des Plantes, seemed to have been for the moment revived. Junot told Laure of his leave-taking with Napoleon the following morning. 'It was Sully and Henri IV,' said Junot. 'Except,' she replied, laughing, 'that you are not quite so reasonable as the minister of the good king, and—' 'And what?' 'And though the Emperor is a greater man than Henri IV, it is by no means certain that he is so good.' 'It is very extraordinary,' said Junot, crossly, 'that you, my wife, should express such an opinion, and that to me.'

FIVE

Caroline Murat and Count Metternich

ONE DAY in the autumn of 1806, while the armies of France marched
deeper into Germany, Junot took Laure with him to hunt deer at
Raincy. The day was perfect, the sun warm, the earlier mist had
dispersed, lingering only along the river. After an excellent chase they
stopped in the park. Laure admired the façade of the château, the
pretty Russian cottage in the grounds, the hunting-box, the orangery,
the stables with their clock-tower, and the charming village at the end
of the avenue of poplars in the great park. The estate, which was once
the property of the Duke of Orleans, had been bought by M. Ouvrard
for the sum of 826,000 francs. Having permission, they went to see
over the house. Laure thought the interior even more beautiful than the
grounds. The bathroom was of unparalleled magnificence, the two
baths being formed from solid blocks of grey granite, the floor of
black, white and yellow marble, the chimney of vert-antique and the
walls of the finest stuccoing. The *salon* was a vast apartment, divided
into three by pillars, between which were statues holding candelabra.
One extremity was the billiard room, the other the music room; the
centre, which had formerly been the bedroom of the Duke of Orleans,
constituted a perfect setting for receptions. The view from the windows
was enchanting; you looked out towards the river over a large lawn,
bordered by the orangery and a summer house; on either side of the
lawn were walks, one of lilacs, the other of acacias. Junot watched
Laure's admiration of both house and grounds with a curious smile.
He asked her how she would like to be the owner of such a property.
When she replied that she could not say, so impossible was it that she
should ever possess such a place, he said simply, 'It is yours.' Many
years later Laure wrote of this moment: 'There are certainly hours of
bitterness in life, and no one has had more experience of them than
myself; but there are also moments, fugitive in duration, but indelibly
engraved on the mind, which are equal to an eternity of happiness.'

When they had settled in at Raincy, Junot's mother came, and from that time she lived with them. Junot rode in to Paris in the morning and returned in the evening for dinner. This was at first, but soon his engagements necessitated him often staying in the Champs-Elysées. The Emperor had left instructions that Paris should be brilliant and gay in his absence and that lavish entertaining should be kept up. Talleyrand announced his orders, 'This is no laughing matter, ladies; The Emperor insists on your amusing yourselves.' Since the Empress Josephine did not dance and the Princess Pauline saw herself as a semi-invalid, Princess Caroline Murat, the Grand Duchess of Berg, alone of the younger matrons of the imperial family in Paris, was the centre of the social life at court. It was not long before rumours were current of her relations with the Governor of Paris. If the Grand Duchess of Berg opened a ball, it was with Junot that she danced; if she went to the theatre or to a fête, it was Junot who escorted her; when she drove out to the Bois, it was Junot who accompanied her in her carriage. His own carriage, with his servants in his livery, was to be seen outside her house at two o'clock in the morning. The truth was that Junot had fallen violently in love with Caroline Murat. Whatever was his sexual feeling for her, his love was added to by his amour propre, by her social position, by the knowledge that she was a princess, the sister of the Emperor. The man who in 1797, in deference to the feelings of his general, had repulsed the advances of Josephine was not the man in 1806 to resist the blandishments of his sister. His head, never stable in these matters, was turned. In becoming Junot's mistress, there was a strong element of calculation in Caroline's actions. She was intensely, insanely ambitious. What if an enemy ball or bullet carried off the Emperor? By the *senatus consultum* the succession lay first with King Joseph, then with King Louis and his sons, then with Jerome. But the Governor of Paris, the commander of the First Military Division, the man on the spot, was a personage of power. If he were to support Murat, might not France, who had accepted a Napoleon, accept a Joachim?

When Junot took to staying the nights in Paris, Laure at Raincy was in despair. At first, weeping, she tried to remonstrate with him. In his infatuation he would not listen to her. Her position was intolerable; she loved Junot, was the mother of his children and was bearing his child; and she had to carry on her life in society, full knowing that all the world knew of her husband's liaison. And furthermore, she was deeply worried. What if the Emperor, to whom they owed everything, were to be informed of Junot's relations with his sister? In matters to do with his own family Napoleon was acutely sensitive. His anger could be terrible. What he allowed himself he did not allow in others. Immersed as Junot was in his affair with Caroline, he was neglecting his duties. On 23 March 1807 the Emperor wrote to him: 'I cannot express to you my dissatisfaction with the way you have despatched the companies of grenadiers and light-infantrymen of the 32nd. Instead of sending 140 men, as I ordered, you have sent only 40 to 60 men; instead of sending them well clothed, well armed and well equipped, you have sent them without clothing.' Again, on 10 May, 'I can only be dissatisfied with your not obeying my orders. I flatter myself that from now on you will fulfill more exactly my instructions and will not regard what I say as idle talk. You have a strange idea of your duty and of military service. I no longer recognize you.'

While Junot was occupied with his love and the constant round of entertainments in Paris, his mother suddenly died at Raincy. During her few days of illness Laure had nursed her tenderly. Junot, who loved his mother deeply, was grief stricken. But his grief did not keep him long from dancing attendance on the Grand Duchess of Berg.

One day the Junots were invited to lunch at Malmaison by the Empress. There, drawing Junot aside, she openly broached the subject of the possible death of the Emperor, and suggested to him in a veiled manner that her son Eugène, who was the Emperor's adopted son and was held in high esteem by the army, might be a suitable successor. Junot affected not to follow the drift of her remarks. Finding him too fixed in his attachment to the *senatus consultum* and to his sovereign, she, laughing, whispered a word in his ear. She alluded to his liaison with Caroline Murat. Junot blushed, quickly looked to see if Laure had heard, and answered the Empress coldly. On their return home, he told Laure of Josephine's proposal, adding that, on the event of the Emperor's death, Joseph would succeed, then Louis and his children. 'And Murat?' she asked, looking him straight in the eyes.

As time passed Laure, pregnant as she was, resigned herself to her position. She learned of other women of her acquaintance to whom Junot had addressed his attentions. She called them her 'relations', and lived in the hope that Caroline would only be a passing one of their number, and that the affair would not come to the ears of the Emperor. The fête-day of the Empress, 19 March, approaching, the Princesses Caroline and Pauline charged Junot with the choice of two plays to stage in her honour at Malmaison. He put the matter into the hands of M. de Longchamps, secretary to the Grand Duchess of Berg. Laure, who with Junot received parts, had the mortification of rehearsing, and seeing and hearing Junot, as the stage lover, reciting verses of love to the Princess Caroline. On the day of the performance Caroline fainted, and the Empress, unlacing her bodice to allow her more air, found there a letter, the writing of which she recognized. 'It is from Murat,' Caroline said, as the Empress, when she had regained consciousness, placed it in her hand. Later the Empress told Laure that it was from Junot.

At the end of the performance the Grand Duchess of Berg invited Junot and Laure to accompany her in her carriage back to Paris. When they arrived at her palace of the Elysée-Bourbon, Junot got out, gave his hand to assist the Grand Duchess in descending, and followed her into the house. Laure, wearied of waiting, went home alone. She spent the night in tears. Junot only returned in the morning.

The victories of Jena (against Prussia) and Friedland (against Prussia and her ally Russia) may be considered as marking the highest point of Napoleon's career. From the Prussian capital he issued the Berlin Decree on 21 November 1806, which sought by a rigid blockade to exclude all British commerce from the continent of Europe; and at Tilsit he had his momentous meeting with the Tsar Alexander. At the end of July 1807 he was back in Paris. His first meetings with the Governor of Paris were cold, and Junot in his extreme uneasiness asked for an audience, which was immediately granted.

It was stormy. Despite his knowledge of the world, and of himself, Napoleon had a naive belief in the essential innocence of his sisters. He did not wish to believe otherwise. But he now roundly accused Junot of having compromised the Grand Duchess of Berg. Faced with the Emperor's anger, Junot could only assure him of his entire devotion to himself. If Marshal Murat felt himself offended, he was ready to offer him any satisfaction. 'My hôtel is near the Elysée,' he said. 'Yes, yes,' said the Emperor, 'much too near.' And he forbade Junot fighting. The latter was very much taken by surprise with the detailed nature of the Emperor's information, until he caught sight of a document on his desk and recognized Savary's handwriting. He declared angrily his intention to chastise his calumniators, beginning with Savary, but again the Emperor forbade him to fight. On leaving Napoleon's *cabinet*, he noticed Savary in the anteroom, but he affected not to have seen him. The result of the affair was, as General Thiard expressed it, that Junot was 'sent to Portugal to take a lesson in etiquette'. He was given the command of the Army of Observation of the Gironde, as the force was called, which was mustering in Bordeaux and Bayonne, preparatory to the invasion of Portugal to enforce the Berlin Decree. Junot felt cruelly his disgrace, and Laure had the wisdom and the restraint not to rub salt in his wounds.

On the Emperor's birthday, 15 August, there was a grand fête at the Hôtel de Ville, and Laure as the Governor's wife had to welcome the Empress as she alighted from her carriage. The ball was opened by the Grand Duchess of Berg, the Princess Stephanie Beauharnais, a lady of the palace, the wife of a mayor, and Laure. She danced with the Grand Duke of Berg. Because of her pregnancy she walked rather than danced. A few days before Junot's departure for Portugal, the Emperor ordered at a moment's notice the Junots to prepare Raincy to receive the Princess Catherine of Wurtemberg, who was to spend a day there, before entering Paris in the evening. The Princess was to marry Prince Jerome, who drove out to Raincy after lunch to meet his fiancée in Laure's drawing room, and to escort her to Paris.

The account given by Laure of the events of the period, and subsequently, in the *Journal intime*, which she later wrote for Balzac, differ markedly from that given in her *Memoirs*. In the latter she expresses her intention of concentrating on public affairs and giving only a minimum of what only affected her personally. In the *Journal* she writes in great detail and with seemingly complete frankness of some of the most significant events in her life. As were many of her contemporaries, she was much affected by the cultivation of *sensibility*, often dealing at great length with the status of her feeling, her loves or her sufferings, to an extent that becomes at times embarrassing, if not boring, to a more restrained or reticent taste.

On the evening before Junot's leaving for Bordeaux the Junots were invited by Their Imperial Highnesses the Grand Duke and Duchess of Berg to dinner, the invitation adding that Princess Caroline hoped very much that Laure would come in spite of her pregnancy. Laure said that the Princess knew very well that she could not suffer the jolting of the carriage. Junot, therefore, went alone, and returned early, at half-past eight, looking Laure thought, very agitated. He joined her in the drawing room, where she was with Cardinal Maury, the Baron de Breteuil, M. de Narbonne, M. de Valence and some women among her friends. Junot left them at nine, saying that he would change out of his uniform, and return. An hour having passed and his not having come back, Laure went to his dressing room. He was not there. She rang, and his Alsatian servant Heldt answered her call.

'Where is the General?'

'Madame, he went out.'

'In the carriage?'

'No, Madame, on foot.'

'Thank you. That is all.'

When the servant had gone, she sank into a chair. It was too clear to her that he had gone to keep an assignation. And he was leaving in the morning at seven.

She went back to the drawing room, and explained that Junot had been unexpectedly called by the Emperor to the Tuileries. Soon everyone left, except M. de Narbonne and her friend from childhood, Melanie, Mme Juste de Noailles. Both knew her position, and in front of her close friends she wept. They stayed until one o'clock, Mme de Noailles furious with Junot and counting on confronting him with his conduct. When they too had gone, Laure went to her bedroom, and throwing herself into a chair, gave way to her feelings. For Junot to leave her at that moment, when she did not know when she would see him again, when she was about to bear his child, without passing the last evening in her company—it was too much to bear. And for whom? For a woman who she thought was unworthy of him. But after the clock struck three her mood of despair and self-pity changed to one of concern. Day was about to break. It came to her that Murat, suspecting that this last night might have been given over to love, had surprised them; that Junot had perhaps been killed. As time passed, her fears increased. She became possessed by a panic fear. At four she could bear it no longer; she went into Junot's room and rang for Heldt. She confessed to him her fears and these were doubled when she understood that he shared them. Without her asking, Heldt told her how Junot had come in to change, that after re-reading a note, he had several times struck his head (a gesture of his when he was agitated), had loaded the pistols that he carried in his pocket, and had gone out by a back entrance giving on to the rue Saint-Honoré. She dismissed the servant and remained in the room, regarding the bed, whose owner might at that moment be already dead. She sat down, but no longer wept. Five struck; daylight entered the room between the thick curtains. A slight noise disturbed her, and looking up she saw Junot enter.

Laure rushed to him, and throwing her arms round his neck,

kissed him on the eyes, the cheeks, the hair, in an access of tenderness and relief. But when Junot tried to kiss her on the mouth, suddenly recalling, she freed herself and stepped back. He did not try to retain her.

'Why have you waited up?' he asked. 'How pale you are, and how changed.' He muttered some words of explanation, but she would not listen, and cut him short. He tried to take her hand, but she withdrew it.

'Why?' he asked gently. 'Don't repell me. I love you,' he added, seeing her move away.

'Oh,' she said, 'then you have some vestige of feeling left.' He blushed, and placed his hand on her breast as if to feel the movement of the child.

'His heart seems already to hear me,' he said, with a sad smile.

'Yes,' Laure said, 'his heart is near mine, and mine has always been yours. He will love you, as I have loved you.'

As he looked at her, his eyes filled with tears. 'Laure', he said, 'you deserve a better lot.'

She came to him and rested her head against his breast, and there wept, no longer with bitterness. His last words had touched her. 'Does my lot have always to be unhappy?' she asked.

'No, no; but how can we mend what has happened?'

'The heart can mend all,' Laure replied; 'and mine is already happy at what you have just said.' She stood back and regarded him.

He moved to take her in his arms, but she drew away, although less brusquely than before. Junot struck his head several times in the way characteristic of him. He was standing in front of her, and looking at her closely. 'I don't want to go,' he said.

'You don't want to go?'

'No!'

'But the Emperor?'

'He won't know.'

'How? What do you mean?'

'That I will not leave today. We are going out to Raincy, where you will be staying in any case in my absence. My carriage and escort will leave, but I shall leave tomorrow at the same time. I can't set out without having first an explanation with you which concerns our future happiness. Yes, our happiness,' he added, seeing her look. 'Now, go and get some rest, then we will leave for Raincy.'

At midday a closed carriage was drawn up in the courtyard, and in this they drove out to Raincy. There, Junot had a little dogcart got ready, and they set out across the park, and took a ride that opened in the woods. Junot was silent for some time; he was very moved when he began to speak, and his agitation did not diminish as he proceeded. He seemed to read her thoughts.

'Yes, I have loved her,' he said; 'but never has she entirely possessed me. She is pretty, she is a princess, sister of my master. All this prestige has turned my head. I have been the cause of your unhappiness, and my own perhaps. What a state I found you in.' He was silent for a short while, then putting his hand in his pocket, he took out a note, which he gave her to read. Laure recognized the handwriting of Princess Caroline.

'I cannot bring myself to think that you are going to set out without our having a last meeting. In entering your own house you will have to put up with bawling and whining. Leave all that and come to your Caroline. Come the ordinary way. All will be open. *But above all, and do not neglect it, come armed and well armed. You understand why.*'

Laure was shocked by the vulgarity of tone, by its complete materiality. Here was a woman who was prepared, to satisfy her own sensuality, to expose at the same instant the life of her husband and that of her lover. She handed him back the note.

'I can imagine what you are thinking,' said Junot. 'And you can imagine what I felt when I received it.'

'But still you went.'

'How could I get out of going? It was impossible. I owed it to you, too, Laure. This woman is a Messalina. But don't complain of the meeting; it has for ever opened my eyes.'

Junot told her how, scarcely had he entered Caroline's room, she examined his pistols to see if they were primed, and drew from its scabbard a Turkish *cangiar* that Junot carried on his nocturnal outings, to test its sharpness. Then she locked the doors, joking on the resistance they could put up, should Murat want to enter. This conduct, combined with her note, produced in him an effect very different from the ardour which her presence usually provoked in him. Instead of understanding the cause of his coldness, she was seized with a sudden access of fury at his continued indifference, and quickly lost control.

'You have returned to that woman! You have returned to her! You little expected that I would have the courage to see you tonight.'

'No,' he replied coldly; 'for she would not have wished it. And what is more, don't mention her name, I have already asked you not to.'

It was in this spirit and on this level, Junot said, that the conversation was carried on. Caroline then tried all her art of seduction to arouse in him a love that was dead. Seeing her thus, powerless and lascivious, acting the role of the prostitute, the effect on him was only to render him impotent. Her rage then had no bounds. She uttered menaces against Laure, and Junot confessed that at that moment she roused in him nothing but horror.

He then threatened to unmask Caroline's conduct to all France and to all Europe, if she did anything to upset the quiet of his wife.

But he did not hide from Laure the disquiet he felt on her behalf. 'She detests you,' he said. 'Your intelligence, your gifts, your reputation as a woman of fashion, with all of which she cannot compete, even though she is a princess—all that wounds and maddens her. Be careful with her. Be on your guard.'

They had come back to the château. It was nine when they went out, and it was two when they re-entered it. They were happy; Laure for having forgiven him and refound her friend; Junot for having freed himself from the burden of his guilt. At five o'clock in the morning he left for Bordeaux. It was 28 August 1807.

Before leaving Paris Junot had been given detailed secret instructions by the Emperor. In Bordeaux he received orders on which he promptly acted, and his army had already passed Alcantara before people in Paris were aware of its destination. Not only were his ministerial orders precise, but in private letters the Emperor was insistent on his using every endeavour, on avoiding any delay, in marching on Lisbon and securing his paramount object, which was to prevent the fleet and ports of Portugal from being surrendered to the English. By force of will and by a display of energy which astounded his opponents Junot entered Lisbon at the end of November, but not before the Prince of Brazil, with the court and the Portuguese fleet, acting on the advice of Sir Sidney Smith, who commanded in the Tagus, had sailed for the New World. The rewards of Junot's outstanding success were his appointment as Governor-General of Portugal and his ennoblement as Duke of Abrantès. At twenty-three Laure was a duchess.

Meanwhile Laure remained at Raincy, only leaving the château on receiving an invitation—it was rather a command—to spend some time at Fontainebleau, where the court was in residence for the months of September and October. Fearing that her confinement might take place while she was at the château, she took a small house nearby, and was carried each day in a chair to the château. In her *Memoirs* she has given a description of the imperial court at Fontainebleau at this time: 'No language can convey a clear idea of the magnificence, the magical luxury, which now surrounded the Emperor; the diamonds, jewels, and flowers, that gave splendour to his fêtes; the loves and joys that spread enchantment around, and the intrigues which the actors in them fancied quite impenetrable, whereas they were perhaps even more discernible than at the Tuileries. When the morning was fine, and in October and November of that year the weather was superb, we went out hunting and lunched in the forest. The ladies wore a habit of chamois cashmere, with collars and trimmings of green cloth embroidered with silver, and a hat of black velvet, with a large plume of white feathers. Nothing could be more exhilarating than the sight of seven or eight open carriages whirling rapidly through the rides of that magnificent forest, filled with ladies in this elegant dress, their waving plumes blending harmoniously with the autumnal foliage; the Emperor and his numerous suite darting like a flight of arrows past them in pursuit of a stag, which showing at one moment its proud antlers from the summit of a mossy rock, in the next was flying with the fleetness of the wind to escape its persecutors. The gentlemen's hunting habit was of green cloth, turned up with crimson velvet, and laced *à la Brandenbourg* on the breast and pockets with gold and silver; it was gay, but I preferred the more unpretending shooting-dress.'

At Raincy Laure was seldom alone, friends driving out from Paris to visit her, among the more frequent being M. Millin, the director of the Bibliothèque and her assiduous friend, Cardinal Maury, Archbishop of Paris, Count Louis de Narbonne, M. Robert de Dillon, and several of her women friends. Once or twice a week she would order a stag hunt, which she followed in a carriage or, driving herself, in the dog-cart. It was M. de Narbonne who brought to Raincy his friend Count Clement Metternich, the Austrian ambassador, who soon became a regular and frequent visitor. Count Louis de Narbonne, who had been a friend of Laure's mother, was the son of a lady-in-waiting of Elizabeth Duchess of Parma, his father being a Spanish nobleman or—some allege—Louis XV himself. At any rate, he was brought up with the princesses of France at Versailles. Emigrating in 1792, he returned to France in 1801 and subsequently entered Napoleon's service. Cynical in matters of love, he rallied Laure for her continued affection for Junot. One day on a walk at Raincy he spoke to her—she gives his conversation in her *Journal:* ' "At your age, charming as you are, are you going to wither in tears, in despair, and finish by dying of grief? Come now. There is a fine resolution for a woman of twenty-three. My beauty, I have seen you born. I have some rights over you; let me direct you. I do not say to you: take a lover. That would be more absurd than shocking. But I will say to you to enjoy your eminent resources, and not to place in this way your happiness on risky ground. General Junot has come back to you, according to you: that is all very well if it lasts, but I do not believe it. If La Rochefoucauld has said that a woman has never one unique fault, it is still truer of a man. Do not allow yourself to be rocked to sleep in a gentle security of which the wakening will be so much more bitter." ' Had she not noticed, he asked that Count Metternich was in love with her? Evidence for the sincerity of the latter's feelings for her was, in his eyes, his giving up Mlle George, the very beautiful actress, who was his mistress.

In her *Journal intime* she relates how, 'Coming back from our walk, we found M. de Metternich and M. de Fuentès, who had just arrived. I noticed in effect that M. de Metternich had an air of profound sadness. In a man who, by his high rank, his position in the world, ought to have the assurance, the manner easy without insolence which characterises the *grand seigneur*, when he finds in himself a feeling which gives him a reserve, a shyness strange to him, the result is an extreme charm.' I noticed this effect, but it was still far from making the impression on me that he would have wished. One walked, but never alone; we played billiards; we dined very late. In the evening Steibelt, who was my piano teacher, Paër, Crescentini, La Catalani played music fit for heaven. We ate ices, we talked, and at midnight we separated, some to return to Paris, to their great regret; we, to retire upstairs to our rooms.'

One day at the end of September Laure arranged a stag hunt, not in the park, but in the nearby Forest of Bondy. She was in her dog-cart, when M. de Metternich came up and asked her if he might accompany her. It was a beautiful warm autumn day, the scent of the woods was in the air. In the course of the drive Count Metternich told her how often he had wanted to talk to her alone, away from the crowd of people who always surrounded her. He said how much he admired her courage, alluding to her marriage—saying that it was common knowledge in Paris how things stood between her and Junot. She replied shortly, not wishing to continue the subject, that she had forgiven him. They had been unable to keep up with the hunt; they could hear the horns in the distance, and the barking of the hounds. After some time Metternich suggested that they return, as it was already becoming damp. They took the road for Raincy. At Livry, turning into a ride in the forest, they saw ahead of them in a clearing a group of horsemen. To her horror, among them Laure recognized Princess Caroline Murat, mounted on a spirited horse.

'We have to search you out, in order to see you,' said the Princess, when she came up to Laure. 'They say in Paris that you have retired from the world, but I see that you have company in your solitude. Good day, Monsieur l'Ambassadeur,' addressing Metternich. 'I come, Mme Junot, to beg dinner, a bed and a hunt tomorrow. Will you have me?'

Laure bowed, without replying. 'Come,' said Princess Caroline, 'Silence signifies consent, but I want a clearly articulated Yes from your pretty mouth.'

'Your Highness cannot doubt that I am sensible of the honour that you do me,' replied Laure, inwardly raging.

They returned to the château, where Laure installed the Princess in a room so that she could change, since she had ridden out from Paris. Her women, who had come by carriage, attended her. As she was leaving the Princess's room, the latter said to her, 'Laure, I have come to you, since you keep away from me. I want to have it out with you, as one ought with a person of intelligence and heart like you. Tomorrow, before lunch, I shall come to your room. By the way, what is that paragon of men, M. de Metternich, doing here? Is he in love with you.'

'No.'

'Bah. Don't tell me that.'

'I am telling you the truth,' said Laure drily.

As she was walking along the corridor to her room, she was overcome with repressed emotion and burst into tears. A door opened, and Count Metternich came out of his room.

'What has she done to you? What has she said to you?' he asked.

'Nothing, nothing. Leave me,' she said, ashamed of her tears. He held her hand. In taking her handkerchief from her eyes, she saw that his were moist.

'It is nothing. Leave me,' she repeated, withdrawing her hand. 'Go down, and above all don't tell Count Louis that you have seen me in tears.'

The next morning Princess Caroline came to her room. It was with difficulty that Laure could contain herself, when the Princess swore her friendship for her and her sisterly devotion. Out of loyalty to Junot she refrained from disclosing what she knew, for she was certain that had Caroline known she would have moved heaven and earth to encompass Junot's ruin. After the hunt the Princess left with the other visitors for Paris.

From that time Laure saw much of Metternich who grew daily in her confidence and affection. She returned from Raincy to Paris, where she gave birth to her first son, Napoleon. The Emperor and Empress were the child's godparents. It was there that she received anonymous letters informing her of Junot's conduct in Portugal. She did not require these, since the scandal caused by Junot's open affairs with Mme Foy and with Mme d'Ega, whose musical evenings Laure had attended in Madrid, was the common talk of Parisian drawing rooms. In her *Journal* she wrote: 'It was then six months since Alexandre [as she called Junot] had left me. From that time I had experienced storms and sufferings. Worn out with worries and tears, never without any doubt would my heart have separated from him, if new injuries had not come to lacerate it. But when I learned that my love could even be ridiculous, when I saw him prefer to me women without honour, without love, whose caresses had even to be paid for—with Mme Foy an epaulette for her husband did the trick, with Mme d'Ega a place for the Count d'Ega, that is what she demanded—it was then that love departed and died.' The predictions of M. de Narbonne were only too quickly verified.

After the Treaty of Tilsit Paris became the most splendid, the gayest capital in Europe. Junot had retained his post of Governor of Paris, and Laure, fully recovered from her confinement, kept open house. There in the Champs Elysées foregathered all that was most distinguished, most elegant in Parisian society, to the complete satisfaction of the Emperor. One day, coming up to Laure at the *petites entrées* in the Empress's drawing room, he said to her, 'Madame Junot, you and M. de Talleyrand, you are the only two persons who know how *tenir un salon*.' She describes her life at this time: 'We lived truly in a whirlwind. Every day balls, every day fêtes. The marriage of young Antoinette Murat to the Prince of Hohenzollern and of Mlle

Tascher to the Prince d'Arenberg gave rise to new magnificences. It was indeed a life of enchantment. Perfectly cured of my fatal passion, I enjoyed for the first time the happiness that a young woman in my position can have, with a fortune of eight hundred thousand livres. For that was the portion of Junot's income left by him so that his wife and his house could be worthily represented. His appointments at this period amounted to fifteen hundred thousand francs. But the Emperor demanded an extreme magnificence, not only in dress but in everything. And all was in proportion.' In this respect the Junots lived up to the Emperor's expectations. According to Mme Georgette Ducrest, Laure spent 200,000 francs on her dress alone. Napoleon called Junot King Marmont II. Marmont's extravagance was well known; on campaigns he dined off silver plate and had a hundred domestics to serve him.

The Grand Duchess of Berg was arranging a quadrille for the court, based on the *Incas* of Marmontel, in which forty-eight persons were to take part. The diamonds of the company were said to have been worth forty million francs. At a rehearsal Laure slipped and slightly strained her ankle. Since she was one of the best dancers, and since her *écrin* was valued in excess of five hundred thousand francs her presence was essential. She was advised to rest her foot on a chaise-longue, so as to be fit for the night of the performance. She had seen Metternich at the Tuileries, at other peoples' houses and at her own house, but always in company. Nevertheless, a tacit understanding had grown up between them. She felt that she was loved, and she rejoiced in the happiness this feeling brought her. The day following her slight accident Metternich called in the morning. She was painting, her injured foot raised on a *tabouret*. She had already discovered that Metternich could be very shy and this shyness could be extreme on certain occasions. Their talk that morning—about things of no importance— was punctuated by long silences. She noticed that his voice was altered; and his hesitancy becoming contagious, caused her to break off in the middle of a sentence. An expression of joy crossed his face, but he said nothing. She, too, was silent. The constraint between them became intolerable. Suddenly, without saying a word, he picked up his hat and rushed out of the room. Hardly had she recovered from her surprise than she saw him re-enter. Taking a chair at her side, he said,

'Really, you must think me very silly?'

'No, why?'

'Why? Because I have a word to say to you, and I am not able to. And unless you say it, I will never be able to speak.'

It flashed across Laure's mind that he was going to say that there was some impediment to their coming together. This thought so engrossed her that she found herself answering him coldly. After a long conversation in which nothing was spoken, although much might have been said, he left her.

When he had gone, Laure took stock of her situation. She realized that for a long time Metternich had attracted her. She liked his tall, slim figure, his fair hair and blue eyes, his aristocratic hauteur—in a word, his undeniable distinction. And his gentleness appealed to her, even his shyness. She knew now, too, that it was essential for her peace of mind that she was loved by Count Metternich. The conflict set up by these ideas deeply troubled her. She gave orders that she was not to be disturbed.

That evening she spent alone by her fireside. Her reflections were of the saddest; what was her future to be? Every way she turned, she found unhappiness. She wept. A knock, and the door of her boudoir opening, her *valet de chambre* announced M. de Cambyse and M. de Metternich. She hastened to dry her eyes. M. de Cambyse came on behalf of Princess Caroline to borrow a beautiful book on Russia, with coloured illustrations of Russian dress, which she wanted, to arrange the quadrille that was to follow the *Incas*. Without getting up, Laure told M. de Cambyse to go to the library and take the book. Junot had built a magnificent library in a wing of their hôtel. He had recently added to his expensive collection a rare *Daphnis et Chloé*, with illustrations by Prud'homme, for which he had paid 30,000 francs. M. de Cambyse left them.

Metternich apologized for his presence. He could not let the day close, he said, without knowing the answer to something which was of the utmost importance for him to know. He had come to the house an hour before, but was refused admittance, being told that Laure was unwell. In his distress of mind he had returned, just as M. de Cambyse, the bearer of an order from the Princess, had been more fortunate than he. He admitted that, seeing her doors open for this man, he could not resist the temptation, and he had followed him.

'Will you forgive me?'

'Of course. But what boredom you will find here. I am dull beyond words,' she said, with an attempt at brightness.

They were silent for some time. Laure poked the fire. Looking up, she found him regarding her with an expression of tenderness that touched her deeply.

'What is wrong?' he said, approaching her and taking her hand. 'You were weeping, when we came in.'

'Me? Certainly not.'

'You were crying; I saw it.' He took her cambric handkerchief, which was wet with tears. 'Here's the proof. Has he hurt you afresh? You are extraordinary; you kill yourself, you weep, you are destroying your health, and all for. . .'

'Not a word on that subject,' she interrupted him. 'Besides, I give you my word it was for quite another thing, fleeting enough. . .'

'Truly? Then it is not for your Alexandre that you weep?'

'Again! No, it is not for him. He no longer costs me tears. From now on I have friendship for him; but anything more, never!'

Metternich listened to her, his face lit up with pleasure. He took her hand and placed it on his heart. It was beating violently.

'There's nothing I can say,' he said in a low voice; 'but you understand me, don't you?'

'Because I no longer love, is that a reason for believing that I can forget?'

'No, no, I ask for nothing. I don't even ask for love.'

That night Metternich wrote to Laure. Some pages from the *Journal intime* are missing, but his letter ended:

' ". . . despair. My reason cannot sustain for long these agitations which are killing me. Laure, have pity on me. I do not know what I ask for. I do not know what I want. I am out of my mind. It is with joined hands, with the feeling of intimate adoration that I have for you, Laure, that I beg you to give me life. At the risk of enduring your anger, I will repeat: And why, why this fidelity for a man who does not appreciate it? Forgive me. A thousand times forgive me. My head has been burning for three days; a fever has not left me. Gall wanted me to stay in bed, but I would not have seen you!

' "This letter, written in the middle of the night, will be handed to you when you wake. It will precede me by some hours. Laure, Laure, let it be that the accent of my despair has not been proffered in vain; that a gentle look give me back my life. I do not want you to reply to me. I do not want letters. I want. . . I want. . . Ah! I do not want anything. But when you can take away or give me life, can you hesitate in your reply?" '

·   ·   ·   ·

The spring came, and with it the balls and fêtes ceased, but there returned the beautiful weather. The Emperor asked the Junots to sell him Raincy, offering them the sum of one million francs. With a heavy heart, for Laure loved Raincy, she complied. No longer possessing a house in the country, she took the Folie de Saint-James at Neuilly, in the part of Neuilly that touches on the Bois de Boulogne. Metternich, or Clement, as she now called him, had a little house in the Bois, and every morning he drove over in his cabriolet to pass some hours with her, while she drew or painted. He went home to dine with his children, then he returned in the evening.

They passed their mornings in a *cabinet de travail*, situated beyond Laure's bedroom, at the end of the house. This bedroom was a little rotunda, furnished with a circular divan, and lit from on top in the vault. A French-window gave on to her private garden, of which she alone had a key, and which was a mass of flowers, provided by the hothouses. These, after those of the Empress Josephine at Malmaison, were the finest in the environs of Paris. Magnolias, daturas, and beautiful orange trees surrounded her retreat, and the flower beds were filled with roses, carnations, jasmine, heliotrope and tuberoses. The delicious scents from the flowers filled her bedroom. The garden was enclosed by a hedge over which honeysuckle grew, and beyond the hedge lay a canal, which prevented persons from approaching from that direction. Beside the canal was a lime walk, again with flower beds of mignonette and roses. This alley led to a grotto, magnificently fitted up, despite its apparent rusticity, as a bathroom, with all the refinements that an unrestrained luxury could desire. It was on this luxury that M. de Saint-James had spent more than six million francs, which had given the house its name. Beyond the grotto the lime walk brought one to a postern gate, leading to the grassy bank of the Seine. At the request of some of her women friends, Laure had erected there a canvas pavilion, from which they might bathe in the river on warm summer evenings.

In her *Journal* Laure wrote of her feeling for Metternich: 'I loved him. I loved him with a true and tender heart. But I had made for myself a plan of conduct, from which all my love could not make me swerve. And yet I loved him; I repeat it, I loved him.'

At the end of June they had theatricals at the Folie de Saint-James. *The Barber of Seville* was put on, Laure taking the role of Rosina. Princess Caroline coming to hear of its success, demanded a repetition, which she would honour with her presence. On the morning of this command performance Dugazon, the actor, who had directed the players, said to Laure, 'It is very necessary for you to have talent; it is very useful in a duchess.'

Metternich came early. Laure, seeing that something was on his mind, asked him what it was.

'It is the Princess who has put me out.'

'And why?'

'If I tell you, you will think me conceited.'

'No, I suspect what you are going to say, and I have already noticed it.' For the truth was that Princess Caroline was in love with Metternich.

'She causes in me a physical disgust,' he said.

'Then we are lost,' Laure said. 'Do you imagine that with her wounded amour propre she will not try in some way to revenge herself?'

'Laure, it is you who will lose us,' he replied. 'If I were happier, I would have more self-restraint. This frenzy which comes over me when your dress touches only my hand, this agitation would be calmed. . .'

'You would no longer love me. Isn't that what you mean?'

'Your heart has never understood me,' he said, and he went out of the room, only immediately to return, and take her hand.

'Laure, take great care. This woman hates you. Take care.'

In the course of the performance Laure noticed the expression on the Princess' face, whenever she was applauded. She played her part well, and the applause at the end was general. After the play, they had supper and then danced. It was one o'clock before the guests left.

Laure was tired, and worried about what Clement had said. Slipping out of the dress she had worn as Rosina, which she had kept on for supper, she put on a muslin *peignoir*, and, opening her bedroom door, stepped out into the moonlit garden. The air was warm, and all was peaceful. She walked along the path towards the grotto, the moonlight through the branches of the limes making patterns on the gravel. The interior of the grotto was not completely dark, but the semi-obscurity caused her to fear, a trepidation which was increased when she thought she heard a noise. She turned, and began to run back along the lime walk. Her fear turned to panic, when she heard footsteps behind her. She was on the point of fainting, when she heard a well-known voice, and she found herself in the arms of Metternich.

'I have frightened you,' he said.

She did not at once reply; at first from fear, then from rising anger. 'What are you doing here?' she demanded.

'I don't know. What I do know is that I cannot go on living like this. I am resolved to die if you do not give me proof that you love me. You love me, you say, and you let me die. You love me and you sacrifice me to stupid prejudices. For all the world I am your lover. No one believes in the purity of our liaison. I see you ever day, they know that I love you, and they cannot believe that we put between ourselves the barrier which exists. Laure, Laure, be mine, or I swear to you, you will be the cause of some catastrophe, the remorse from which will poison your days—very different from having made my happiness.'

Laure wept. He was on his knees before her. Bending down to speak to him, her tears fell on his face.

'Oh! you weep,' he said, 'you weep and you let me suffer!'

Laure described the scene in her *Journal:* 'Soon my agitation became convulsive; he got up to support me, his mouth met mine. I do not know what became of me, but he carried me in his arms into the grotto, which was only a few steps from us, and when I came to myself, I had committed a fault which I must expiate with tears of blood. His delight was so great, his happiness so profoundly felt, that I would have reproached myself, if I had let him see all that I experienced...

'I am yours,' I said to him, 'now it is to you to dictate your will. I am your property. My heart is avid for happiness, and it has suffered so much! I give it into your hands.'

SIX

Junot—Othello

IT IS NOT to be thought that a liaison between personages so prominent in Paris as the Duchess of Abrantès and the blond young Austrian ambassador should pass unnoticed. Soon all were aware of Laure's happiness; and news of the affair was not long in reaching the Tuileries. The Emperor was displeased; the 'little pest' which he had often called her jokingly, was becoming something of a threat; if she wanted to take a lover, why could she not, like other women, find one among eligible Frenchmen? This connection with the *foreigner* could be politically dangerous; not that Napoleon rated Metternich highly at first; it was only later that he came to take him at his true worth. With Laure's earlier friend and now rival, the Grand Duchess of Berg, the matter took on a more serious aspect, with results that were evident only too soon. One day at the beginning of October 1808 (Laure records in her *Journal intime*) Metternich announced to her that he had been invited by Princess Caroline to luncheon on the following day.

'And you are going?'

'Of course. You have nothing to fear; my heart is only too firm.'

The next day he arrived at the Folie de Saint-James in the early afternoon. 'It was somewhat warm work', he said, smiling. But Laure did not consider, with such a woman, that it was a smiling matter. He told her that after a luncheon, which she had arranged as if it were a supper for four libertines in a *maison de filles*, she had taken him into a small bedroom, the floor of which was strewn with rose petals. She made him sit down beside her, took his hands, and behaving towards him with complete abandon, asked him if he did not find the place charming. He had replied coldly that he thought a woman's bedroom ought to recall something other than *one thing only*, and that books and musical instruments were a pleasant addition. As for the poor roses, it was truly a pity to have despoiled all her hothouses, for roses at that season were rare.

Princess Caroline found Metternich's indifference to her beauty and charms highly offensive, and there followed a scene.

'But, Madame,' he said at length, 'how can you reproach me? I have not even the honour of being your friend. No relation, even of society, exists between us. You are the Emperor's sister, and as such I respect you. We have hardly spoken to each other. On my side I have made no advances to you. You can hardly hold me culpable.'

'I know,' she said, pale with fury, 'I know well what causes your contempt.'

'But, Madame, if you are so certain that I love elsewhere, why this scene?'

'Yes, I know it. I know that every evening at ten o'clock your cabriolet without armorial bearings pulls up near the bridge, that you follow the edge of the water and that you enter the postern by the grotto, of which she has given you the key. That you leave at three o'clock in the morning, that in order that your cabriolet makes no noise in returning home, you have one with a horse which you have bought, and which you keep with a servant in a house that you have rented. Am I not well informed?'

'Yes, Madame, and I blush for you.'

At this she lost all control, raged, wept, flung her arms around his neck and tried to kiss him. He extricated himself with difficulty, and spoke in a tone of which the *sang-froid* must have been very insulting.

'I advise you, Madame, to put a stop to this scene, which is humiliating for both of us. I love, I love with passion, I love a person whose happiness you destroyed. As you are in possession of our secret, think that I am in possession of yours. And if need be, I shall divulge it.' And on this he left her.

Laure's first reaction, on hearing this recital, was to fear the revenge Princess Caroline would take on her. On her, for it was on Laure's account that two men had humiliated her. Within a few days of this incident Princess Caroline was named Queen of Naples. Before she left Paris, she had a meeting with Laure, a meeting in which she displayed a crudity that would be unbelievable, if we had not the latter's own account of it in the *Journal intime*. Even if the pen is an inimical one, the account, taken with other events which follow, has the accent of truth.

'Some days after this singular interview with the Prince [he was, in fact, then Count] Metternich, I received a message to go to old Neuilly, where she then was. In entering the first *salon* I met General Sebastiani, who saluted me in an ironic manner and asked me if I would be visible on the following morning. I had known him a long time. This request made me smile and I said Yes, adding that he had no need of permission —keep this well in mind.

'Entering the Princess's room, I found her alone. She had just lunched. Rumour has it that sobriety was not her virtue. In fact, she was flushed, and her eyes were starting out of her head. Having indicated a chair with her hand, she began this singular conversation:

' "It is said, Madame Junot, that you pretend I am jealous of you. And of what, good God, would I be jealous? You are pretty, but I don't think I am at all bad. Riches? As for that I hope we won't be rivals; my *écrin* is finer than yours."

'I listened to her with an air of astonishment which would have been comic to a third party. I believed her completely insane. She went on:

' "And even for M. de Metternich. . . If I wished to give myself the trouble, I would take him away from you, for certain. . ."

'I got up immediately.

' "Madame," I said, interrupting her, "When Your Highness will have a conversation with me becoming to us both, she will find me disposed to listen to her with the respect that I owe to the sister of the Emperor. But when she forgets herself to the point she has just done, for fear of forgetting myself, I retire."

'I had in fact opened the door and I was going away, when she recalled me.

' "What are you doing? Don't you see that I am joking?"

' "These pleasanteries, Madame, are in too bad taste for me to welcome them. I shall remain, but on condition that we speak of things which can be said by you and listened to by me."

'I resumed my chair, and she went on:

' "You were really angry then! What would you say, if I asked you what you thought of all that was said of me and Junot?"

' "This, Madame, is only painful for me, I will listen."

' "Well, then be so good," she went on, "as to explain for me a point where you alone are wrong, for Junot has never been my lover, and your jealous rages have persuaded all Paris that it was so."

'I smiled in replying that I had to help me in that task two powerful auxiliaries, herself and Alexandre.

'She went on, with a lofty air: "Oh! I will not go so far as to discuss with you, I will only say that, having so handsome a husband, one will not believe that I have taken for a lover an agreeable man, but one so much his inferior."

' "Without accepting that, Madame," I replied, "I will limit myself to replying that it is a pity that you think so. For all that you prove, is that you have had bad taste."

'She bit her lips and, after a moment's silence:

' "Do you know, Madame Junot, it is you who have a singular taste. You who have teeth which are pearls, how is that those you love have always bad teeth? M. de Metternich's are frightful."

'I rose, and looking at the clock, said,

' "Your Imperial Highness will forgive me, but it is late. I must be home at two o'clock and I have only just time to get there."

' "Some assignation, perhaps?"

' "The hour would be a little inopportune. It is not an assignation."

' "By the way, do you know," she went on, "that General Sebastiani is in love with you?"

' "In love with me? Good God! What whim has taken him. I have known him since my childhood, and he has never thought. . ."

' "Well, it is nonetheless true."

'I withdrew, my mind filled with indignation and disgust.'

Laure found Metternich waiting for her at the Folie Saint-James. When she had recounted to him her interview with the Princess, he looked serious. 'Take care,' he said. 'I will be on the watch. But take care of yourself.' She told him of her meeting with General Sebastiani; they laughed, and gave it no further thought.

The following day Laure was scarcely risen, when General Sebastiani was announced. The General was a Corsican. Mme Permon had known him, and liked him well enough, but with her social pretensions had rather looked down her nose at him as the son of a cooper of Ajaccio. Laure had always known him, and regarded him rather with her mother's eyes. Treating him as an old acquaintance, she had him shown into an inner room, where, having finished her dressing, she joined him. No sooner was she there than he launched into a declaration of his love for her. It took her so much by surprise that at first she thought he must be out of his mind. She burst out laughing at this ridiculous scene. But it ceased to be ridiculous, when he suddenly advanced on her and caught her up in his arms. Freeing herself, she sought refuge in her bedroom. 'General,' she said, 'your behaviour is revolting, whether it is on your own initiative or whether it has been dictated to you, never again will you see me alone.' Opening the door, she stepped out into the garden.

Sebastiani was not discouraged. He called on several occasions, and the *valet de chambre*, on Laure's instructions, showed him into the drawing room. Then one morning, the names of General Sebastiani and the young Duc Gustave de Coigny, his brother-in-law, were announced. Ascertaining that they had come together, Laure had the *valet de chambre* show them into her rotunda. Three rooms separated her from the rest of the house. She had her back to the door, but turned round, when she heard the footsteps of one person approaching. 'Where is the Duke?' she asked, as Sebastiani came into the room. 'He will be here in a moment, Madame. I have sent him to Suresnes to Mme de Vaudemont, to tell her that we will be dining with her this evening. He will be back.'

'We will wait for him, then, in the garden,' said Laure, going to the French-window.

Before she could reach it, he had hurled himself on her, with an agility astonishing in a man of his age, and seizing her hands so roughly that she let out a cry of pain, threw her on to the divan.

'Understand me well,' he said, 'I am not going out of this room, until I get, if necessary by force, what I would still ask you on my knees. You are in my power. While you kept me waiting, I went out to the concierge, on your behalf, and told him that, having important business to discuss, you were to be disturbed by nobody, not even M. de Metternich. Say what you like of me, it is all the same to me, but I am going to have you now—because I wish it!'

Laure struggled with all her force. She would have torn his face, but he held her hands in the grip of a vice. As she tried to scream, he covered her mouth with his. Breathless, panting, crying she found him on top of her. With a superhuman effort, she managed to free herself, and in turning hit her breast on the edge of a bedside table. She let out a scream of pain. For a moment he relinquished his hold, and she, springing up from the divan, flung herself on the bell rope, which broke with the force of her tug. But the bell sounded, and her *valet de chambre* came.

'Show this gentleman the door,' she managed to say; 'and give orders to the concierge that he is never, never, not even with a member of my family, to be allowed to enter this house again!'

When she was alone, she dissolved in tears. It was clear to her that Sebastiani's actions had been dictated to him from above. The Queen of Naples, now that she occupied a throne, could always find persons low and corrupt enough to satisfy her Corsican sense of revenge. She had wanted to profane, to degrade her. . . Laure had not time to change her torn dress, when Metternich arrived. He had passed Sebastiani at the beginning of the wood. When she had told him, through her sobs, what had occurred, he wanted to run after Sebastiani and accost him there and then. But she stopped him. She already realised that, in the position that they found themselves, there was nothing that they could do that they would have to accept all in silence.

Laure had had no direct word from Junot from Portugal for more than two months. The news she had of affairs in that country, which she received from Metternich, who relied on information coming by way of England, was that matters were very serious there for France. The Emperor was in Bayonne in the summer of 1808, arranging Spanish affairs to the disadvantage of the Bourbon rulers. A civic fête was to be held in the Hôtel de Ville, where Laure in her capacity as *Madame la Gouverneuse* was to receive the Empress. In her anxiety about the fate of Junot she felt that she could not be present at this fête. She sought and received an audience of the Emperor, who had returned from Bayonne and was at Saint-Cloud. In seeking to absent herself from an official function at this juncture, Laure was clearly in the wrong. As the wife of the commander-in-chief in Portugal, it was her duty to be present and show a brave front to the rumours of serious setbacks there, to alleviate the fears of many women who would be at the fête and who had husbands and sons in Portugal. The Emperor was right in insisting on her attendance. With Marshall Lannes, Laure was one of the few persons who dared stand up and speak their minds before the imperiousness of his will and his awe-inspiring rages. In her *Memoirs* she gives the words of her conversation with Napoleon on this occasion at Saint-Cloud.

It was nine o'clock in the evening; the Emperor was in his study, looking upon the little private garden reserved for his use. On her coming into the room, he asked with a show of petulance why she did not believe the reassuring message he had sent her about Junot by Cambacérès. 'Your husband is perfectly well—what the devil do you mean by these conjugal jeremiads?'

'Sire, my mind is relieved since Your Majesty has had the goodness to send me word that I might be easy; but in the situation in which I stand at this moment I am come to entreat Your Majesty to permit me to decline going to the Hôtel de Ville tomorrow.'

'H'm! What do you say? Not go to the Hôtel de Ville? And pray why not?'

'Because, Sire, I feel that some misfortune has occurred to Junot. I beg Your Majesty's pardon'—she saw his expression, which presaged a storm—'But, I repeat, I have no news of Junot—nor has Your Majesty any—and I am unwilling to expose myself to hear, perhaps of his death, in a public ballroom.'

'I have told you that your husband is in good health—why don't you believe me? I cannot prove it, but I give you my word.'

'It is certainly enough to satisfy me, Sire, but I cannot write a circular to communicate this satisfactory assurance to the four thousand persons who will be present at the city fête, and who will think it very extraordinary that I should present myself so publicly when I have such a strong cause for uneasiness.'

He took several steps towards her in his anger, and exclaimed in a terrible voice, 'And what should those four thousand persons know about your cause for uneasiness? This is the result of your drawing-room council, your letters, and all your gossip with my enemies. You attack all my actions. What was that which the Prussian minister, one of your friends, was lately saying at your house about my tyranny towards his King?' This was about the tenth time since Laure's return from Portugal that Napoleon had reported what was said at her house. Most often he was truly informed, but this time it was not true.

'Your Majesty has been misinformed. The Prussian minister has never uttered those words in my house.'

'So I have told an untruth.'

'I have the honour to answer that Your Majesty is misinformed.'

'Oh! to be sure. That is what you all say when you are spoken to as on this occasion.'

The Emperor fixed on her a steady gaze, his displeasure shown in his expression. She averted her eyes, not from fear, but as if it were not becoming of her thus to dispute with him.

'What are Your Majesty's commands?' she said, making to withdraw.

The Emperor did not reply immediately, but after a moment he said, 'I forbid you to repeat what has passed here—do you understand me? See that you obey! or I will let you know who you have to deal with.'

'I shall obey you, Sire, not for fear of your anger, but that I may not have to blush before conquered foreigners at letting them see our family misunderstandings.' But she had still not settled the question that had led her to seek the audience, and she asked the Emperor if it were not more suitable for her to stay away from the Hôtel de Ville, when such reports were current respecting the army of Portugal.

'And what are those reports?' the Emperor asked.

'They say that it is lost—that Junot has been compelled to capitulate like Dupont, and that the English have carried him to Brazil.'

'It is false! It is false, I tell you,' and he struck his fist on a table, dislodging some paper. 'It is false!' and he uttered an oath. 'Junot capitulate like Dupont! It is a tissue of lies, and precisely because it is said you must go to the Hôtel de Ville. You must go—do you hear? Even if you were ill, still you would go. It is my will. Good night.'

In her carriage on the way back to Neuilly Laure wept like a child. The Emperor, she thought, was more than severe towards her and Junot. Home at the Folie de Saint-James she found Metternich awaiting her, to hear the result of her audience. Walking by his side along the lime walk in the summer evening she felt calmer. The next day she was present at the Hôtel de Ville.

In Portugal, however, on 21 August 1808 Junot had been defeated by Sir Arthur Wellesley at the battle of Vimiero, and this was followed on the 30th by the signing of the Convention of Cintra, whereby all French forces were to be withdrawn from Portugal. They were to be repatriated on board English ships to French ports. Laure learned of the Convention from Metternich, who had reports from Holland.

Immediately on receiving the news, Laure asked for an audience of the Emperor, who was at Saint-Cloud. Very naturally he wanted to know the source of her information. Laure was silent. 'I suspected as much,' said Napoleon. 'Well, Junot can make what he will of it. I wipe my hands of the matter.' In her *Journal intime*, she goes on: 'If he had limited himself to these few words, all would have been well. But he added some things which derogated from the nobility of my feelings. I replied to him with the pride that those feelings evoke, and it is this which he has had written himself, in the memoirs of Las Cases —that I *treated him like a small boy*'. It is unfortunate that she does not enlarge on this, since Las Cases, still smarting after nearly twenty years from an injury he felt he had received from Junot, is a prejudiced and inaccurate witness. In his *Mémorial de Sainte-Hélène* he wrote: 'The Emperor added that, less still as a sovereign than as loving Junot,

guided also by the connection of birth in Corsica, of which his wife was
a native, he had her come one day in order to give her some paternal
advice on the inordinate expenses of her husband, on the profusion of
diamonds that on her return from Portugal she, Madame Junot, had
thoughtlessly displayed; on her intimate relations with a stranger . . .
which might have political repercussions, etc. But she indignantly
brushed aside this advice dictated by her interest alone. She became
angry, said the Emperor, and I was treated like a small boy. It only
remained for me to send her packing and to abandon her to her own
devices.'

Junot had been forbidden by the Emperor to come to Paris. On
arrival in France he was to set out straightway for Spain. Laure was
waiting to hear at which port he had landed, so that she might go to
meet him, when the Emperor sent for her on 15 October to come to
Saint-Cloud. He informed her that Junot was at La Rochelle; then,
with that petty malice which was characteristic of him, he said, with a
smile, 'He is not alone. Here, read this,' and he handed her a translation
from an English newspaper:

> 'We are always happy to bring back to France one of the brave
> generals of the Corsican, but he is not alone, and we have been able
> again this time to convince ourselves that the East has inculcated in
> him its customs. His seraglio was still more numerous than in 1801.
> Mme Foy and Mme La Comtesse d'Ega hold there the first rank.'

Laure went to La Rochelle, and found Junot very much changed.
General Thiébault in his *Memoirs* says that Junot in Lisbon had given
evidence of the first onset of what was to become general paralysis of
the insane. Laure's *Journal intime* records this unfortunate meeting
between husband and wife. She knew that Junot was aware of her
relations with Metternich and was also conscious that she had been
informed of his behaviour in Lisbon. He asked her to invite Mme Foy.
She refused.

'Still the same jealous Laure,' he said.

'No, I am not jealous. Nor do I any longer weep,' she replied.

The first evening he came into her room. 'What,' she said, smiling,
'do you want an old married couple to celebrate their wedding
anniversary? Don't be funny. Kiss me and take yourself off.'

'But I am going to sleep here. There are two beds.' Laure had
already noticed them. 'I had them brought in,' he said. 'This morning

I was deeply struck in seeing you again. I find you prettier than ever. You well know, and you abuse, your power over me.'

'No, I certainly do not,' she replied; 'but the position of the two of us is absurd. You should go away and leave me.' She saw his face become suddenly disturbed.

'Is it true that M. de Metternich is your lover?'

His voice was uncertain, his eyes were wild. He frightened her. She hastened to approach him. 'My friend,' she said, 'we are playing here singular parts. You affect the jealous husband, when it is I who should be the one to complain. Is it in this way that we are to pass the first night of our reunion?'

They spent an unhappy fortnight together in La Rochelle. Laure felt under a constant restraint, while on Junot's side there was a renewal of love, or rather desire. It was a frenzy, an amorous fury that repelled instead of attracting her. Often she freed herself from his arms in pain from a bite or too powerful an embrace. She felt that the senses were all, love nothing. She could not love in that way. They separated; Junot, who thought he was to have a chance of redeeming his tarnished laurels in Portugal, to take command of the 3rd Corps at the siege of Sargossa; Laure to return to Paris.

There she found herself very much alone. Metternich had been recalled to Vienna. There were reports that Austria was secretly rearming; all presaged renewed war. When Metternich returned after two months his reception by Napoleon was cavalier. The authorities were ordered to close their doors to him; scandalous references to him appeared in the newspapers. Laure alone continued to receive him each day on the Champs-Elysées, and when Duroc called to warn her not to brave the Emperor, she replied that she was not an authority. Finally Metternich was obliged to depart, leaving behind him in Paris his wife and children as little short of hostages.

News reached Paris of the terrible battle of Wagram, fought on 5 and 6 July, 1809 and the defeat of the Austrians. The victory, however, was dearly bought; in the two-day battle 23,000 Frenchmen were killed or wounded and 7,000 missing. Particularly heavy were the casualties among the troops under Macdonald's command. In an attack by 30,000 men only 3,000 reached the enemy, whose guns tore huge gaps through their mass, leaving a dreadful carnage of dead and dying bodies, that shook the morale of even the bravest. This was the reality behind the talk of glory. Laure, too, was guilty of this veiling of the truth.

Every week Laure received two letters from Metternich, who had found a secret channel for their correspondence through the agency of the Comte des Audrouins. She sent her old maid Josephine, who had been in her mother's service and had been present at her birth, to send and collect her letters. From them she learned that Metternich had been appointed Foreign Secretary by the Emperor Francis II. The agitations of these disturbed times brought on a nervous illness, and on medical advice she went to take the waters at Cauterets in the Pyrenees. She returned to Paris in October, her nervous complaint apparently cured, but with a pain in her chest and a tendency to spit blood which frightened her. Shortly after her return Junot returned, back from Saragossa. Her worst fears of the state of his mind were confirmed. His temper was uncertain, his mood being constantly sombre, at times wild. His remarks to her were often sarcastic; his attitude was ambivalent; it was clear that love was corroded with jealousy.

The King and Queen of Naples arrived in Paris on a visit to the Emperor, to attempt to put right the serious differences that had arisen between him and Murat, who had taken it into his head that he was the ruler in his kingdom. On 2 December, the anniversary of the Emperor's coronation, a grand fête was to be held at the Hôtel de Ville. Junot, Duke of Abrantès, and Laure, as Governor of Paris and his wife, were to receive the Emperor and Empress. In spite of her being very unwell, Laure went, arriving at four o'clock. Shortly after her arrival a message was brought to her from the grand-master of ceremonies, M. de Ségur. It informed her that he had received orders from the Emperor that the Empress was not to be received by Laure and her ladies at the entrance, as was the custom. This was the first public intimation of the coming divorce, and it saddened Laure, who had a real affection for Josephine. The Emperor arrived, accompanied by the Queen of Naples, the Duke of Abrantès and Prince Berthier. During dinner, from her place near the Empress, Laure could see her attempts to hold back her tears. After dinner the ball was opened, the Duke of Abrantès dancing with the Queen and Laure with the King of Naples. When the dance was finished and Laure was retiring, she suddenly felt faint. Junot was at her side, and noticing her extreme pallor, he was able to catch her as she fainted. He carried her into the nearby room of the Prefect of the Seine, where she vomited blood from a broken blood-vessel, staining her court dress. Medical assistance was quickly found, and she came to. She asked Junot to send for her carriage to take her home, and then insisted that he resume his official duties. The Queen of Naples had seen all this, had observed Junot's concern, and found an occasion to speak to him. Laure was afterwards certain that it was from this moment, convinced of Junot's continued love for her, that Caroline decided on her revenge.

For a long time Count Marescalchi, Minister of Foreign Affairs for the Kingdom of Italy, had requested the Emperor that he be allowed to give a reception in his honour. With this end in view, he had had built a pavilion in the garden of his hôtel in the rue d'Angoulême. The Emperor at length accepted, and the day was fixed for 13 January 1810. For this fête the Queen of Naples arranged a quadrille to represent a game of chess; it was devised by the dancing master Despréaux, and was pronounced charming. Sixteen pieces took part, all ladies of the same height; the two Queens were the Duchess of Bassano and the beautiful Mme de Barral; Laure was one of the pawns. Waxed canvas, marked with the squares of a chess-board, was placed on the floor; and each piece danced, when two opposing magicians armed with wands, touched the dancers lightly on the shoulder.

Although Laure and Metternich had been separated for a year, their love for each other seemed only strengthened. On the day of the Marescalchi fête she received a letter from him.

'"I cannot live without you," he wrote; "I feel that I cannot. Surrounded here by glory and honours, I do not wish to retain them if I am not to see you. If you do not promise me to have yourself ordered to take the waters of Carlsbad and come this year, I will leave my ministry and have myself named ambassador to France."'
She rang for her maid Josephine, and giving her the letter, bade her place it with the other letters in a precious box of Chinese wood, which had been given her by Metternich for this purpose, and of which Josephine had the key.

Laure gives the events of this fateful night in her *Journal intime*. At eight o'clock she left the house, but before doing so she went into the drawing room to find Junot.

'How do I look tonight?' she asked. He regarded her without replying. 'Do I look awful, then?' she said, surprised at his silence.

'Awful? Oh, no; you look only too pretty.' And he went up to her and seized her hand with violence. 'Sometimes I feel a desire to give you a wound that will disfigure you. Then you would no longer please.'

These words which at another time would have only produced laughter, made her shiver. However, forcing a smile, she showed him the dress she was going to change into after the quadrille, so that he could recognize her. It was a domino of rose satin, with a broad white band. She left him, setting out in her carriage to pick up a fellow-pawn.

After the quadrille, which was a great success, she, like the other dancers, were obliged to go quickly to change, to avoid the pleasantries, such remarks as 'Look, there's a pawn. Let's queen her.' Putting on her pretty rose domino, she came back to the ballroom. As she entered, she ran into the Duc de la Vauguyon, the Queen of Naples' current lover. He recognized her immediately. She recounts this curious conversation in the *Journal*:

' "Since I have not been clever enough to disguise myself, you will give me your arm," I said. "But as I do not wish your Queen to take umbrage, I am going to take off my mask. . ."

' "That will allow me to see your eyes," said the Duke, "and you know what I think of their regard."

' "Take care," I replied, laughing. "Those whose slave you are will launch on us their lightnings which will pulverise us; and, however used you are to the eruption of Vesuvius, in comparison with them I believe that is a small matter."

' "Yes, and beware of taking it too lightly," said a voice near us.

' "It is the Queen!" I said in a low voice to M. de la Vauguyon.

' "What does it matter?" he replied. "It is odious to be spied on in this way. When slavery is no longer prestige," he added in a loud voice, "it is necessary to snap out of it."

' "Quiet, in heaven's name! Be quiet for my sake, if not for yours."

'I was trembling. Her perceived it and pressed my arm.

' "What are you frightened of?"

' "I don't know, but I don't feel well."

' "Come, let us go into the first Throne Room, and it will pass off." '

They went into the room, which was so filled with people that they could move only with difficulty. Laure was laughing at a remark of M. de Vauguyon's, when she felt herself seized by the arm with such force that she let out a cry. She turned and saw a large figure in a black domino; his face was covered with a black mask which was agitated by his heavy breathing. M. de la Vauguyon was just about to remonstrate with the man for the insult when Laure recognized Junot. Leaving the Duke's arm, with a sad smile, she took that of her husband.

To her utter astonishment she was immediately dragged away and led across the room and hurried through the corridors to the vestibule, where Junot shouted in a voice of thunder for his carriage. His servants were not there, but Laure's were, and she found herself in the carriage. Then, Junot tore off his mask, and began cursing and uttering imprecations against Count Metternich. He was beside himself with rage, in his fury breaking the windows of the carriage. In this way they reached the Champs-Elysées.

Inside, he forced her up the stairs and through the rooms, until reaching her bedroom, he flung her in an armchair. Shutting the door and locking it, he stood in front of her, his arms folded. He then accused her of betraying him, of dishonouring his name. He abused Metternich.

'He used to visit you at Neuilly', he said. 'He entered by the postern gate by the grotto. You gave him the key. He writes to you, sending his letters through the Comte des Ardrouins. You received one this morning, saying that if you did not come to Carlsbad, he would come to Paris. You see I am well informed.'

When Laure tried to speak, he silenced her. On one condition, he said, he would forgive her, forgive them both. That is, if she would that instant put in his hands the sandalwood box, in which were Metternich's letters and a bracelet containing a lock of his hair. Laure, seeing that he knew everything, rose mechanically from her chair, took a lamp, and going up to Josephine's room, returned with the box and gave it to Junot. He was very pale, and his hand trembled.

He would forgive her, he said, if she swore never to have anything further to do with Metternich. Laure swore, but begged him to throw the box and the contents on the fire, as reading the letters would do neither of them any good.

'No,' he said, 'by these I can tell if you were well loved.'

Laure sighed, and Junot, interpreting this as a sign that she still loved, was moved to fury. 'Don't tell me that you still love him!' Her reply was to burst into tears. At the sight of her tears, Junot's anger quickly changed into tenderness. He took her in his arms. He blamed Caroline Murat for their separation. Would she not come back to him? Weeping she did not reply. He kissed her eyes, her cheeks. His lips trembled as they reached hers. His tenderness suddenly changed to passion and he tried to make love to her. She struggled against his too violent embraces. A bite on her lips gave her the strength to break away. Pointing to the box, which lay on a table, she said, 'Actions like these will not wipe out the past.' He looked at her with hate, then, picking up the box, he left the room, slamming the door so that it resounded throughout the house.

Never had Laure passed such a night as this. She threw herself on the bed, but her anxiety and her fears prevented sleep. It was scarcely daylight when she heard a carriage leave the house. Ringing for Josephine, she learned that Junot had left for the Tuileries. Stanislas de Giradin says in his *Journal* that a 'furious husband' had a chilling reception from the Emperor. ' "Ah, my dear fellow," he said, "I would not have time to occupy myself with the affairs of Europe, if I took on the task of revenging all the cuckolds of my court." '

It was nearly nine when the sound of carriage wheels announced Junot's return. She heard his footsteps in the next room, then he came in, locking the door behind him. His face, changed from its usual heightened complexion, was of ghastly pallor; it looked as if it had caved in. He approached her bed, and told her to read a letter he held, but first of all to hold out her left hand. He wrenched off a ring, which was inscribed with the date of her meeting Metternich in the lime walk at Neuilly. Apparently he had recognized it earlier as not his. The letter was a challenge to Metternich. Laure, who was lying on her bed, clothed only in a light cambric dressing-gown, tore up the letter, after glancing at it, and, getting up, threw the pieces in the fire. 'What did you do that for?' he asked.

'You have not kept your word,' she replied. 'Last night you swore that you would say no more of this affair. And what right have you to reproach me for loving, you whom I loved with all the single-mindedness of first love? You who have humiliated me before the eyes of all Europe. Who are you to recriminate against me? And now you threaten with death a man, who, like you, is the father of a family, and for what crime? For loving sincerely, genuinely—a thing you have never done.'

Junot came up to her, and caught her by the arm so roughly that his nails dug into her flesh. 'Have you finished?' he said. 'It is not to come back to me that you wanted my forgiveness, but to go on loving that man. You still love him, don't you?'

Laure did not reply, but the tears rolling down her cheeks, she slumped on a sofa. Junot walked up and down the room, then stopped in front of her and demanded if she possessed anything else of Metternich's. She shook her head. 'Just as well,' he said, 'or I would have brought it back to you, but covered in his blood.' At this, Laure rose, and throwing her arms around him, begged him for her sake, and that of his children, not to fight. 'Return to yourself,' she said, 'and if you have ever really loved me, put out of your mind all thought of vengeance.' He looked at her, then flung her with violence on to the sofa. 'Your fears are not for me,' he cried, 'it is not my death you fear, but his. It is not me you love, but him.' He bent over her, taking her by the hair, 'Say that you curse him! he cried, beyond himself with passion, 'Say that you hate him!'

'Ah, never.' she replied.

Immediately, picking up some gold sewing scissors that were on her work-table, he struck her six blows on the chest. Standing back, his eyes wild, he stared at her. Blood oozed from the wounds and from her mouth. She had burst another blood vessel. Then, flinging himself on top of her, he put his hands round her neck, as if to strangle her. His face was twisted and discoloured with demented rage. Laure, with no sense of fear, awaited death, when she felt his hands relax their grip.

'I can't do it,' Junot said.

Opening her eyes, she saw him standing over her, his face and clothes covered with blood. He stumbled across the room and threw himself into an armchair. She heard him groaning. He remained seated for some little time. Suddenly he rose and went to a bureau, where he took up a pen and wrote. He was quite calm. Next he went to the washstand, and taking a sponge, wiped the blood from his face and clothes. He rang, and went to the door. Laure heard him speaking to the *valet de chambre*. 'When she comes,' he said, 'just knock and show her in, but don't come in yourself.' He then sat down again, covering his face with his hands. Later Laure thought that the scenes that she had witnessed were an early access of his madness.

Scarcely ten minutes had passed, when there was a knock on the door. Junot opened it, and there entered the Countess Metternich. He had written to her in Laure's name, and she, living only a few steps away at the hôtel de Courlande, had come immediately. Seeing Laure pale, dishevelled and covered with blood, she hurried to her side. Junot stopped her; seizing her by the arm, he pushed her into a chair.

'Listen to me,' he said, 'Your husband is this woman's lover. She is my wife. I loved her and still love her. What I felt when I heard that she was your husband's mistress, was nothing to what I felt last night, when I read his letters. I have the right to demand satisfaction from him. But if I killed him, would I have satisfaction for what I have felt? I know a means of making him suffer. They say he is a good father. I will kill his children. On your side you can take your revenge on this woman. I leave her to you. Just now I could have killed her, but something restrained me. . .'

During Junot's demented talk the expression on the face of Mme de Metternich was one of incredulity, stupefaction. The sight of Laure, lying half naked and covered with blood, the sound of his distracted voice, filled her with something approaching terror. 'My God,' she said, 'My God.' Coming to Laure's side, she enquired what she could do for her. Laure, with a feeble voice, asked her to forgive the wrong she had done her. Turning to Junot, she said, 'Monsieur le Duc, the part of Othello hardly becomes you, you who have scandalised France with your behaviour. To have acted in this way is criminal, the action of a madman. Poor woman. . .'

Junot cut her short, with a mocking laugh. 'You are tarred with the same brush,' he said, 'to sympathise with the mistress of your husband.'

'Monsieur le Duc,' she replied, 'I shall remain no longer to listen to your insults.' She came up to Laure, and bending down, asked again what she could do. Could she send help?

'No,' Laure said, 'I only want to die.'

When the Countess had gone, Junot sat down on a chair beside Laure's sofa, and took her hand. She shivered.

'I revolt you,' he said.

She did not reply. From the sound of his heavy breathing she suspected that a fresh outbreak was imminent. By her words, in fact, she provoked it.

'What does it matter, since we must separate?' she said.

'Separate?'

'You don't imagine after this that I can remain in the same house as you?' This question brought on a new paroxysm of rage from Junot, in which was mingled not a little fear. He tried to make her swear she would not leave him. When she refused, he insisted. He got up, flinging the chair from him.

'Alexandre,' she said, 'your anger does not terrify me. I repeat that it is my intention to leave you.'

For some moments he stood, looking at her. Then he bent down and took her in his arms. Kissing her, he said, 'We shall never leave each other. You once loved me; you will love me again. You will come back to me. You must.' Feebly she tried to fend off his kisses, but her weakness was too great. All she was able to do was to turn away her mouth, to close her eyes. Holding her inert body in his

arms, he became increasingly amorous. She could do nothing but submit to his passionate embraces. For an hour she remained in a condition
of physical and moral agony, then gradually he came to his senses.

He got up and rang for Josephine, to fetch the doctor. When
M.Magnien arrived, she was unconscious. Dr Dubois was sent for.
By the time he came they had got her to bed and had dressed her
wounds. At last, well after midnight, she fell into an uneasy sleep.

The following day she was visited by Madame Mère, coming on her
own account and on behalf of the Emperor. Terrified by her threat of
leaving him, Junot had been to the Tuileries, and the Emperor had
sent for his mother and had told her on his part to convey to Laure that
he did not wish the separation to take place. Madame Mère, who
loved Junot for his loving Napoleon, and Laure for being her mother's
child, used every means to reconcile them, and her solicitations were
added to by their friends—and by the tears of the children, who,
without knowing why, came to ask her 'to forgive Papa'. And forgive
him she did, although, she said, with an 'ulcerated' heart.

Far different were her feelings towards the Queen of Naples, when
she discovered the part that she had played in 'this bloody tragedy'.
Princess Caroline, knowing that Laure was communicating with
Metternich, sent for her maid Josephine and extracted from the old
servant, by means of a very large bribe, knowledge of the existence of
the casket of letters and the part played by the Comte des Ardrouins
in his rôle of agent. Then by means of anonymous letters she informed
the Duke of Abrantès. Junot, not sufficiently the *grand seigneur* to
overlook in his wife extra-conjugal intimacies that he permitted
himself, waited until Laure had left for Count Marescalchi's ball before
assuring for himself that Josephine was in possession of the precious
box. The sequel was the result of his insane jealousy, but, in justice to
him, he was already not always the master of his own actions.

The day after she had forgiven Junot she learned that all Paris was
talking of the affair. The channel most likely would have been the
servants. Laure concludes her *Journal intime* for Balzac:

'The following Friday the first performance of *Fernand Cortez* was
put on at the Opera. . . I felt that I did nothing if I did not by my
behaviour put paid to the rumours, which by their nature were
damaging. I said to Junot that I would go to the Opera. . .

'He resisted for form's sake, but I saw that he was happy with my
resolve. I got up only at six o'clock. . . I put on some rouge to hide my

extreme pallor and, thus adorned, having in my box only devoted friends, I took myself to the Opera.

'Scarcely was I in my box than every regard was directed on me. I was in torment. Soon a sort of murmur arose and I heard some phrases directed against Alexandre which could only have irritated him. To remove all suspicion I smiled at him, and spoke to him as naturally as I was able to put on. What an evening! . . .

'I finish this narrative. A short time after what I have just said, Junot was appointed to command the 8th Corps in Spain.

' "I will depart also," I said to him.

' "That is impossible."

' "I wish to go. If I remain in France after such an *éclat*, I would have to retire to the country, far from Paris. I cannot remain here after what has just happened. If I separate from you at this moment, I know that hate could rise up between us. I am frank and am not able to dissemble what I feel. If we set out together, painful memories will be effaced. Alexandre, I want to go."

'He was moved and embraced me without speaking.'

1 Madame Junot in her wedding dress 2 General Buonaparte, engraved from an original painting by Cossia, Verona 1797 3 Josephine as wife of the First Consul, engraved from a miniature by Isaby 4 Madame Mère

5 Malmaison: the lawn on which the First Consul played games
with his guests 6 The Library at Malmaison 7 General Junot,
Duke of Abrantès 8 Caroline Murat

9 The coronation of Josephine, by David   10 Count Metternich, by Sir Thomas Lawrence   11 The Duchess of Abrantès, from a miniature by Quaglia

12 The Duchess of Abrantès *c.* 1830, by Gavarini 13 Honoré de Balzac as a young man 14 Maurice de Balincourt

SEVEN

War and Peace

THE JUNOTS set out for Spain at midnight on 2 February 1810. It was excessively cold. Laure, who had cropped her hair, wore a grey cashmere riding-habit, a well-furred Polish cap, fur boots and a large travelling cloak. They made a short stop at Bordeaux, where Laure paid a visit to the aging mother of her childhood friend Laure Caseaux. Junot also paid a visit, an expensive one. He called on an actress, and for this one visit paid 12,000 francs. The lady was henceforth known in Bordeaux as Mme la Duchesse. At Bayonne he received orders to make all speed for Burgos and, despite his protests, Laure insisted on accompanying him much of the way on horseback. She was dismayed to see, when they entered Spain, the ravages of war everywhere in the beautiful countryside through which she had passed so few years before on their Portuguese embassy.

In the evening of their fourth day in Spain she was tired, and suggested that they rode in the carriage. Junot immediately settled himself in a corner and was soon asleep. Laure, a prey to sad thoughts, watched the changing landscape through the window. The road, which was steep and winding, ascended a hillside covered with boulders of brownish granite interspersed with groups of stunted oaks. She recalls the scene in her *Memoirs:* 'I looked out vaguely in front of me, and saw slowly disappear each detour of the mountain, for the road was steep and dangerous. Suddenly, arrived on a level, I saw in front of me an oak of a strange form and aspect. Its branches appeared to me broken and to move heavily in the wind which, at this spot on the mountain, blew more violently. My sight, which is very short, did not allow me to distinguish completely the appearance of this tree. While I looked for my glasses, the carriage had climbed the slope and had arrived immediately below the tree. The postilion, almost asleep from the slowness of the mules, only half turned round. I advanced my head in order to see better and, in the movement, my forehead received a kick from the foot of a horrible corpse, naked, bleeding, mangled, and hanging from the tree as a warning of French justice. Nor was it alone; there were three more!

'At my cry Junot awoke and the postilion stopped the mules. He stopped them in front of the four corpses which I did not wish to see, but which, by a horrible attraction, I could not stop myself from looking at. Oh! for how long afterwards have I seen in my dreams those figures, whose last expression had been that of rage, but of a demoniacal rage. I still see their mangled and clotted limbs, and the mules, their ears straight, their nostrils dilated, drawing back in dread of death—of those corpses more horrible than all that horror can present us.'

At Laure's distress Junot complacently remarked that she should reserve her sensibility for other worse evils. A few days later at Pancorvo, among the bushes of juniper and box that grew, with thyme and lavender, between the rocks, the soldiers found a corpse that had been hacked to pieces. On one of the arms they recognized the remnants of a French uniform. Laure was not to be spared any of the horrors of this most cruel, as it was the most unnecessary, of wars. She was seeing at first hand the consequences of Napoleon's thirst for glory.

At Vittoria there were letters from Paris, with the news that the children were well. By the time they reached Burgos Laure was badly in need of rest. Her presence there among all the savagery of this war was a source of amazement and admiration to the French officers. It was at Burgos that she learned of the forthcoming marriage of the Emperor Napoleon with the Archduchess Marie-Louise of Austria. The headquarters of the 8th Corps was at Valladolid and there they installed themselves in the magnificent house, or rather palace, built by Charles the Fifth. A ball was given in Laure's honour by General Kellerman, the commandant, and she in turn gave another for the ladies of Valladolid. As in Paris, she kept open house. Not long after their arrival despatches from Paris informed Junot of the appointment of Marshal Masséna, the Prince of Essling, as commander-in-chief of the French forces in the Peninsula. Junot limited the expression of his injured feelings at this news to remarking that the Emperor did not consider Marshal Ney or him fit for trust and was placing them under tutelage.

Considering that the palace was sufficiently spacious to accommodate the two staffs, Junot counted on surrendering half to the Marshal, but he had forgotten the latter's habits of campaigning. When he and his staff galloped out from Valladolid to welcome the commander-in-chief, they found in the carriage beside him what appeared to be a young subaltern decorated with the cross of the Legion of Honour. Masséna was surprised and clearly embarrassed at hearing of Laure's presence, and that he was to share the palace with the Junots. Junot, when he discovered that the 'subaltern' was the Marshal's mistress, was not at all put out. Laure was, however; and at dinner that evening, when she came down and saw the young lady present, she found that she was suddenly feeling unwell, and excused herself. For the rest of the time that the Junots spent at Valladolid Masséna's mistress remained in her own apartments. Relations between Junot and his chief were difficult from the outset, and friction from their staffs' having to share accommodation did not help matters.

In fact, bad relations between the generals and Masséna boded ill for the success of the French in the Peninsula, where they were opposed by a general of the calibre of Wellington. Masséna wanted to send Ney home to France, and Junot had great difficulty in disuadings him from doing so. Troops were seconded from the various commands to undertake the siege of Ciudad-Rodrigo, held by the Spaniards. One day in June Laure, who finding herself pregnant had kept to her room, was disturbed by Junot, who came in beside himself with rage. These uncontrollable accesses of anger were of frequent occurrence. They were then in Salamanca. 'It is necessary to finish it,' he muttered, 'all this bores me. A good cut of the sabre will settle it.' He picked up his hat and sabre and was about to leave the room, when Laure barred his way.

'Where are you going?' she asked with a tone of authority that she found necessary to employ with him.

He took her by the arm and pulled her aside. 'Leave me, Laure, there are questions that do not concern you. My honour is attacked by the Prince of Essling. He knows my character, he knows that I will not support an injury, and it is one to take troops from my corps without warning me. It is not the first time either, and I have an account to settle with him. Leave me, I say.' He grasped the hilt of his sabre.

'You will not go out of this room,' she said, ahead of Junot at the door.

Fortunately in an adjoining room were members of Junot's staff, and Laure was able to warn them what was afoot. But the paroxysm of his rage had already passed. He realised that he could not fight with the old veteran of Rivoli.

On 11 July Ciudad-Rodrigo surrendered to the French. Little more than two months later, on 15 September, Laure arrived to live in this war-scarred town, while Junot advanced with the army into Portugal. There, in a house whose roof was half destroyed, among the ruins of demolished buildings, the air heavy with the smell of fire and the stench from bodies buried so close to the surface of the ground that dogs dug them up to feed on the flesh, Laure gave birth to her son Alfred. Junot wanted at first to call the child Rodrigue. This boy, born almost on a battlefield, was to die on a battlefield; he was killed at the battle of Solferino in 1859. Ten days after his birth Laure left Ciudad-Rodrigo, insisting on travelling on horseback, through a countryside overrun with guerillas, for the comparative safety of Salamanca.

Salamanca was then commanded by General Thiébault, who had been Junot's chief of staff in Portugal, and who has left most interesting memoirs. The General had been informed of Laure's setting out from Ciudad-Rodrigo, but he also learned that the celebrated guerrilla leader Don Julian planned to waylay and capture her in the wood of Matilla. Knowing that the escort with which she was travelling was too weak to withstand an attack from the formidable band commanded by Don Julian, General Thiébault despatched two columns, one to the right, the other to the left of the wood, while he put himself at the head of two squadrons and advanced directly to meet her.

General Coüin, who commanded the detachment in escort—Laure and the little Alfred proceeding in a light carriage and the sick and wounded in carts—had so badly timed their progress that they approached the wood of Matilla when it was already dark. The road was only a rough track cut through the wood, covered with tree stumps against which a carriage could be easily upset and which caused the horses to stumble. The soldiers were foolhardy enough to gather the dry heather, which they found beneath the oak trees, and from it to kindle torches, to light the way. General Coüin was too far ahead at first to give the order to put out the torches, which would betray their presence to the guerrillas. Suddenly, in the wood, they were aware of the sound of horses. A voice cried 'Halt!' Laure, hearing the voices and tumult in front of them, had given herself up for lost, when she recognized the sound of French. Then in the darkness she heard someone enquiring for the Duchess of Abrantès. It was General Thiébault. Spending the night at Matilla, the next morning they were safely at Salamanca. After this episode, Wellington, learning of Don Julian's intention to capture the Duchess, sent instructions that he should desist, since, he said, 'they did not make war on women'.

General Thiébault had prepared for Laure a house, formerly occupied by Marshal Ney, furnishing it as well as he could in the conditions in which they found themselves. There she entertained the French officers, who were delighted to find in Salamanca a house which offered the amenities that they associated with home. 'It was,' wrote the General in his *Mémoires*, 'an inconceivable fortune the society of a lady so distinguished in the depths of Estramadura. Desirable everywhere, it was inestimable in the middle of these provincial Spaniards, the smartest of whom did not approach in instruction and manners our *femmes de chambre* in a good household. It was then all that which our century could produce in amiability, in education, in brilliance; it was one of the first *salons* of Paris transported into the midst of a population which seemed to belong to a past age; and more still than a society, it was a woman whose character equalled her merits.' When Marshal Bessières offered to escort Laure to the comparative safety of Valladolid, and General Thiébault added his recommendation that she avail herself of his offer, she refused to leave Salamanca, saying that she had promised Junot that she would await him there. 'It was necessary to have found oneself there,' wrote Thiébault, 'to appreciate the courage of this resolution. I was very much struck by it. In putting herself in this way above the considerations which would have persuaded all other women, the Duchess placed herself above her sex . . . and she showed that she could raise her character, her force of sentiment, to the level of so many other qualities, of a merit which the world has judged, to which posterity will pay homage.'

She had as companion Mme Thomières, wife of the general. Alfred was doing well; news of her other children was good. She was therefore content, but, as she herself wrote, 'I was young then and I did not yet know what I have since learnt: it is that it is necessary never to build on what one believes a certainty of happiness.' As was always her way, she put her heart into entertaining. General Thiébault paints a pleasant picture of these evenings *chez la Duchesse d'Abrantès* in Salamanca: 'The evenings of the Duchess were occupied with music, chess, reading letters or newspapers from Paris, the news of Spain, rumours from Portugal, and conversation. Chess retained only the Duchess and me, if not always at least very often. Music was provided by the Marquis de Valença and [General] Fournier as singers; the

Duchess singing at times, but usually she played the piano, as accompanist or to play some little sonatas which she had composed for her daughters; and myself, putting to music some romances of which she or her brother, M. de Permon, had furnished the words. Letters kept us in touch with the news of Paris and the Tuileries, and made us forget for the moment the land of exile, which began to give us more fears than hopes. Conversations, which were fed by these subjects and a thousand others, were enhanced by all the seduction, which the Duchess brought to them by the grace and facility of her speech, by the clarity of her ideas, the choice of her expressions, and I will say almost the profundity with which she treated the most varied subjects. Often she astonished us. One evening among others, the talk turning on the art of the theatre, the Duchess holding forth on the subject brought up the parallel between the theatre of the ancients and that of the moderns. She spoke for more than an hour and left us, M.Luuyt and me, confounded with the erudition and the indescribable power of observation of which she gave proof, but more with the order that she put into her account, of the linking together of her ideas and the elegance of her choice of expressions. "My word," M.Luuyt asked me, as we were leaving, "what more could say a professor, who, all his life, had studied the matter?" And I would have asked the same question.'

The rumours of reverses became a reality; it was learned that Masséna's army, unable to break the English lines at Torres-Vedras, had fallen back and was now in full retreat. It was retreating on a countryside despoiled by the inhabitants of any vestige of food or fodder, and infested with guerrillas, who were in communication with Wellington. Indeed, he was in possession of full information of what went on behind Masséna's lines, including the sorry condition of the French forces. It was at this time that Laure learned that Junot had been wounded at Rio-Mayor, a ball striking him in the face, breaking his nose and embedding itself, from which it required a painful operation to extract it. Wellingtom wrote to Junot, whose troops were in actual contact with the English:

'Headquarters, January 17th, 1811

'Sir,—I learn with great regret that you have been wounded, and I beg you will let me know whether I can send you anything that may be of use in dressing your wound or accelerating your recovery.

'I do not know whether you have lately heard from the Duchess. At the end of last month she was delivered of a son at Ciudad-

Rodrigo. She has left that place for Salamanca, and intended to proceed to France at the beginning of this month.

'I have the honour to remain, Sir, your very obedient servant.

Wellington.

'Monsieur Duke of Abrantès.'

Marshal Ney, who ill supported being under the orders of Masséna, after withdrawing his forces out of the reach of the enemy and leaving them in safe quarters, took it on himself to return to France. Arriving in Salamanca, he called on Laure and did not spare her accounts of Masséna's incompetence. He also brought news of Junot who, he said, would soon be rejoining her. When Junot reached Toro, where Laure had gone in company with Mme Thomières, Laure was horrified at his appearance. It was not only his recent facial wound, but she saw that he was suffering from wounds within—from the failure of the French army, the faults of Masséna (he was to be replaced by Marshal Marmont in May 1811), the successes of the English, and by a letter he had received from the Emperor in which he sensed a coldness towards him. But their stay in Spain was nearly over. There came orders from the Emperor that the 8th Corps was to be merged in a reorganized Army of Portugal, and that Junot was to return to France to take up a new appointment. Laure recounts the excitement at this news: 'It is necessary to have undergone a long exile, far from one's country, to appreciate the harmonious magic of these words: "Laure, we are returning to France." I made a bound from my carriage on to Junot's neck. I embraced him, weeping and laughing at the same time. There is a sweet folly in such a moment. All griefs were forgotten. All.' Before they left Toro, Marmont, on his way to take up his command, came on a visit to his old comrade-in-arms.

Junot himself commanded the escort to the returning columns. Mme Thomières accompanied Laure, tearful at leaving her husband in Spain, whom she feared she would never see again. Her fears were realized; General Thomières was killed at the battle of Salamanca. The first part of the journey was uneventful, but at Bribiesca rumours of guerrilla actions in the north gave them cause for alarm. It was said that the bridge at Bidassoa had been destroyed by the guerrilla leader Mina, that the town of Vittoria had been sacked, that General Caffarelli had been murdered. They heard of the fearful massacre at Salinas de Lecy, which was on their route. At Vittoria General Caffarelli advised them to wait, but Junot, thinking that the guerrillas

were unlikely to strike again so soon, decided to press on. Salinas was
a narrow defile in the mountains, through which flowed a stream, the
Eva. In the middle of the defile they came upon the scene of the
ambushed French columns the bodies of men, women and children
lying where they had fallen. Arms gnawed by dogs, half putrefied
limbs, heads whose faces and hair were matted with blood, and over
all a fetid stench which sickened—it summed up for Laure all the
horrors of the war in Spain. At Bidassoa they found that the bridge
was still intact, and on foot she re-entered France.

Back once more in Paris, Junot went off to take the waters at
Barèges, while Laure resumed the mode of life to which her talents
were so particularly suited. She took up again her service with Madame
Mère. To a person so socially sensitive as she it did not take long to find
the cause of the subtle change which pervaded the atmosphere of Paris.
This was the new ascendancy of the Faubourg Saint-Germain, which
had now gravitated to the Tuileries. There a new court was already
fully formed, a court which, in the phrase of Saint-Simon, 'sweated
hyprocrisy'. But first Laure had to undergo the formalities of a fresh
presentation, to the young Empress Marie-Louise, whom she found as
insignificant as reports had prepared her. Like her mother, Laure felt
the need of constantly having people around her. Before long her
salon on the Champs-Elysées had become once more the best known
and most distinguished in Paris. It has been said of Laure de'Abrantès
that she, more than any other single hostess, set the tone for post-
Revolutionary French society, even that she was 'the first modern
woman'. The drawing rooms that later Proust frequented were in a
tradition first formed by her. In her *salon* she gathered about her those
whose distinction in one walk of life or another marked them out.
Once a fortnight she gave a purely military dinner party for eighty
guests in the great gallery, that Junot had had built in the garden—
marshals, generals and colonels and their wives, others of lower rank
coming for the reception afterwards. But it was in the intimacy of her
inner rooms that her peculiar qualities and graces were most in evidence. One of these rooms was that whose walls she had frescoed with
the portraits of famous women of all ages. It was about this room that
the Emperor mocked her, 'Your ancestors, I presume?'

In 1808 Metternich had sketched Laure's portrait in the manner
that was fashionable at this period. The novel *Adèle de Senange* had
superseded *Paul et Virginie* in popular favour, and all the Virginies

were then Adèles. 'Adèle has talents,' he wrote; 'they are not as remarkable as those of an artist, but they are what they should be in a woman of her rank. What she does, moreover, she does well and in a manner to make her house more agreeable than any other. She is a good musician, a marvellous dancer, speaks several languages, and possesses to a rare degree of perfection all those little womanly graces so agreeably necessary in the intercourse of life.

'I have never seen in any country a woman who conducts a *salon* so well; there is never gaming, but she has the art of engaging each person of her society according to his particular taste and of making her own conversation so interesting that the evenings spent in her drawing room seem always too short.

'If it is necessary to sum up my judgement on Adèle, I will say that I have never known a woman more attractive nor more made to interest, because she flatters at the same time one's heart and one's self esteem.

'One fault, however, spoils in my eyes all that she has of charm. This is her *coquetry*. This extreme desire of pleasing, which is rather an eccentricity of mind than of heart, but which she will not correct. In order to do that, she would have to meet someone who was sufficiently superior to her to dominate her to the point of making her renounce herself. This fault, though, does not prevent Adèle from being one of those charming and adorable beings of which nature is unfortunately too sparing, and *even* with this imperfection there is no mother who would not glory in having her for a daughter, no man who would not be a thousand times happy to be her friend, her lover or her husband.'

If from her position as *Madame la Gouverneuse* Laure knew everyone, it was with her intimate circle that her rare conversational powers were seen at their best. There a topic was raised and tossed from one to the other like a ball, never being allowed to fall to the ground. All was touched with the spice of an intriguing malice, few things were held sacred, few holds barred. It was on this account that Napoleon feared her, accusing her of habitually siding with his enemies. These, however, were mostly of the Faubourg Saint-Germain, whereas the circles around Laure d'Abrantès extended over the whole gamut of Parisian Society. Foremost among the *habitués* was Cardinal Maury, the Archbishop of Paris, that coarse old trimmer, who every day, whether Laure was at the Champs-Elysées, Raincy or at the Folie de Saint-James, sat himself down at her table doing full justice to her exquisite food and Junot's well-stocked cellar. The Junots' chef was

Harvey, one of the best in Paris, who is said to have acquired a fortune of 300,000 francs during their embassy in Lisbon. Laure did not really care for the Cardinal; he was rather better appreciated by Junot, their having much in common. Among the older frequenters of her house were some who had known the *ancien régime*: MM. de Cherval, de Courtomer, and Louis de Narbonne, the last-named calling twice a day. Then there were his two daughters, Mme de Brancamp and Mme de Rambuteau; and the Duchesse de Raguse, the Comtesse de Bréhan and Mme de la Marlière. Others were M. de Montbreton, chamberlain to Princess Pauline, MM. de Montrond, de Breteuil, de Sainte-Foix, de Saint-Aulaire, Decazes, Greffulhe, de Lavalette and Alexandre de Girardin. Among the intellectuals were Dussaulx, the critic; Millin, the librarian of the Bibliothèque Impériale, one of her oldest friends; and Legouvé, the Academician. Legouvé was the author of a work on the merits of women. One day he was giving a reading of his thesis and prefaced it by announcing its title, *Le mérite des femmes*. 'So much the better,' was heard murmur M. de Ségur, 'it will not take long.'

Among the *savants* were Geoffroy Saint-Hilaire, Denon, and the doctors Hallé, Corvisart and Desgenettes; among the painters, Gérard, Girodet, Augustin the miniaturist, and Hubert-Robert. Above all the *salon* of Laure d'Abrantès was known for the excellence of its music. She herself played the harp and piano, and composed. Mme Permon's old friend the singer Pierre-Jean Garat, who had been music teacher to Marie-Antoinette, frequently sang. Nadermann, whose famous duet was known at the time all over Europe and was dedicated *A Madame Junot*, played duets with her. Other musicians who were intimate to the house were Félix Duvernoy, Crescentini, Boïeldieu, Steibelt, Nicolo Isouard, Drouet, Libon and Hullmandel. To name all those who were received by Laure would be to name all the élite, in so many different walks, of Paris—and many distinguished persons from abroad. All this entertaining required a great deal of money, and the large annual income of 1,500,000 enjoyed by the Junots was insufficient to meet their extravagant demands. To this they seldom gave a serious thought. The Emperor would provide. But the result was a *salon* without rival in Paris.

In the winter of 1811-12 political events presaged the coming war with Russia. 'The prospect of a new war,' wrote Laure in her *Memoirs*, 'cast a gloom over society in general, but particularly around the

court. It was in vain that the Emperor ordered balls, fêtes, and quad-
rilles. Marie-Louise was surrounded by young and beautiful women
who were commanded by Napoleon to exert every nerve to render
her gay; but these ladies had brothers, fathers, husbands and lovers, so
that the joys of the court were forced pleasures, and not joys springing
from the heart.' In the spring of 1812 Junot was gratified at being
posted to Milan to take command of the troops mustering there, and
march them north. When the Emperor left for Germany to place
himself at the head of the great army about to enter on the Russian
campaign, the condition of Paris was such as described by Laure: 'At
this time Paris presented a curious but melancholy spectacle. Husbands,
sons, brothers and lovers were departing to join the army; while
wives, mothers, sisters and mistresses, either remained at home to
weep, or sought amusement in Italy, Switzerland or the various
watering-places of France.' Laure was one who sought the waters.
She did not go as usual to Cauterets. On the suggestion of the late-
Empress Josephine, whom she visited at Malmaison and found regret-
tably coarsened, she resolved to take the waters at Aix-en-Savoie.
Placing the two elder girls in the Abbaye-aux-Bois, and leaving little
Alfred in the care of his English nurse, on 15 June 1812 she set out for
Aix with her four-year-old Napoleon, her friend Mme la Baronne
Lallemand and her brother-in-law M. de Geouffre.

Forseeing the crush, and wishing to place herself in the most desirable
light (it had become second nature with her), she had booked in
advance and had secured herself the finest house in the town, that
owned by M. Dommanget on the Place Centrale. Aix was packed; the
Court, Parisian society and the theatre were all represented there. The
last was in the person of the leading actor of the day, François-Joseph
Talma, the friend of the Emperor. Madame Mère had taken a house,
sharing the expense with her half-brother Cardinal Fesch, a circumstance pleasing to one like her who liked to live frugally, with an
economical eye on the family's future. Princess Pauline Borghese was
living a short way out of town, on a hill among the vineyards, so that
'it was necessary to get a little mud on one's boots in going to visit
her'. She monopolized the attention of Talma and of M. de Forbin—
the latter described by Laure as 'without gainsaying the most agreeable
man of the society of France, that means of Europe'—and of the
hussar Colonel Duchand, who was about to become her lover. Across
the *place* from Laure, in a less prepossessing house than hers, was Julie
Clary, wife of Joseph King of Spain, and her sister Desirée, whom

Napoleon once thought of marrying and who was now the wife of Bernadotte, recently elected Prince of Sweden. In her *Memoirs* Laure is reticent about much of what went on in Aix at this time. However, she does say: 'The Princess of Sweden had with her a very agreeable person, Greek by birth, very beautiful, and who died tragically a short time afterwards. She was named Mme de Flotte.' This Mme de Flotte was indeed Greek, but a Greek of Marseilles, the widow of a naval officer who, dying in 1806, left her and her two children in extreme poverty. Returning to Marseilles, she was first befriended by a bank clerk and then became the mistress of General Cervoni, commandant of the city. The latter was a friend of the Clarys, themselves natives of Marseilles, and it is likely that it was through him that Mme de Flotte was taken up by Desirée Clary, whose intimate friend she became. 'One says strange things of this friendship,' Laure hinted enigmatically. She and Mme de Flotte were to become deeply embroiled.

The first shot in what was soon to be open warfare between the two women was fired on the day following Laure's name-day, 10 August, the feast of St Lawrence. She, with a brilliant party of friends, went on an outing to Bonport on Lake Bourget, not yet famous as the setting for Lamartine's *Le Lac*. A sudden storm having sprung up, Talma, shaking the water from his drenched hair, grasped the mast with one hand and entertained the company with a scene from Shakespeare's *The Tempest*. The evening was beautiful; and on their arrival back under a starlit sky, Laure had arranged a firework display on the border of the lake, whose still waters reflected the lights in the heavens and on shore. The next day she called on Madame Mère. Much to her astonishment, after several hesitations, the old lady voiced her disapproval of this little fête, by reason she said, 'of the firework display held in a place where the imperial family resided'. Knowing Madame Mère's own benign temperament, Laure felt sure that this rebuke had been prompted—not by Queen Julie, who was far too placid and kind, but by the Princess of Sweden and her faithful friend Mme de Flotte. It was a few days after this incident that the Empress Josephine arrived and took up residence in Aix.

A week later, on 17 August, Laure and her friends became aware of the arrival at the house across the square of a strikingly handsome young officer. This was the Marquis Maurice de Balincourt. Maurice de Balincourt was born at the château of Champigny on 24 July 1789, descending in the direct line from the Duc d'Elbeuf, and was the grand-nephew of Marshal de Balincourt. His mother, *née* Claudine de Bernard de Champigny, had died under the Terror in the prisons of Sens on 6 November 1793, the eve of her execution, and the little Maurice and his sisters were brought up by their maternal grand-mother, the Marquise de Champigny. His fortune, carefully looked after by a relation during his minority, amounted to some two million francs. Now aged twenty-three, he was tall, with a fine figure, a mass of wavy fair hair and eyes of a steely blue. With his air of innate distinction, Maurice de Balincourt was regarded by common consent as the best-looking of a remarkable generation of martial young men. Among his gifts was a talent for painting, quite beyond the ordinary. When Balzac wrote, 'romantic lovers have had, under the Empire, their finished model' he might have been writing of Maurice de Balincourt. For six months he had been the lover of Mme de Flotte, and it was she who, through the Princess Désirée, had Queen Julie invite him to join the house-party at Aix.

Laure had retained her regard for Metternich (and always would), but he was far away, and inextricable difficulties lay in the way of their meeting again. In Aix she shared the attentions of Forbin with the Princess Pauline. Towards the end of August, she planned another excursion on Lake Bourget, or rather she persuaded Forbin to have Princess Pauline command one. In this way she would serve two purposes—by the imperial presence of the Princess she would avoid the censures of her previous fête, and she would have among the company Maurice de Balincourt. Everything was duly arranged; on a beautiful hot summer's day the party gathered at the landing-place of Puer. The men, who included MM. de Rambuteau, de Sémonville, Doumerc, Talma, de Forbin and de Balincourt, were all dressed in the frockcoats and top hats, which were *de rigeur* for taking the waters at Aix,—all except Colonel Duchand, who was in full regimentals, with a dolman of brilliant sky-blue. Among the ladies, besides Laure, were Mesdames Rambuteau, Sémonville, Lallemand, Doumerc, Mlles Menou, Jellon and Brigode. Laure took the arm of M. de Forbin. Some twenty persons were gathered on the shore, awaiting the arrival of Princess Pauline. Time passed and still she did not come. She appeared at last, languishing and beautiful, carried in a palanquin. Laure describes her dress with some pride, since she had designed it—all with the exception of the hat: 'It was a skirt of cambric, richly embroidered and with magnificent lace of Valenciennes, and on top a shorter dress, opening in front, which we called a "Polonaise". This second dress was similarly embroidered, and also with Valenciennes lace. So far nothing too much. But she had on her head, a hat of Italian straw, turned up with three immense feathers of carnation red, with similar ribbons.' She was a sight to behold. At length, when the Princess had settled herself becomingly in the boat they set out...

As they rowed over the lake Princess Pauline took it into her head to recite some verses of Petrarch, written to his Laura, as she was at pains to remark—this strangely she did well:

> *Che fai? che pensi? . . . che pure indietro guardi*
> *Nel tempo che tornar non puote ormai . . .* ★

The party went ashore at Haute-Combe, Forbin still giving Laure his arm. But it was at Balincourt that she kept looking, and she felt a lightening in her heart when she noticed how he too was observing her. Their eyes meeting, she smiled at him. When they came back and were seated in the boat she found him at her side. In her *Memoirs* she goes on: 'Our return was ravishing. The Princess recited still. I no longer listened. I was seated by the side of the boat, overtaken by a sort of enchantment which can only be evoked by the aspect of a country itself enchanting. The return appeared to me only too quick. I would have liked to float all night on this lake so calm, with its blue waves, its edges of flowers and shadow, which presented to me the image of one of those delicious solitudes of the New World, in which one forgets everything, even one's country.' In these same *Memoirs* Laure draws a veil over her own wakening love for Balincourt, referring instead to the feelings that were passing through the heart and mind of Princess Pauline. She adds, 'This was the day that proclaimed the favour of M. le Colonel Duchand.'

In September of the following year she was to write to Balincourt: 'It is today the 7th, Maurice. I wager that you do not remember that it is today a year ago that we went to walk beside the lake. I remember it well—also the 10th! As for that day, arrange it as you will, but it is necessary that I see you. If you do not come, no matter how nor when, I shall not for the life of me forgive you.' Maurice de Balincourt had touched Laure more deeply than she knew. He awakened in her a love whose depth she had not thought possible.

·   ·   ·   ·

★What are you doing? What are you thinking? . . . . That indeed you look back on a time that can never return.

7 September 1812. On the day that Laure discovered her love for Maurice de Balincourt beside the still waters of Lake Bourget, in Russia there was fought near the River Moskva the battle of Borodino in which, in a single day, the casualties amounted to the appalling number of 63,000 men. This was glory indeed.

On Saint-Helena Napoleon remarked to Las Cases, 'Junot, in the Russian campaign . . . gave me grave cause for displeasure; one no longer recognised him; he made some capital faults which cost us dear.' Napoleon was referring chiefly to the actions near Smolensk in August. Two Russian armies, commanded by Bagration and Barclay were trying to form a junction near Smolensk, pursued by the French under Murat and Ney. The Russians were being driven into a marshy *cul-de-sac* formed by the River Dnieper. Junot, with the 8th Corps, was within marching distance; if he went to Ney's assistance, the Russians would be irretrievably cut off. It would be another Austerlitz, Moscow would fall, the campaign would be gloriously over. The aides-de-camp Chabot and Gourgaud were sent to his headquarters with orders for him to march immediately. He refused, alleging some inexplicable difficulties. Murat, pocketing his pride, went himself to this man whom all Europe knew to have been his wife's lover, to plead personally with him. 'Go on, Junot, march, your marshal's baton is there!' But Junot was in the grip of an attack of his madness, and stubbornly refused to budge. When he finally did move and the artillery was brought up, the Russians were already out of range. It was too late. The Emperor's anger was clear to everyone in the bulletins, especially that from Smolensk dated 23 August 1812, in which he rated 'the inept Junot' for 'his lack of resolution'.

In her *Memoirs* Laure makes out that she was ignorant of the incriminating bulletins, her friends having kept them from her. But in reality, after reading them she put off a planned visit to Geneva. From everywhere the news was bad; in Spain the French had lost the battle of Salamanca, fought in July, when Marmont was seriously wounded; in Russia, in spite of the glowing reports of the *Moniteur*, news received in letters was of the gloomiest. Maurice de Balincourt, awaiting his expected appointment as chamberlain to Queen Julie, accepted her invitation to return with her to Mortefontaine. With them went Princess Désirée—and Mme de Flotte. Mortefontaine was two hours' distance from Paris. Concealing her true reason for leaving, Laure wrote to Junot: 'I quitted Aix to return to France on 28 September. One begins already to be anxious; news arrives from Russia which speaks of marvels, but then private letters say quite the reverse.' She travelled north by way of Lyons, not to see Cardinal Fesch, as she alleged, but to visit the exiled Mme Récamier, a meeting that could have only been displeasing to the Emperor. After four days in Lyons she resumed her journey to Paris.

In Paris Laure was disturbed by Junot's letters from Russia; some were lucid enough, but others indicated that the Emperor's displeasure weighed heavily on his disturbed mind. Evidence of his periods of normality is given by the touching letter he wrote to his younger daughter two days before the battle of Borodino:

'It is not long since I wrote to you, my dear Constance. My letter was for your sister and for you. I have just received two letters from you, dear friend, one of 24 July and the other of 14 August; the first is better written than the second, but both gave me pleasure.

'You are now with your mama. Be happy, my dear children! This happiness is wanting to your father. In the meanwhile, give contentment to your mama, be very wise and very good. On his return, your papa will be so very happy, if he hears from your mama, from everyone: Your charming daughters, M.le Duc, are very well brought up, very amiable, very well instructed. With what pleasure he will embrace them, and how much will he tell them that he loves them with all his heart. . .'

But not all Junot's and Laure's letters reached their destination; increasingly they were intercepted by the Cossacks. The Emperor Alexander was interested to read those communications of exalted members of Parisian society. The letters of one bundle, written by Junot to Fissont, his secretary, were written at one time and from the same place but had different dates and addresses. They consisted of two letters to Laure and love-letters to the Baronne Lallemand and Mme Foy. Precise instructions were given to Fissont how these letters were to be handed to the respective recipients. Even in the depths of Russia he remained the incorrigible Junot.

But Junot was only on the periphery of Laure's preoccupation. She was deeply, insanely, hopelessly in love with Balincourt. Moreover, she suffered from a racking jealousy. Maurice was at Mortefontaine, in the same house as Mme de Flotte. He came to Paris, where he had kept his bachelor's flat, and he saw Laure. She had given him the key that allowed him access to her bedroom by a private passage. She wrote to him daily, at times more than once a day. Her letters and a diary she kept, into which she poured the minutiae of her exacerbated sensibility, the *Livre rouge*, were only made known, when excerpts from the papers in the possession of the Balincourt family were published by M.Robert Chantemesse in 1927. They reveal the passionate depth of her love for Balincourt.

'To wait for you and then to regret you, there is my life. . .

'You have developed in me faculties of love which up to this moment were unknown to me. . .

'This occupation with you, so strong, so constant, which agitates my blood, which carries me to delirium when I am away from you, that is love. . .

'You have seen me in your arms bathe your breast with tears, which flow from a happiness no doubt comparable with that of the angels. Why this excess of sensibility? Who could move my whole being in this way? It was my love, this ardent, unique love, that makes my sight troubled when I see you, my whole body shiver when you press me to your heart. How many times have I cried out to myself in your presence: Oh, how happy I am to love!

'I do not know if one will ever be able to give me a moment of intoxication like that which I experience in hearing your step and when one pronounces your name in announcing you.

'Adieu. I am going to try to sleep. See to it that my awakening is happy. . .'

Laure uses here her words exactly; it was a delirium, a state of ecstasy, her love for Balincourt. Her diary, the *Livre rouge*, was kept for him. In it was placed a sheet of writing paper, accompanied by a note, which read: 'Keep the promise that I am adding here. It is nothing but the exact truth. I desire you to keep it and to be able, a long time ahead, to thank me for having said in advance something that is true. My well-beloved, this blood which I have just used is all yours, there is not a drop that does not belong to you.

'I would like to have my book only for an hour. Send it back to me, and add there only one word—one only, you understand: "I love you".

'That is enough for some hours of happiness.

'Adieu. I press you to my heart and I love you more than my life.'

On the sheet of paper Laure had written a letter in her own blood. She had opened a vein in her left arm; a blot of blood stains the top of the paper.

'So long as there runs in my veins the blood which I am using to write this promise, so long as a breath of life will make my heart beat, I swear at the feet of God who hears me, I swear by my most holy and sacred affections, that you will be *the most and the best loved*.

'Never a love like this has filled my soul, and I repeat here, what you have already remarked: *If I am not yours, I belong to the grave*.

'Yes, Maurice, either you or death.

'This is the cry of my heart, it will be its last feeling, as its last beat will be for you.

'I swear it again and I will renew the oath that nothing will make me break.

'Laure.'

But her love was marred by the continued presence of Mme de Flotte at Mortefontaine; she was racked by the fiercest tortures of an insensate jealousy. Here her extreme sensibility was her undoing. In turn she tried to excite jealousy on his side by maintaining a close relationship with the attractive Forbin. Balincourt met him at Malmaison, and some words dropped by Forbin gave colour to a closeness that did not in fact exist. She hinted, too, that General Alexandre de Giradin, who had once declared his love for her, was persistent in his attentions. She went further; she confessed to him her affair with Metternich; and, hinting at the continuance of the feeling on his part, sent him a copy of the *Portrait of Adèle*. This came into the hands of Mme de Flotte, who ridiculed it, saying that it had not been composed by Metternich, but by Laure herself. To show Maurice that she was quite capable of writing such a piece, she sent him a *Portrait of Gracieuse*, of Mme de Flotte. In this two friends are talking of a woman:

' "Depict her to me. Is she young?"
' "No."
' "Is she pretty?"
' "No."
' "Then she has a good figure?"
' "No, she is very bent, and walks almost like me."
' "What sort of eyes has she?"
' "Small and rather bloodshot."
' "And teeth?"
' "Still less beautiful than her eyes."
' "Her throat?"

' "Neither beautiful nor ugly; she hasn't one." '
' "Her skin?" '
' "Frightful. She is very marked by small-pox." ' '

And so on in this strain. 'And it is for her that you have wished to
sacrifice me,' added Laure in a letter to Maurice. But matters soon
took a more serious turn. Laure's jealousy was proportionate to her
love. Maurice's appointment as chamberlain was almost fixed, and
Queen Julie, pressed by her sister and her friend, wished him to break
with Laure. The figure of the Emperor was conjured up in the back-
ground. Laure, however, declared that she had no fears of him. Her
affairs are no concern of his. There were respites in her jealous feelings,
when she seemed alone to enjoy the full flowering of Maurice's love.
They exchanged rings. She gave Maurice a chain on which was
engraved *Doux souvenir, bonheur présent, seul espoir d'avenir**. But her
fear of Mme de Flotte's influence over Maurice was always there. She
complained that her health was suffering and confessed that she had
recourse to increased doses of laudanum. Then in the first weeks of
December she discovered to her joy that she was pregnant. It was at
this juncture that she heard that Mme de Flotte was wearing the ring
which she had given Maurice. There was nothing that that woman
would not do to hold Maurice, she protested. She became hysterical
in her despair. 'Oh! Maurice, you whom I have loved so much, whom
I adore still at this instant with so much love, would it be possible for
you to be perjured!' Maurice pleaded that he was innocent, that he had
simply mislaid the ring, and Mme de Flotte had somehow got possession of it. But the strain on Laure—the continual anxiety, the tears,
sleeplessness and the laudanum—became at length too great for her
to bear. Her nerves were strained to breaking pitch. On Saturday 19
December she could bear it no longer. She had horses put to her
carriage and drove out to Mortefontaine.

What happened there, in what precisely consisted 'her unfortunate
step' (*sa malheureuse démarche*), has never been revealed. Memoirs of
the time and the police records make no reference to it. But the
scandal was immense. Ultimately, through his watch-dog Savary, it
came to the ears of the Emperor.

Back in the Champs-Elysées from Mortefontaine, Laure sat down
at two o'clock in the morning to write to Maurice: 'I have arrived at

---

*Sweet memory, present happiness, only hope of the future.

this instant in the most pitiable state, overcome at one and the same time by feverishness, shivering and faintness. I find my poor brother who was dying with worry and who, above his tears, seems by his eloquent silence to thank you for having saved his sister from despair.

'Maurice, the *éclat* of my unfortunate step can only be justified by you. Your love is my protection and my defence against all that will be said. If you abandon me, I am lost, and I will be so for having loved you too much.

'Adieu. I can bear no more. I will write to you tomorrow.'

And then the unexpected happened. While she was driving back from Mortefontaine, all unknown to her, the Emperor had returned from Russia. In her *Memoirs* she reports: '. . . on 19 December, a quarter of an hour after midnight, he arrived before the front gate of the Tuileries. . . The Empress was about to retire to bed when the Emperor's *calèche* stopped at the gate. . . Before daybreak on the following morning (20 December) the cannon of the Invalides announced to the city of Paris that the Emperor had returned.'

EIGHT

The End of the Affair

ON THE DAY following the Emperor's return from Russia, 20 December 1812, Laure was too distracted to go herself to the Tuileries and she sent her brother Albert in her stead. But in the crush he was unable to speak to the Emperor and returned with no news of Junot. Savary, however, had a long interview with Napoleon. In spite of Laure's brave words to Balincourt, she feared the Emperor's anger, when he heard of the *éclat* of Mortefontaine, as hear he must. And in her present despair Maurice failed her. It was clear that the inmates of Mortefontaine likewise feared the Emperor's wrath. The Princess Désirée was being watched by Savary's police, as the wife of Bernadotte, whose politics were under suspicion. (Shortly after he went over to the allies.) There was no reply to Laure's frantic letter to Maurice. She wrote again. 'I can only die,' she wrote hysterically. 'That is what you wish, is it not true? But to condemn me to death with so much cruelty? Since yesterday my agony is frightful; my life would have ended long ago, if one had not deprived me of the means. But can one stop an unfortunate woman as desperate as I am? Before the end of today you will be satisfied. I will have ceased to exist, but do not force me to curse you with my last sigh, come for one moment only, and in dying my last thought will be forgiveness if I can rest my eyes only once on yours. . .'

Still there was no word from Maurice. He did not come.

On 23 December Laure took an overdose of laudanum. But the effect of such a dose was not to produce the death she sought; her stomach reacted so violently as to evacuate the poison. She was obliged to live and to face what her future held in store for her.

From the side of the Tuileries there was silence. Maurice got in touch with her; he wrote and came to see her. Hope returned, as the days passed and there were no overt reverberations, no sign of the storm she feared. Napoleon was immersed in the immense task of raising a new army to replace that lost amid the snows of Russia and of repairing the political fabric of the Empire, threatened by the secession of Bernadotte and perhaps the Murats. In January 1813 Laure received a letter from Junot, written from Elbing on the Vistula on 22 December, asking her to solicit an audience of the Emperor, which he would not refuse her. Junot wanted permission to return to France, since he was so ill that he could not walk without a stick or mount a horse. He complained of the bitter cold. Laure, resolving to put on a bold front, wrote to Duroc to request an audience, which was granted for the evening of the following day.

When Laure wrote her *Memoirs* in 1832, she gave a detailed account of this long and, for her, momentous interview with Napoleon, which not only obscures the true facts, but omits entirely the principal consequence of her interview. Although in 1832 she was writing for the general public, avid for facts about Napoleon (the cult had already begun), it is curious that she should have employed this mystification, since there were still alive persons, Savary and Balincourt among them, who would have been well aware of the circumstances in which the audience took place. We may imagine that there were hard words on both sides, but on this occasion Laure was very much on the defensive. Two points, however, are clear—she obtained permission for Junot's return; but for herself the sentence was social death—it was that she should join Mme de Staël, Mme Récamier and Mme Chevreuse in exile. In the first matter Napoleon wrote on 28 January 1813 to Prince Eugène, in command of the armies in the East on the defection of Murat, ordering him to send Junot home—it would be 'one embarrassment less for the army'. He was, moreover, 'no further use' to him. With Napoleon men, even the most faithful, were expendable. About the second result of her audience Laure wrote on the same evening to Maurice in the overwrought style which had become habitual in her writing to him:

> 'I said to you that this fatal love would be the death of me! I must go, I must leave my country, my friends, all that is dear to me, to go dying as I am to perish in a strange land. If I refuse, my husband will know of the fatal scene and its distressing causes. The silence *of him who is all-powerful and who commands all* is the price. That is what I have learned today, and I shall sacrifice myself for your safety and your tranquillity. I will go. I will quit my dear country to go to seek the death which, moreover, I will bear from here in my heart;

in leaving you, the mortal blow will be struck. Maurice, I repeat it
at this moment, never have I loved anything like you; to be separated
from you is death for me. Yes, I shall not survive so cruel a trial.'

The Emperor, who felt perhaps that he had been too hard on the
unfortunate Junot, had in mind for him the appointment to the first
distant governship vacant; and Laure would accompany him in this
his virtual exile.

Gradually the news percolated through of the terrible losses in the
East. Black, Laure thought, had become the national colour. She
awaited Junot's return, continuing to see Balincourt. 'Maurice,' she
wrote to him, 'I can do everything, except cease to see you, I am
willing, however, out of caution as regards you, out of interest to
your peace of mind, to agree to what you appear to desire. Come
sometimes to my *salon;* you can justify more frequent visits than you
have made this last month. That will be easy for you. The Duke's
return will be the most plausible pretext, because your staying away,
precisely at that time, would only confirm the rumours that are current
about you and me.' On receiving a letter from Junot, she immediately
wrote to Maurice: 'I am sending you a letter that I have just received.
Read it with attention and you will see that it is necessary for us to see
each other, not tomorrow, but this very day, no matter what time
you return from Malmaison, be it in the middle of the night. Tomorrow there would already be danger, but this evening there is none,
and it is necessary for us to profit by it to say a long adieu, perhaps even
an eternal one. Maurice, I am in despair, and I have not even the
consolation of admitting to myself all my grief, since he is my friend,
the father of my children, and I am criminal in shedding tears. Come
immediately. He speaks of the 6th, but it is not necessary to rely on
that. His letter has arrived today and I have a firm idea that he will
arrive tomorrow, in the evening or night. Adieu, Maurice, come to
console and say good-bye to your poor Laure.'

Junot arrived, but it was no longer the same Junot. In place of the
young Governor of Paris, the first aide-de-camp of the Emperor, the
officer whose fine figure and splendid turnout were the admiration of
all, there appeared a coarsened, aged man, bent, walking with difficulty
supported by a stick, dressed carelessly in a shabby greatcoat. Even the
presence of his children failed to rouse him from his lethargy. 'He was
in a strange state,' Laure wrote, 'often in a condition of somnolence
during the day, the night brought him no sleep. He so strong, so much

master of himself, wept like a child.' Napoleon's words, 'that he lacked resolution' preyed incessantly upon his mind. Laure, playing on his snobbishness—'he always liked to have about him persons with sixteen quarterings,' said the Emperor—had Balincourt to the house, and the two men met. She herself was in a highly nervous state; troubled by Junot's mental and physical illness, her love for Maurice left her open to all the torture of her jealousy for the continued presence of Mme de Flotte at Mortefontaine. Balincourt's appointment as chamberlain to Queen Julie was officially announced. Laure's jealousy on his behalf was to have other objects than Mme de Flotte. Queen Hortense showed Maurice marked attentions, as did Mme du Cayla, and others still. The unfortunate Mme de Flotte was to die of her love for Maurice de Balincourt. Meanwhile Laure continued to see him, to write him passionate letters and to carry his child. As soon as she could with propriety do so, she informed Junot of her pregnancy. Unsuspecting, Junot made her swear that she would bring up his son, if it were a son, in the service of the Emperor. Then in the spring of 1813 the Emperor announced Junot's appointment to the dual post of Governor of Venice and Governor-General of the Illyrian provinces. At the end of May he was already in Trieste; Laure and the children were to follow him.

The Governor-General came directly under the orders of the Emperor, who was fully engaged at the time with the armed struggle in Germany and preparing for the abortive Congress of Prague. Nominally Junot was under the Viceroy of Italy, Eugène de Beauharnais. It quickly became apparent that Illyria was governed by a madman. A grand ball was given in Dubrovnik in honour of the Governor-General, to which were invited the civil and military authorities and their wives and the leading ecclesiastics of the province. At ten o'clock in the evening the rooms were crowded with dignitaries in splendid uniforms and their ladies dressed in what for a province was their finest array. It was given out that the Governor-General was still dressing. At length a footman in gilded livery threw open the double doors of the apartments of M. le Duc, announcing in a loud voice, 'Monseigneur the Duke of Abrantès, Governor-General and Lieutenant of His Majesty the Emperor and King!' All heads turned towards the entrance. There stood Junot, his hair curled, wearing white gloves and dancing pumps, under one arm his sabre, under the other an immense plumed hat—and for the rest as naked as the day he was born. Then, we are told, the tumult broke out, mothers dragged away their daughters, the bishops veiled their eyes, 'and in an instant the rooms were deserted'.

This was not the only untoward incident. Rumours were rife. Junot gave a dinner party, at which he had the honours of the table performed by a young lady of between twenty or twenty-five, who was clearly not used to the part she had to play. The Governor-General took it into his head to vary the liqueurs by introducing a decanter of sulphuric ether. When his guests politely refused this unusual drunk, Junot filled a glass and emptied it at one draught to the somewhat embarrassed plaudits of the company. At another time, it was said, he mustered two battalions of Croatian troops, had the bells rung and the drums beat to arms, to deliver the town of a nightingale. Again, it was reported that he suspected a conspiracy among the sheep of Illyria and had alerted the police, the troops and the administration. The stories were endless. He awarded an imbecile with the grand cordon of the Legion of Honour, and, finding his conversation agreeable, accompanied him through the streets of Gorizia. On 25 June the police reported that the Governor-General gave a luncheon party which, beginning at midday, went on until seven-thirty in the evening. The drink flowed. On getting up from the table Junot called for his carriage, dismissed the coachman and mounted the driving seat, whipped up the postillion, and drove furiously through the town, calling out pleasantries to the women who appeared at the windows. A favourite servant accompanied him, who from time to time threw bottles into the air, which Junot brought down with a well-aimed pistol shot. Returned to his palace, he made an assignation with the sister-in-law of one of his servants, who immediately fled; then ordered dinner for twelve. He gave orders to the police and soldiers of the garrison 'to arrest them' wherever 'they found themselves'. No one knew who 'they' were. At dinner he boasted of his horses, his warlike deeds, his own beauty and then began to sing. Eventually to his staff's infinite relief he retired to bed. Next morning at nine o'clock he had an apoplectic fit. Seguier, the French consul in Trieste, took it on himself, in place of the resident, the Count Chabrol, who was ill and unable to leave his bed, to acquaint Prince Eugène and the Emperor with Junot's condition.

Before his final collapse Junot wrote three letters: one to Prince Eugène, in which he expressed his desire for peace, and went on, clearly out of his mind, to divide up the countries and the riches of the world among named individuals; another letter he addressed to the

English admiral of the Adriatic fleet, proposing a meeting to discuss peace; and a third to the Emperor. Laure, in her *Memoirs*, gives an extract from this, 'pruned of its incoherencies':

> 'I who love you with the adoration of the savage for the sun, I who am *all for you*, this eternal war that it is necessary to make for you, *I no longer want it*! I want *peace*! I want at last to rest my tired head, my suffering limbs in my house, in the middle of my family, of my children, with care for them, no longer to be a stranger to them. I want, at last, to enjoy what I have bought with a treasure more precious than the treasures of India, with my *blood*, the blood of an honest man, of a good Frenchman, of a true patriot! I demand at last tranquillity, acquired by twenty-two years of effective service and seventeen wounds through which my blood has flowed for my country, first, and then for your glory.'

The glory was turning sour.

The Emperor, who was in Dresden, gave orders on 6 July to Prince Eugène to have Junot conducted under safe escort to his parents' house at Montbard in Burgundy, and to have the Minister of War in Paris acquaint Laure, who was to set out immediately to take charge of her sick husband. In her *Memoirs* she states categorically that it was Savary, out of malevolence towards her and Junot, who suggested this course to the Emperor and came to the Champs-Elysées to inform her of Junot's collapse and the Emperor's orders. There are several reasons for these falsifications, but chief among them is a desire to draw the veil over her relations with Balincourt. It was first thought that Junot would return to France *via* Geneva. Laure says that she set out on 17 July, accompanied by her brother Albert and her close friend, Mme Thomières, and travelled without stopping to Geneva, where she 'alighted at Sécheron at the house of the good Déjean on the 21st at 10 o'clock in the morning.' In reality she met Maurice at Melun. One wonders how he, an officer—when the death-struggle was about to take place in Germany—so long evaded military service. From Melun he went on to Vichy, to join Queen Julie, Mme de Flotte, Mme Regnault de Saint-Jean-d'Angely and Mme du Cayla. Laure had double cause for anxiety.

Laure, waiting in her hotel in Geneva, by an administrative mischance missed Junot. Lieutenant Poiré, who commanded his escort, on the plea of superior orders, ignored the order awaiting him at Lyons to take his patient to Geneva. At two o'clock in the morning of 22 July he handed over Junot to his distracted parents in Montbard. A few days later in her hotel bedroom, from which she could see the lake and Mont Blanc, Laure gave birth to a stillborn child. Every day she wrote to Maurice. On 26 July she wrote:

'Lying on a bed of suffering, shedding tears of despair in the fear of having caused the death of my child by this unfortunate voyage and perhaps also from the unreasonable anxiety to which I abandoned myself for three days in receiving no letters from you, agitated by a bad fever—that is the state I was in this morning, when your letter arrived.

'Oh, power eternal of an entire, exclusive love; all the accidents have not ceased, but they have diminished at the very moment, in measure as I read. I felt a gentle balm descend on my heart and expand over my whole being. I laughed, I wept, and when I had arrived at the end of your letter, where you tell me *that my place will always be on your heart*, that it is that which is always destined for me, *at least so long as I shall wish it*, I burst into tears and I said to Agathe [Thomières] that I was very happy.'

Laure went on to tell Maurice that *He* was at Montbard, where she, unable herself to move, had sent Albert. She suggested that Maurice come to Lyons for eight days. From there he could easily visit her. At the moment of writing she had no precise news from Montbard. She was unaware of what had happened. She did not know that Junot, who hardly recognized his relations, had escaped the vigilance of his attendants, jumped out of the window of his room, run the length of the garden, climbed a wall and fallen into the road, suffering a compound fracture of the leg. In some reports it is said that he tried to amputate his wounded leg with a pair of scissors. Seven days later, on 29 July 1813, he was dead.

Napoleon was moved by the news of Junot's death. Writing to Savary, he said that Junot had lost his esteem in Russia, but that he could now see that his lack of resolution at Smolensk was the result of his illness. His children were to be looked after and provided for, but for Laure there was to be no reprieve from the sentence of exile. Savary sent her brother-in-law Geouffre to Geneva to inform her of the Emperor's orders—she was not to come within fifty leagues of Paris. Geouffre also brought a letter from Junot's brother, one of his trustees, telling how Savary had gone to the Champs-Elysées and, breaking the seals that had been placed on the contents of the house, had removed the Emperor's and Caroline Murat's letters from a strong-box. Laure never knew how he had come into possession of a key, which Albert Permon had seen in Junot's room at Montbard, or opened the combination-lock, the letters of which Junot and she alone knew. In her *Memoirs* she gives the date of Geouffre's arrival in Geneva as 25 August. This is inaccurate. Whether this was from lapse of memory is uncertain, but more probably it was part of her intentional mystification. On 19 August she wrote to Maurice from Lyons, telling him that she was on the way north, that the place she had chosen for her exile was Rouen, and asking him to meet her on the 23rd at Versailles, where she would be staying with Mme Raimbault.

It is not clear what decided her to defy the Emperor and return to Paris, but on 25 August (not 17 September, as she says in the *Memoirs*) at 9 o'clock in the evening she arrived back in the Champs-Elysées. There had forgathered a group of her closest friends: MM. de Montbreton, Decazes, Alphonse Perregaux, de Forbin, de Courtomer, de Brigode, Millin, Mme La Marquise de Bréhan, her husband, M. de Cherval, her uncles MM. de Comnène, M. Suchet, and others. She relates the scene: 'When I descended from the carriage and saw myself surrounded by this friendly group who wished to spare me the first moment of my return to this house, where I re-entered furtively for the first time after the death of its master, I was not able to restrain my tears. But they had judged with their hearts. There was nothing of bitterness on those tears. They had saved me from the terrible impression of the first moment.' Knowing how tired and moved she must be, her friends left her early.

It was ten-thirty and she was about to retire, when there was a new arrival. The *valet de chambre* announced the Duc de Rovigo. It was Savary. There proceeded a long altercation, but in wordy warfare Savary was no match for an outraged Laure. She was supported too, by the welcome she had been given by her friends. Her presence in Paris was well known. His first threats dissipated under her calm determination. The scandal which had led to her exile was now her saving. 'Oh, the linnets can sing while the master is away,' Savary said. 'But I am here, and we shall see.' Savary, however, had too much on his hands to occupy himself other than intermittently with one determined woman. Events in the East moved irrevocably to the disastrous defeat at Leipzig on 16 October 1813. The frontiers of

France were open to the victorious allies. Laure remained unmolested.

She herself was occupied with disturbing matters. A family council was held to consider Junot's estate, when it was discovered that his debts amounted to the huge sum of 1,400,000 francs. The family was divided on the course to be followed. The Junot side, accepting the advice of Laure's old friend Millin, who had been called in, were for realizing the assets, which would leave her and the children an annual income of 60,000 francs. The Permon party, of which Geouffre was the prime mover, was for holding on, primarily in the hope that the Emperor would be bound to make adequate provision for the family of one of his generals and oldest friends. Unfortunately for Laure, the latter advice was adopted. It was only later that she was to discover how Geouffre had profited greatly from her and her children's property. Income to maintain Junot's Duchy of Abrantès had come from estates (*majorats*) scattered in many parts of Europe, those in Prussia being already under threat.

But as her supreme consolation she had Maurice, whom she saw and, when she could not see, wrote to constantly:

'Today 7 September
'When I think that I have been able to live until last year without knowing you and without loving you, I do not believe myself, Maurice.

'You ask me the details of my manner of life. . . Nothing is more boring. First, all my morning is consecrated to men of business, whose society is not very amusing. I dine mostly alone with the children; then my family and some friends like Calo, Agathe, Madame de No[ailles], the white cat, *the lady who resembles you* . . . come to pass the evening with me in my little grey *salon* until eleven. Then everyone goes and before midnight every night I am in bed. As for that, I have taken again my tiny little room of last winter: how much I have suffered there. Do you remember that, Maurice? But do not let us speak of it, you have made up for it since!'

Then she went on to recall (what we have already quoted) the events of that time the year before, when they were both at Aix-en-Savoie.

It was decided that she would have to sell some of her belongings. Princess Pauline Borghese, who was immensely rich and whose finer feelings did not extend to her friend's distress, bought 10,000 francs worth of wine from Junot's cellar ('after it has been carefully tasted') and tried to get hold of Laure's sapphires, the most beautiful in Paris. Maurice de Balincourt, as mayor of Champigny, was in the country to raise troops for the Emperor. His meetings with Mme de Flotte from time to time could still stir Laure's jealousy, and her letters to him were full of warnings of her enmity and dangerousness. She had been saddened by news of the deaths of Bessières and Duroc, killed in the campaign in Germany, and now she was shocked at hearing of her and her mother's old friend Count Louis de Narbonne's death from typhus at Torgau, where he was governor. It was Narbonne who had introduced Metternich and who had written to her on hearing of Junot's death, 'Dispose of me as of your father, of your brother, I warn you that if I were in misfortune, it is only what I would ask of you. How a word from you will make me happy.' Now he too was gone. All part of the glory. Meanwhile the Empire was succumbing. The Allies crossed the frontiers. The battle of France was being fought. 'General Bonaparte was trying to save Napoleon'.

The Allies were in Paris. On 30 March, the day King Joseph abandoned Paris, one of the young men who rode through the streets of the city, distributing white cockades and shouting *Vive le Roi! Vive les Bourbons!* was the Marquis Maurice de Balincourt. He had been nominated to the staff of General Dessoles. On 11 April 1814 the Emperor Napoleon signed the deed of abdication. Suddenly Laure Duchess of Abrantès was one of the queens of Paris. But so was Princess Désirée, wife of the victorious Bernadotte. And she and Mme de Flotte had still a shot in their locker. One day Laure had gone out for a breath of air and returned to find her servants in a state of alarm. A French officer, on behalf of the Prince of Sweden, had come to requisition the house. She sat down immediately and addressed a letter to His Royal Highness:

'For a fortnight foreign troops have occupied Paris, I have received no offence from the officers nor from their inferiors, whatever their ranks. I confess that it appears to me as strange as it is vexatious that I should have experienced the first insult at the moment when Your Royal Highness arrives in Paris. Certain that it is not you who have ordered that my house, respected by all parties, should be violated by someone of your household, I complain to you about what has been done at my house this very day, with the hope that you will give me entire satisfaction.'

Within an hour of this letter's being sent to the Princess Désirée's residence in the rue d'Anjou-Saint-Honoré, where Bernadotte was staying, his principal aide-de-camp, M. le Comte de Brahé, was at the Champs-Elysées house with the Prince's profound apologies. The Duchesse d'Abrantès was a power in the land.

Laure was delighted to meet Count Metternich again, who, within a few days of his arrival, called on her. In the course of conversation the matter of the *majorats* was raised, these being largely in Prussia, Westphalia and Hanover, and Metternich was doubtful whether she could recover them. Those from Illyria were safe. However, he would speak to Count Czernichev, an old friend of hers, the foreign minister to the Tsar Alexander, the person best able to help her. Alexander had great influence over King William of Prussia. The next day Czernichev came personally to the house, and Laure requested him to obtain for her an audience of the Tsar. 'I will mention your wish,' replied the Count laughing, 'but I doubt very much whether he will grant it.' 'Why not?' asked Laure, hurt at his response. 'I don't know, but I am willing to bet he won't.' The following day he returned. 'It is as I thought,' he said, 'the Tsar will not receive you at the Elysée.' He paused. 'He will not see you at the Elysée, since he wishes to do himself the honour of calling on you.' Alexander would call the next day between twelve and one—'if it suited her'!

The Tsar Alexander came, in a carriage alone except for one servant, and spent some considerable time chatting *tête-à-tête* with the Duchess of Abrantès on all manner of subjects—Napoleon, the Empress Josephine, Junot, Savary and Caulaincourt—and the *majorats*. He would personally intervene with the King of Prussia on her behalf. Like Madame de Sévigné, when King Louis XIV did her the honour of dancing with her, Laure was overcome with the greatness, the graciousness of the Tsar. 'Everyone must acknowledge the charm of this sort of affability in a sovereign; it carries with it a *prestige*, the influence of which must be felt by persons of the coldest temperament. Besides, in 1814 Alexander was really great.' But when, some time later, the Baron Hardenberg brought her the letters of investiture and the arrears of revenues from the Prussian *majorats*—to be received on condition that the Junot children took on Prussian nationality—she flatly, proudly refused. A few days after his first visit Alexander called on Laure again, this time walking, dressed in a green coat and wearing a round hat, accompanied only by Boutiagine. After he had left, Savary appeared—he had the habit of appearing at the most unlikely moments—and it was then that there occurred to her the thought that Alexander and Napoleon, who was still at Fontainebleau, might meet in her house and reach an accommodation. Historians are inclined to disbelieve that she wrote to Napoleon and gave the letter to Savary. In her *Memoirs* she states that she did write but that the letter was never delivered, remaining in Savary's pocket.

Laure's *salon* now resumed its place as among the most distinguished in Paris. At the periods of the first and second restorations she reached the pinnacle of her social acclaim, this was the time of her glory. She was the most sought-after woman in Paris. Metternich called every day and frequently had tea with her. Wellington too, and it was at his request, and that of the Tsar, that Lord Cathcart, English ambassador to the Russian court, took possession of the ground floor of her house. On the first floor she made over apartments for General and Lady Cole, and their *protegée* Miss Eliza Bathurst, daughter of the Minister of War. With her brother Albert and her uncles the MM. de Comnène, her household was very full. Lord Cathcart was most friendly disposed to her, and she had to put 'the old tom-cat, the old monkey', as she told Maurice de Balincourt, firmly in his place. The Empress Josephine called her to Malmaison and the Cardinal Maury sought her out, both wanting her to intercede for them with her highly placed friends and acquaintances. Blacas d'Aulpe, the Bourbon chief of police, was another who found her services of use. What precisely she performed for him is not known, but she received from his sources a remuneration of 1,500 francs a month.

Her differences with the late Emperor were known to all, and this made her position with the restored Bourbons highly favoured among those who had served Napoleon. It was arranged by the Prince Comnène that she should be presented to Louis XVIII and to the Duchess of Angoulême. She was presented to the latter first, making her curtsy between Mme Juste de Noailles and the Duchess of Hamilton. The King had been previously acquainted by Prince Comnène with Laure's alleged claims on the State, particularly the 200,000 francs inscribed on the *Grand Livre* on behalf of her eldest son, now tactfully called Léon. His Majesty was graciousness itself. He confirmed her in her title, and promised that the money should be paid and that her present needs should be helped by the purchase of the house on the Champs-Elysées. In fact, those promises were never kept. All that Laure saw of the royal bounty was 80,000 francs, which was paid for the Bible of Belem, part of Junot's loot from Portugal, and much later a pension of 6,000 francs. The bible was redeemed to be returned to its rightful monastic owners in Portugal. The poor prior had been exiled for three years as penalty for being robbed. Despite the rents paid by the Allies for their lodgings in Laure's house, she was in actual need, and it was not long before Maurice de Balincourt had to come actively to her relief. Her entertaining was still on the same prodigious scale, her butcher's bill for the month of January 1814 amounting to 2,040 francs. A widow of a *grand officier* received an annual pension of 3,000 francs.

Laure gave a dinner party for the Duke of Wellington. Among the men she invited were Sir George Murray, the Duke's quartermaster-general, the Comte de Luçay, Maurice de Balincourt, Princes Wenzel and Maurice of Lichtenstein and a French lieutenant-general. The ladies included the Countess de Luçay, the wardrobe-lady to the Empress Marie-Louise; Mesdames Duchâtel, Doumerc, Lallemand, and the Baroness Thomières. She says in her *Memoirs:* 'We were all as elegant as we could be; and in those days this was saying something. My house, always excellently furnished, was on this occasion decorated with particular care, and seemed to join in our female coquetry. There were flowers everywhere—and flowers in the month of May—a month redolent of roses! "It seems," said the Duke, "that you have adopted our fashion of dining late. Is it not a delightful one?" ' But where was the money to come from to pay for all this lavish entertaining?

During the Hundred Days Savary came to the Champs-Elysées to require Laure to present herself at the Tuileries. She refused. Then in the spring of 1815, finding herself again pregnant, she retired, with her two boys, to Maurice's property at Champigny. This lies on the Paris to Sens road, some six miles beyond Montereau. From this delightful retreat she wrote to Maurice, who was in Paris: 'The countryside is ravishing; the lilacs are in full bloom and the park is truly a little paradise at this moment. The syringas are in bud and are going to flower in a few days. I have a rose-tree on which there are perhaps a hundred buds already formed; the tulips are still beautiful, but the hyacinths are completely over.' It was all too idyllic to last. On the fateful 18 June 1815 was fought the battle of Waterloo. The Allies again swept towards Paris. There was fighting in the vicinity of Champigny, but the Tsar Alexander had let it be known, out of regard for Laure, that the property and its inhabitants were not to be molested. The German official who informed Maurice of this sent his compliments to the Duchess of Abrantès. It is Fouché who, as much as any one single person brought about the act of the second abdication of Napoleon. Under the influence of Maurice, Laure had become, as she said, 'more royalist than napoleonist'. In her *Memoirs*, written at a time when the cult of Napoleon was growing—in fact, they contributed much to this growth—Laure has hard words to say about those who 'dress Napoleon in a tiger's skin', forgetting what she wrote to Maurice in July 1815:

'*And the Tiger*, what is he doing? Have they put him in a cage yet? If he has not been put there, it is necessary for those who neglect it to do so. Have I not the appearance of being a cannibal, in short, to say such a thing? But then, to what have we not been reduced? To what have we not been forced? The state of the oppressed and the victims finishes by not being very agreeable when it is prolonged, and one is not to be too much blamed, it seems to me, to wish a little evil to those who have done so much to us!'

In August she was back in Paris, and wrote to Maurice, who was at Champigny, how she had been invited to a small informal evening with the Tsar and the Duke of Wellington. Wellington, who was staying in a house opposite hers, saw much of her. Her pregnancy did not seem to hinder her social activities, or to excite comment. Then she retired to the country, to Champigny, where she gave birth to a daughter, who was named Laure. It died shortly afterwards. In October 1815 Maurice was appointed captain in the Lancers of the Guard. Laure was soon sufficiently recovered to return to Paris and to be present at the grand ball given by the Duke of Wellington, which she described to Maurice, with very apparent satisfaction at the treatment she had received at the hands of the gallant Duke. She was accompanied by her daughter Josephine, who was only fourteen, and her neice, Clotilde Chodron. 'The ball was extremely numerous. The list was of eight hundred persons. Josephine has been the queen of the occasion. . . The Duke asked me, as a favour, to dance a quadrille with him and I did so opposite my daughter. All the ball came to place themselves around us to watch us, and those poor English . . . say that I am the Gosseline of the *salons*. There was a time when that could have been said, but now the praise is a bit exaggerated. While we were dancing, supper was announced. The Duke had it wait and, signaling to Prince Paul to give his arm to the Duchesse de Richemont, he came to offer me very gallantly his and made me sit at table on his right.

Geouffre gave his arm to his niece and I made him a sign to place her as near as possible to me.

'The Duke, seeing this, said to Lady Webster, who had just sat down next to him, "I beg your pardon, Madame, but a young lady cannot be too near her mother. Would you then yield your place to Mlle d' Abrantès?"

'Josephine, as beautiful as an angel, modest as a little virgin, red as a strawberry at being thus the object of general attention, came to place herself at the left of the Duke, who found himself thus between her and me. I will say that all the *crème de la crème* of the Faubourg Saint-Germain who came at that moment to sit at the Duke's table, around which were arranged twelve other tables, have been a little suffocated at this marked preference for our family. After supper, during which the Duke was very amiable, he asked Josephine to dance a *contredanse* for him, he found so much pleasure, he said, in seeing her dance—all in all, maternal vanity apart, she was charming. . .'

Later in the evening Laure was taken somewhat by surprise, when the Marquise de Coigny brought up to her a tall woman, 'very white, very fat' and introduced to her the Princess Bagration, the widow of the Russian general killed at Borodino. She too had been a mistress of Metternich. Laure finished her letter to Maurice: 'Adieu, my dearest angel. Adieu, well-beloved of my soul. This is a long letter, but I have the self-esteem to believe it will not bore you. Adieu.'

For the first half of 1816 Laure tried to stem the pressure from her crowd of creditors. But all was unavailing. The house on the Champs-Elysées was let to the Baron Ville d'Avray for 26,000 francs a year, and her remaining furniture, pictures and the library had to be sold. She, with the children and some servants, sought refuge with Maurice at Champigny. On her name-day, 10 August, she was fêted by the villagers and the estate workers. She was presented with orange-trees in tubs, decorated and with inscriptions in gilded paper—'*To Laure, the well-beloved,*' '*Today is the fête of the Graces and Friendship*'. All went well, while the money lasted. But her creditors pursued her to Champigny. She tried to sell seven pictures in London; she began to dispose of some of her jewels. She began, too, to borrow from Maurice. He stood loyally by her, and paid her most pressing debts. From Champigny she moved back to Paris and rented an hôtel from Mme de Kercado in the rue Saint-Lazare. In this difficult period of the Restoration she saw how many others, celebrities under the Empire, were now impoverished. 'The misery is general,' she wrote, 'There is nobody who is exempt. M. le Duc d'Esclignac has seen his furniture sold by court authority a week ago. I have seen the day before yesterday 18,000 francs of protested notes of hand, signed however by L. de Tarente, Prince de la Trémoille; Sémonville . . . owes my lawyer a note for 4,000 francs, which he is unable to pay him. The same lawyer has been with his colleague, Fournier-Verneuil, to the house of Mother Dufour, who has an estate which is worth three millions. The debts are such in this house that M.Fournier was obliged to get up at seven o'clock in the morning to go and kill a rabbit if he wished to lunch. . .'

In a letter to Maurice she complained that her brother-in-law Geouffre had 'eaten' in two years more than 72,000 *livres* of her and her children's money. 'Oh, what a man! what a man! I knew him to be light, but to lack the heart and the honour to the point of robbing the widow and orphan, I would never have thought that.' She still saw many of her old friends in Paris, and she gave Maurice at Champigny news of them. She rebuked him when she thought she had reason to suspect that he was seeing other women—Lady Erskine, for example. He was; but he still remained loyal to her in many ways. Financially, above all. He paid—she was incapable of economy. She thought she had found one day an excellent means of saving money. This was a restaurateur who for 30 francs a day, would feed five persons. 'I have four *entrées*, four *entremets*, soup, remove, a roast and bread. The dessert and wine are on me.' She wrote, telling Maurice, that for her pictures in London 75,000 francs had been offered. 'Adieu, my adored angel, adieu. Alas, when will we see each other again? If you wanted to do so—that would be if my *bitches of affairs* did not hold me in a chain of iron. . .' She even proposed wild-cat schemes for Maurice to buy life-annuities. Laure seemed to be fated financially; she squandered money and anything she touched failed.

In the summer of 1817, with the help of Metternich, she went to Italy in a vain attempt to secure money which she alleged was owed Junot by the Holy See. Meeting Metternich in Florence and armed with his introductions, she went on hopefully to Rome. There she visited Madame Mère and the Princess Pauline Borghese. Blacas d'Aulpe, then Minister in Rome, looked on this with disfavour and did nothing to help her suit with the papal authorities. An old Sicilian, Prince Raffadetti, whom she had met in Paris, now a widower, wished to marry her, but she would not hear of it; his money was only his during his children's minority. On her journey home she visited the field of Marengo and made two sketches of it, one from the tree where they had carried the dying Desaix. She returned to Paris, all the expense of her travel for nothing. Her creditors were on the watch for her. Then the blow fell. Maurice was obliged to sell Champigny. He had done all he could do on behalf of his mistress.

'Oh, my friend, I, I, whose life belongs to you, I who would give all my blood for you without knowing why you demanded it, that it would be me who could be the cause of an anxiety which you could not appease. My God, my God! that I had not died on the day I had the weakness to speak to him of my affairs. He would not have come to my help, he would still be what he was, and I, I would not have become odious to him. Ah! Maurice, I see it only too well. This is the reason for the coldness and for the end of our love, unfortunate woman that I am!

'Adieu. My poor head aches and my hand is so trembling that I can scarcely write.'

This source exhausted, Laure turned again to the Tuileries: 'If Your Majesty has judged me too presumptuous in demanding this sum of eight thousand francs, will you deign to do that which you think fitting; but in pity for four children and an unfortunate woman, Sire, in pity, do not abandon me.' The response is not known, but it appears that it was negative, since soon after she bought a diamond on credit and then immediately sold it. Maurice, for the last time, came to her rescue and paid up.

The lovers had spoken of parting so often that neither could really believe it true when at last it happened. It was in the summer of 1818. They returned their portraits, their rings, their gifts. It was the end of the affair. Laure left her hôtel in the rue Saint-Lazare, for a small apartment, No. 18 rue Basse-du-Rempart, where she remained for part of the year 1819, before installing her family in the village of Orgeval, near Saint-Germain-en-Laye.

On 14 February 1824, at the Tuileries, the marriage contract was signed between Maurice de Balincourt and Euphrosine de Lisleroy, in the presence of His Majesty and all the members of the Royal Family. The married couple retired to their estates in Provence.

NINE

Honoré de Balzac

IN 1819, when Laure, with her four children and the servants, took a house at Orgeval, the village, which lay a few miles due west of Saint-Germain-en-Laye, was set in a delightful unspoilt countryside of fields and woods running down to the Seine, which here forms one of its great serpentine loops. It was typical of the beautiful landscape of the Ile-de-France. After the turmoil, the endless receptions, the comings and goings, of Paris, it was a charming rural retreat, sufficiently near to the city for her friends to visit her and for her to drive in, which she did two or three times a week, to see old acquaintances and to lunch with M. de Cherval or the Duc de Valmy. She has left us an account of how she passed her summer days at Orgeval: 'In my pretty retreat I occupied myself with flowers, with botanising. . . I walked for whole days in the Forest of Saint-Germain; or at times I descended as far as the Seine and set out in a boat with all of my young family. We took with us provisions, dined in the forest, and made also long excursions, leading almost a nomadic life. Then I returned home to have my peasants dance. . . The rest of the time I worked with my daughters; we had readings in common. Then my friends came to me, those true friends whom distance and the reversal of my fortunes have never separated from me. In a life so pleasant and peaceful one understands that I did not have a great desire to return to this country of courts that one showed me from afar as a paradise over which a woman, with a little wit, could hope to reign. . .' One cannot but feel that she was very consciously making a virtue of a necessity.

Yet even in these idyllic surroundings, in her country pavilion—her 'hermitage' she called it—very different from her extravagant town house and its lavish entertaining, she could not restrain her expenditure. Her 'bitches of affairs', her creditors in person, followed her. She applied to the Duke of Orléans, now in Junot's old command of Colonel-General of Hussars, for a pension. He, with a view to the future, wishing to make himself agreeable in circles which owed everything to the Emperor, looked favourably on her request and wrote to the Minister of War. The minister, Marshal Gouvion Saint-Cyr, no friend of Junot, acknowledged the request, saying that he would abide by the decision of the Committee of War. When, however, she was awarded a pension of 12,000 francs, which was cut by the War Office to 10,000, Gouvion Saint-Cyr by a stroke of the pen, reduced it to 6,000 francs. Against this seemingly arbitrary decision she appealed in vain. She had as well, it will be remembered, Napoleon d'Abrantès' *majorat* of 6,000 on the *Grand Livre*, giving her a sizeable income, when it is considered that a colonel's active pay was an annual 6,000 francs. But money ran through Laure's hands like water. Still, when in January 1819 the Hôtel d'Abrantès in the Champs-Elysées, which was valued, together with Junot's added gallery on the rue Saint-Honoré, at 419,500 francs (the mirrors alone being valued at 53,758 francs), was sold for 280,000 francs, she had settled the bulk of Junot's (and her own) debts. But her *dot* and much of her jewellery had been disposed of in the settlement. She had the children to educate. At the beginning of 1821, putting Napoleon (Léon) in the Collège Henri IV, with a view to a diplomatic career, and the younger Alfred at the military school at La Flèche, she moved with the two girls, Josephine and Constance, from Orgeval and took a house in Versailles, at No. 69 rue du Grand-Montreuil.

Later, in *The Woman of Thirty Years* Balzac was to describe Laure's house in Versailles. It was, he wrote, 'a *maison de campagne*, situated between the church and the barrier of Montreuil, on the road which led to the Avenue de Saint-Cloud. . . Built formerly to serve as the resort for the passing love-affairs of some *grand seigneur*, this pavilion had very extensive outbuildings. The gardens in the middle of which it was placed stretched away to the right and to the left of the first houses of Montreuil and of the cottages which were built in the neighbourhood of the barrier. Thus, without being too isolated, the owners of this property enjoyed, with the town almost at its gates, all the pleasures of seclusion. By a strange contradiction, the facade and the front door of the house gave immediately on to the road, which perhaps formerly was little used. This hypothesis appears likely if one comes to think that it passes a delicious pavilion built by Louis XV for Mlle de Romans, and that before reaching it the curious may recognize, here and there, more than one *casino* whose interior and décor betray the spiritual debauches of our ancestors who, in the license which is laid at their charge, sought to invest it nevertheless with shadow and mystery.' At the beginning of this century, according to M.Turquan, the house was still standing among market gardens and utilitarian institutions, but then was occupied by *five* families.

No longer did she possess her own carriage. Once a week, at least, she went to Paris, if not on business or pleasure, then to visit Léon at the Collège Henri IV, behind the Panthéon. She travelled by a kind of diligence or omnibus, known as the *gondola*, which picking her up at the Place d'Armes in Versailles, deposited her in an hour and a half in the Cours-la-Reine in Paris. She wrote of these journeys: 'It is in the *gondola* that one learns to know the moral state of the country. It is there that one learns things without make-up, that truth reveals itself in its nudity. I have known more about France perhaps in the seven years that I have passed at Versailles than I have done before, and that by a journey in the *gondola*.' After talking to her son in the visitors' parlour, she went to call on Mme Sophie Gay in her friendly house in rue Gaillon.

Like Mme Hamelin, Mme Gay had made her name under the Directory; she had shone under the Consulate and Empire, and now in the autumn of her days under the Restoration held a *salon*, where met many of the leaders of the Parisian literary world—the poets Arnauld and Béranger, Benjamin Constant, Philarète Chasles, Sainte-Beuve and others. Daughter of a financier in a small way, she had married *en seconde noces* M.Gay, the receiver-general of the department of the Ruhr. During the Empire their receptions at Aix-la-Chapelle were celebrated for their splendour and gaiety. Mme Sophie Gay herself wrote—rather badly. She was outshone by her daughter, the charming fair-haired Delphine, whose poetry as a young woman had taken both Paris and Rome by storm—to the extent, in the latter city, of her being crowned on the Capitol. Delphine Gay was to marry in 1831 Emile de Giradin, a son of an old flame of Laure d'Abrantès, General Alexandre de Giradin, and Mme Dupuy, wife of a Parisian lawyer. It was in Mme Sophie Gay's *salon*, in 1825, that Laure met Honoré Balzac. He was then twenty-six, an unprepossessing figure at first sight, short, plump, badly or over-dressed, with an unruly mop of black hair. But when he spoke one's first impression quickly and totally changed; he talked brilliantly, full to over-brimming with exuberant life; one forgot the squat nose, and one's attention was drawn to his full, sensuous lips and to his eyes which blazed fire.

Laure had another point of contact with Balzac. The latter's sister, also named Laure, had married a M.Surville, who about this time had been appointed civil engineer to the department of Seine-et-Oise, and they lived in Versailles, where their daughter Camille went to school with the younger Junot girl. The two Laures became friends, and Balzac, who was very close to his sister and often visited her, soon had opportunities of calling on the Duchess of Abrantès in rue de Montreuil. Up to this time Balzac had had few opportunities of meeting, apart from Mme de Berny, women of Laure's social standing or worldly experience. At the outset he saw her through the eyes of an enthusiastic admirer of Napoleon and of the Empire, of a man who, above all, admired grand ideas and energy. One evening, soon after he met her, he said with great warmth to Mme Ancelot, who has left us her memoirs of the period: 'This woman has seen Napoleon as a child [she had not], she has seen him as a young man, she has seen him occupied with the ordinary things of life. Then she has seen him grow and rise in the world until it resounded with his name! For me she is like one of the elect who comes to sit at my side, after having lived in Heaven, in the presence of God himself!'

Honoré Balzac was born at Tours on 20 May 1799, his father being of peasant stock from Canezac in the department of the Tarn, an intelligent man who had bettered himself and had obtained official administrative posts during the Revolution. His mother, Anne Charlotte Laure Sallambier, was an heiress and something of a beauty. Honoré only adopted the *particule* in about 1830, possibly under the influence of Laure d'Abrantès. (Laure was vain of being a duchess. Her uncle was always the Prince de Comnène in her correspondence, and her brother Alfred, the former commissioner of police in Marseilles, became about this time, unaccountably enough, M. le Comte de Permon. It must be remembered that it was, although so largely parvenu, a peculiarly snobbish period, when a General Fournier could adopt for reasons of his own the high-sounding surname Fournier-Sarlovèze—simply from having been born in Sarlat in Burgundy.)

At the other end of the village of Villeparisis, near Versailles, where the Balzacs moved from Tours, lived the Bernys. Mme de Berny, who had married during the Terror, had been born Laure Hinner, the daughter of a musician of German extraction and of Laure de Laborde, a lady-of-the-bedchamber to Marie-Antoinette, who, with King Louis XVI, were god-parents to the child. Brought up in close relation with the Court, she had absorbed and retained much of its refinement

and manners. Honoré, twenty-two and struggling to become a writer,
had been engaged as a tutor to the Berny children. In this humble
position he was very much attracted by Mme de Berny, although she
made no attempt to disguise the fact that she was forty-five. She had at
first teased him about his ambition, his uncouth manners and appearance. He little cared. To him she represented the cultivated society of
the *ancien régime*. Respect gave way to sexual desire. In the spring of
1822 he declared his love for her, and she, hopefully, thankfully
accepted this love of a young man in whom she already sensed the
making, the mould of genius. Balzac, who owed much to women,
owed an enormous debt to the love, the sexual always mingled with
the maternal, of Mme Laure de Berny. She watched over him, recounted to him and lived for him a form of life he had never experienced, advised him on manners and dress, criticized his work, lent him
money. Above all, she gave him faith in himself. She loved him.

Laure d'Abrantès, with her knowledge of the best that Paris had to
offer of intellect, of the arts and literature, realized at once, when she
met Balzac, the power that was in this young man, who was already
crippled by debts, who worked some sixteen hours a day and who
flitted from house to house to escape his creditors. Even in their debts
and fecklessness with money they had something in common. Laure
had translated a novel, *Casti et Inès*, from the Spanish and had ideas of
novels of her own. From her youth she had taken to jotting down her
ideas and impressions on paper. She could now use her pen to make
money, which she was so desperately in need of. She showed her work
to Balzac, who praised it, while he criticized it. If Laure was immensely
impressed by Balzac, he was dazzled by her—by her appearance (she
was forty-one, but still very attractive), by her intellect, by her spirit
and fire, by her knowledge of Napoleon, of courts and society, by her
extraordinary amiability and gaiety. By the fact, too, that she was a
duchess. When she offered him friendship he first seized it with both
hands. But the observant Mme Ancelot soon noticed: 'The marvels
of the Empire then exalted Balzac to the point of giving to his relations
with the Duchess a vivacity which resembled a passion.' It was soon
not limited to resemblances only. It became, on both sides, a passion.
But first it was friendship; she wrote offering it to him. He replied:
'Friendship is a mirage that I still pursue despite many disappointments.
Since my schooldays I have sought not for friends but for one friend.
I share the view of La Fontaine, and I have not yet found what my
romantic and exigent imagination depicts to me in such glowing

colours. . . Yet I like to think that there are souls that know and understand one another at a glance. Your proposal, Madame, is so pleasing and flattering that I cannot but grasp your extended hand. . .' But how could the young man accept friendship from an attractive woman, the young Balzac who had propounded the axiom: 'A woman is never so moving and so beautiful as when she renounces all dominion and humbles herself before a master'?

With a woman so passionate as Laure friendship was bound to give way to love, passionate love. There was the difference of fifteen years in their ages, but there was no denying Balzac's deep feeling for Laure. And she returned it to the full measure of her generous and highly responsive nature. But she soon learned that he was 'in silken fetters' to Mme de Berny and taxed him with this lady's dominance over his feelings and actions. He replied with warmth: 'If I have any quality it is that of energy. . . To be dominated is intolerable to me. . .' He painted a realistic portrait of himself as a young man in his mid-twenties: 'In my five feet three inches I contain every possible inconsistency and contrast, and those who find me vain, extravagant, obstinate, frivolous, illogical, fatuous, negligent, idle, unpurposeful, unreflective, inconstant, talkative, tactless, crude, unpolished, crochety and of uneven temper are no less right than those who would say that I am economical, modest, courageous, tenacious, energetic, neglected, hardworking, constant, reserved, full of finesse, polite and always cheerful. The man who calls me a coward will be no more wrong than the man who says that I am extremely brave. In short, learned or ignorant, talented or incompetent, I am astonished by nothing more than myself. I conclude that I am simply an instrument played upon by circumstance. . .' It seems that the friendship offered in August 1825 had turned into love by September, when he was writing to her, tutoying her and addressing her as his 'Dearest Marie'. There were already too many Laures in his life—his mother, his sister, and Mme de Berny. He called her 'Marie the Scold' (*la Grondeuse*). From Tours he wrote:

'I forgive you all your scoldings, my beloved angel, and I hope soon to be intoxicated by that dear gaze and to see that heavenly face. I cannot leave here before 4 October, and so there is time for another sweet letter from my Marie to reach me—but not the scolding Marie, Marie the adored, the Marie I love. I do not want to fly to you, my dearest, without having had a letter of love and reconciliation. I shall come to you in gratitude, and you can now count upon my return. . .'

But Mme de Berny, suspecting that something was afoot, and perhaps warned by Madame Balzac, who had eventually recognized the former's relation with her son, now stepped in, and for a moment seems to have won Honoré back. Not for long. Laure, with her personal fascination, and with her endless funds of the kind of information that the incipient novelist was so eager to possess, had weapons too at her disposal. One was scorn. She wrote to him:

'Your distaste for coming here is more than ridiculous. To put your fears at rest I may tell you without anger that the most complete indifference has succeeded anything that may once have existed between us. And since the word "indifference" is to be interpreted literally you may not have any fear of scenes or reproaches. But I must see you. However strange this may be, *it is the case*. If the interests of my family and my future were not involved, and even your own interest, I assure you that I should treat all relations between us, past, present and future, as though they did not exist.

'Will you therefore remember for the last time that I am a woman, and simply accord to me the strict courtesy that any man owes to the humblest of creatures. And if you are still so weak as to be on the defensive, poor man, then you are even more pitiable than I thought! . . . .'

He came back, but Laure had to share him with Mme de Berny, his *Dilecta*, who at this time was helping him financially and practically in his ill-fated printing venture in the rue des Marais-Saint-Germain, today the rue Visconti. His conversation with Laure had begun, and continued, on literature. He criticized her *Casti et Inès*: 'Now,' he said, 'I will ask you a question: Why have you not recounted the story of Inès as it happened? Why have you put between your sensations and the truth a glacial old man? . . . I find that the third person of this old man takes away the charm, especially in an account given from one ear to another and where the *I* can only have grace. Didn't we agree the other day that nature is the only object that we should aim at? . . .' Elsewhere he discussed the characters of Laure's heroines in the novels she had written and shown him, and which he subsequently helped her to publish. 'There are,' he said, 'two great classes among women: the Isadoras (allow me to take this touching symbol of grace and submission) and the de Staëls, whose masculine ideas, daring conceptions—force, in a word—find themselves joined in a bizarre fashion to all the frailties of your sex. Clarissa, in Richardson, is a girl in whom the sensibility is at every moment suffocated by a force Richardson calls virtue. There are then, in my way of thinking, two kinds of sensibility, as there are two kinds of suffering.' He goes on to contrast the male, intrepid, forceful woman with the submissive, self-abnegating one, to say that the superiority lies with the latter. He then propounds his axiom which we have already seen—that a woman is never so attractive as when she acknowledges a master. One may wonder how Laure received this analysis and this preference. Nor is it clear under which category Balzac considered she fell—or wished her to fall. One may remember Metternich's comments on Adèle's character, that she required a superior man to dominate her. Balzac wrote to her:

'Let me believe that the terrible agitations of your life have only been measured for you on the force of your character; that this force gives you high and fine thoughts on the changing spectacle in the centre of which you have found yourself; that at this moment the retreat in the midst of which you live is for you only a new night which awaits the dawn. In fact, the more I have considered your destiny and the nature of your intelligence, the more I have been struck with this idea that you were one of those feminine talents which are able to extend their dominion further than ordinary laws allow them; that you could make of a brilliant epoch what Mme Roland has only tried of a time of grief and glory. I do not know if you have felt often those impetuous movements which rise up from the depths of the heart and master you at the appearance of a multiplicity of scenes, heroic figures, great characters, but I like to believe it, for it seems to me that nature has set a special seal on you. Would chance alone have launched you across all the countries of our old Europe stirred then by a Titan surrounded by demi-gods?'

No-one was better equipped than she, argued Balzac, to write an account of the periods of the Consulate and the Empire—she who had lived so close to their central figure and knew at first-hand both persons and events. He would help her with his adivce, and would undertake to find a publisher for her and see her *Memoirs* through the press. In 1826 she harnessed herself to this immense undertaking, which was to run into eighteen octavo volumes. These, together with her *Mémoires sur la Restauration* and her *Histoire des Salons de Paris*, amounted to thirty volumes. Throughout her adult life she had been collecting material. Many nights, before going to sleep, she had written down scraps of conversation, expecially of Napoleon's, overheard that day, sketches of people, impressions of memorable happenings. There was the mass of Junot's papers; there were letters kept, cuttings from the *Moniteur* and other journals, accounts of campaigns from those who had played a leading part in them, and, above all, there was her remarkable visual memory, that could remember a dress, the furnishing of a drawing-room, a reception, scenes. She had a knack with words, her pen flowed. Too facilely, in fact; the *Memoirs* would have been better if they had been curtailed by half. But she was to be paid by the volume, and she was always so short of what Balzac called 'the needful', 'living money' (*argent vivant*). It is clear that in the earlier volumes Balzac played a very considerable part; when in the later volumes their relationship had become less close, the quality of the writing slackened.

The first four volumes appeared in 1831, the eighteenth and last in the first edition in 1835. They were a great and immediate success, especially the earlier volumes. Laure herself remarked: 'My *Memoirs*', such as they are, badly put together, boring, are the fashion, by one of those freaks that one sees to often. They sell. If one buys them to make cornets for pepper, ah well, they give a hand to Lamartine, to Chateaubriand, in their bad luck, poor chaps! Then they had made themselves a name. They are the *Memoirs*, the *Memoirs* of someone *who has seen*. Mme de Motteville will be known a thousand years from now.' *Oh, oh! Ah, ah!* as Balzac would say. He was hugely gratified by the success, but when he went so far as to seek a little of the credit for it, Laure would have none of it. She wanted the triumph for herself, did she not need it, every penny of it? She refused to divulge his part in their writing. 'You are piqued', she wrote to him, 'by my refusal, by my announcement that you have not worked on these *Memoirs*. What would you wish me to do? I have to act in this way. The success of this work has been great. Just or not, it is a fact. I have in my bureau newspapers—French, English, Italian, Spanish, German, etc.—which all speak of the *Memoirs*, and speak well of them. Why do you want me to shed the little merit that this poor work has?' Balzac behaved generously and was silent.

The partnership of Laure with Balzac was not all one-sided. Their correspondence shows the depth of their love for each other. In 1831 he wrote to her, in spite of a wisdom tooth which was causing him agony: 'Dear Marie, your silence has been very painful to me. . . . Do not believe that you are not loved. Oh, that I could make pass over into you the confidence that is in me! Believe especially that never has any-one let himself be moved by his own heart, in speaking thus by letter with her whom he loves. Oh! no, it will never be me whom one can accuse of putting grandiloquence, affectation, rhetoric into these letters whose negligence betrays the abnegation. Oh! Dear, you know nothing of me, I have even seen it in those two letters. . . . Don't imagine, Dear Marie of grace, that my love is not full of pain. Oh, dear, have I not already told you that it was for you to add unhappiness to unhappiness. I have made this clear to you, and this perseverance in loving me has astonished me, I have admired it, it has touched my heart, and I love you.' But here Laure's age told against her. With the years her figure lost something of its earlier grace; she put on weight. Her face, too, took on an appearance which in time became almost vulturine, as can be seen in the lithographs of Gavarini. She developed what her enemies called a ginny voice—she who never even touched wine! But despite her frequent illnesses—she suffered much from abdominal troubles for which she had always had recourse to laudanum, which she now took in increasing doses—she retained her enthusiasm for life, her irrepressible gaiety. Her smile never lost its power of charming; a succession of men had been captivated by it.

She took a small apartment in the Abbaye-aux-Bois, so that her living at Versailles would not cut her off too much from the society she could not forgo. At this convent, where the nuns let rooms to those who wished to live lives in only semi-retirement from the world, the 'divine Juliette', Mme Récamier, held her *salon* frequented by people of all shades of opinion and of social rank. Chateaubriand was the lion, and he could be found chatting to such literary figures as Lamartine and Benjamin Constant. Laure introduced Balzac to this select circle. An Academician who was present noticed Balzac's naive, child-like wonder at finding himself among such people, and thought it very touching. Sitting down beside him, he found his spontaneity and the intelligence of his conversation remarkable indeed. Laure described him at this time: 'Take a good look at this young man with the charcoal eyes, with hair the colour of jet; regard his nose, his mouth above all, when a mischievous smile comes to lift up the corners; do you see a kind of disdain and malice master his look, where however there is kindness for his friends? This is M.de Balzac. Although he is only thirty, many books have already issued from his pen.' He read to Mme Récamier's *salon* his *La Peau de chagrin*, and she was so delighted that she asked him to read it a second time. Through this introduction Balzac had secured an influential circle of admirers. Laure, with her physical attraction, her habitual buoyancy of spirit (when she was not 'scolding' or feeling neglected), her knowledge and her valuable connections, had become indispensable to Balzac. Mme de Berny was there, but Laure held for the time the first place in his intellect and in his amatory feelings.

In 1829 there had appeared Balzac's *La Physiologie du marriage*, which established his success as a writer, as a profound analyst of the feminine heart. If it owed something to his own experience and the talk of his Voltairean father, it owed even more to the confidences of such women as Mme de Berny, Laure d'Abrantès, Mme Hamelin, Mme Sophie Gay, and to that old philanderer and sceptic of the *ancien régime* Villers-la Faye. In this work Balzac speaks of Laure almost by name. He speaks of his conversations with 'a Duchess', who had been 'one of the most human and *spirituelle* of the Court of Napoleon', who, 'having formerly reached a high position in society, the Restoration had overtaken and ruined', and who 'had made a hermit of herself'. French literary critics have found it an engrossing occupation to trace in the *Comédie humaine* the influences of women on Balzac. Among the most significant must stand Mme de Berny and Laure d'Abrantès. It is generally agreed that Balzac took his models where he found them, and that many of his characters have the actual characteristics, even if compounded, of those persons whom he had met and observed in his life. He worked very close to nature.

It will be agreed that in *La femme abandonnée*, which he published in 1833 and dedicated to the Duchess d'Abrantès, the appearance and character of Mme de Beauséant is singularly like a portrait of Laure. 'The figure of the Vicomtesse de Beauséant rose up suddenly before him with gracious thronging associations. She was a new world to him, a world of fears and hopes, a world to fight for and to conquer.' 'In the brilliant eyes of this *grand dame*, was all the courage of her house, the courage of a woman strong only to repel contempt or audacity, but full of tenderness for the softer sentiments.' 'The contours of her small head . . . the characteristics of her beautiful face, her fine lips and her mobile countenance, guarded an expression of exquisite prudence, a suggestion of assumed irony which gave the appearance both of guile and even impertinence. It was impossible not to forgive her these two feminine sins in thinking of her misfortunes, to the passion which had nearly cost her her life. . .' 'This woman separated from the whole world who, for three years, lived at the bottom of a small valley, far from the city, alone with the memories of a brilliant, happy, passionate youth, formerly filled with receptions, constant homage, but now given over to the horror of the void. This woman's smile announces a high opinion of her own value.'

Laure wrote her *Journal intime* for Balzac. Was he not thinking of her affair with Metternich, when he wrote of Mme de Beauséant in *La femme abandonnée*, '. . . after an *éclat* that most women envy and condemn, above all when the seductions of youth and beauty almost justify the fault which has brought it about. . .'? Was he not alluding to Metternich's 'language of flowers', which he taught all his mistresses (this was to decorate their rooms with the flowers that for the particular moment gave expression to their mood), in the first sentence of his description of Mme d'Aiglemont in *La femme de trente ans*, a portrait of Laure d'Abrantès in her early forties?

'In her house the setting was in harmony with the thought which dominated her person. The coils of her hair largely plaited formed on the top of her head a high crown in which mingled no ornament, for she seemed to have said farewell for ever to all care of the *toilette*. . . Also one never surprised in her those little calculations of coquetry which spoil many women. Only, however modest her bodice, it did not entirely hide the elegance of her figure. The luxury of her long dress consisted in its extremely distinguished cut; and, if it is permissible to look for ideas in the arrangement of a piece of material, one could say that the numerous and simple folds of her dress communicated a great nobility. Nevertheless, the not insignificant frailties of women were perhaps betrayed by the meticulous care she took of her hands and her feet. But if she displayed them with some pleasure, it would have been difficult for the most malicious rival to find her movements affected, so involuntary they appeared, or owing to a habit formed in childhood. This remains of coquetry would be even excused for her careless grace. These characteristics, this *ensemble* of little things that make a woman plain or pretty, attractive or disagreeable, cannot be indicated, especially when the personality is the link in all the details and imprints on them a delicious unity. Her bearing also accorded perfectly with her figure and her setting. At a certain age certain favoured women alone know how to give a language to their attitude. Is it grief, is it happiness which lends to the woman of thirty years, to the happy or the unhappy woman, the secret of this eloquent bearing? It will always be a living enigma which each interprets in accordance with his desires, his hopes or his theories. The manner in which she held her two elbows supported by the arms of her chair, and joined the tips of her fingers of each hand, giving the impression of playing; the curve of her throat, the negligence of her languid but supple body, which appeared in the chair elegantly exhausted, the indolence of her limbs, the carelessness of her pose, her movements full of lassitude, all reveal a woman without interest in life. . .'

At moments, yes; moments when she felt the reversals of her fortune and her present position were too much for her; but only for moments. Then the natural resilience of her character reasserted itself, the gaiety which was second nature to her revived, and that sanguine expectation of present pleasure in persons and things was restored. But her extreme sensibility ensured that she would have sombre moments.

After 1830 and the July Revolution, she realized that a change of regime would not alter her position in relation to the Tuileries. Her Napoleonic memories revived as she composed her *Memoirs*. At the time of the July uprising she heard the cry *Vive l'Empereur!* and saw again the *tricolore* on the streets. She described a scene she witnessed: 'I was then at the Abbaye-aux-Bois. It was Thursday. The Parisians had just taken the Swiss' barracks, rue de Babylone, and cries of victory were heard on all sides. I was then on the terrace of the Abbaye-aux-Bois, which is in front of the convent, and I rested on the shoulders of my eldest son. Suddenly on my right I perceived an object, lit up by the beautiful July sun, and shining with the colours cherished in my childhood, my youth, and which all my life I have cherished and venerated. Immediately my heart was seized by one of those measureless joys which Heaven reveals. I burst into tears and threw myself into my son's arms. I could only clasp him convulsively to my breast, pointing out to him with my hand the flag, whose sight took me back to the most beautiful days of my life. ' "Take a good look at it,' I said to him. There's the flag under which your father fought for twenty years. There are the colours France should love, for those colours are sanctified with the blood of its children."

'And I bowed before the flag.' The Napoleonic cult had already begun.

In the *Correspondance* of Balzac there is a letter headed 'Paris, Thursday 1831', which suggests a connection with a passage in *La Femme de trente ans*. The letter refers to an evening spent with Laure at Versailles. The story relates how 'one evening the two lovers sat alone and side by side, silently watching one of the most beautiful changes of the sky, and cloudless heaven taking the colours of pale gold and purple from the last rays of the sunset. With the slow fading of the daylight, pleasant thoughts seem to awaken, and soft stirrings of passion and a mysterious sense of trouble in the midst of calm. Nature sets before us vague images of happiness, bidding us to enjoy this happiness within our reach, or grieve for it when it has fled. In those moments filled with enchantment . . . it is difficult to resist the heart's desires grown so magically potent. Cares are blunted, joy becomes ecstacy; pain, intolerable anguish. The splendour of sunset gives the signal for confessions and draws them out. Silence grows more dangerous than speech. . . And for speech, the least word has irresistible force. . . Is not heaven within us, or do we feel that we are in heaven?'

Balzac wrote to Laure on that Thursday:

'I have returned in the most unfortunate manner. I waited a half-hour at the gate of Versailles, and then I saw appear in the avenue a wretched one-horse conveyance which was only able to carry me as far as Sèvres. At Sèvres I hoped to be able to find a second conveyance, and I walked towards Paris by the light of those magnificently beautiful stars which you contemplated, and, like you, I enjoyed the imposing silence which filled the spirit. But I walked! At length, about Auteuil—and there I thought of the mysterious pavilion—I heard afresh the health-giving and snuffling sound of another cab, which set me down at midnight on the Place Louis XV; and from the lack of a carriage, I had to use my poor flat feet to regain my lodging.

'In getting into bed, I admitted to myself that the quarter of an hour extra that I spent at your window compensated for all these trials and tribulations, and, as I went to sleep at almost half-past two, I soothed myself by thinking of this vague resemblance between us, of knowing that you slept also perhaps, and that you wrote to me that you had suffered!

'Here, this morning, they have given me your last letter. I will say nothing about it; that which I had received had so moved me. You suffer, you say, and without hope of waking again to a beautiful

morning. But think that, for the spirit, these are spring times and
fresh mornings at all times; that your past life has no name in any
language; it is scarcely a memory and you cannot judge your
future life by the past. How many persons have started all over again
on beautiful and pleasant lives much further on than you in life!
We are only what our personality is: do you know if yours has
received all its development, if you breathe in the air by all your
pores, if all your eyes see? Plants, flowers themselves have a grada-
tion, and how many saplings, in the forests, have not seen the sun!

'In your letter there breathes a melancholy which seems to escape
from a spirit which has never known happiness, and I do not believe
it is like this. It seems to me that happiness, this shining happiness,
leaves a long luminous path, a milky way in our lives, and that its
reflections multiply in all our situations, even the most terrible. The
fallen angel does not speak like men; has it not seen paradise? There
is in my words a seeming contradiction of which you cannot accuse
my thought. In reflecting, you will see that I am consistent, and that
one can have been happy, without knowing the most perfect
happiness. . .'

He continued in a cheerful, thankful tone and suggested that she
show him all there was to see at Versailles, Trianon, Marly, etc., of
which he knew nothing. He concluded: 'To thank you for your friendly
cooperation. I can only truly draw from the bottom of my heart one
of those *Thank you's* that I count among my treasures of tenderness,
and I send it to you with a holy recognition of what you have done.
Let me remain in the fullest expression of this feeling, especially in
thinking of this evening that I keep in my heart like a dear memory.
I shall say like you: *Adieu and au revoir.*'

On 5 October 1831 Balzac replied to an unknown correspondent.
It was to the Marquise de Castries, who had written praising his
Physiologie. 'Such sympathy inspired at a distance is my most cherished
possession, my whole fortune, my most pure delight.' If the Marquise
was of the Faubourg Saint-Germain (at last he had reached it!), she had
led an adventurous life. By two extraordinary coincidences she was
connected with Laure's past. She had had an affair with Metternich's
son Victor, the consequence of which was the birth of a son. Later,
under his grandfather's influence, the Austrian Emperor created the
boy Baron von Aldenburg. Further, her uncle was the Duc de Fitz-
James, the descendant of James II and Arabella Churchill, whose father

had built the Folie de Saint-James, once lived in by Laure. Balzac, although fascinated by the Marquise, whom he went to meet in Switzerland in 1833, never achieved with her what he so very much desired. She led him on, played with him, and left him unrequited. But from this time there was a more formal note in his letters and dealings with Laure. The friendship, with which his affair with Laure had begun, resumed its more placid way. But not on her side. As in her relationship with Maurice de Balincourt, Laure was a demanding mistress. With Balzac she reverted at times to Marie *la Grondeuse;* she continued to express in her letters her unhappiness at his apparent desertion of her and her lively desire to see him. She tempted the *gourmet* as well as the *gourmand* in him with delicious dinners and coffee from Havana, the most exquisite to be procured in Paris. As he inhaled its fragrant aroma he would think of her. She invited Mme Wyse, the estranged daughter of Lucien Bonaparte, whom she tried to help, to meet him. Then in 1832 Balzac received a letter postmarked from Odessa, addressed to him *chez Gosselin éditeur,* Paris. It was from l' *Etrangère;* and behind the anonymity of the signature lay the voluptuous form and the intriguing personality of Madame Hanska.

Laure was forty-nine and Balzac thirty-four when she saw the inevitable parting of ways. 'She had been pretty,' wrote the Countess Dash about this time, 'she no longer appeared so.' She had the courage herself to make the break. He must have told her that he was using the excuse of going to Besançon in search of paper and that from there he would slip across unknown into Switzerland. She must have, too, suspected his motive in doing so. It was to be his first meeting with Mme Hanska at Neufchâtel, which took place in October 1833. He was to marry her only in 1850, the year of his death. From Versailles on 21 September 1833 Laure wrote to Balzac: 'When I think of what I all but said to you yesterday, it turns my heart cold. However, it is *necessary* that I say it to you. Never was this will so far from my thought than yesterday evening, and it was one word of yours that made me change my opinion. My God! After so many years to see a mystery rise between us! For mark well my words, it is of the greatest importance, and it is not so much the fortnight that you are going to spend in Switzerland that will get me used to the thought that I must speak of. This is a little in the style of the *sphinx,* but patience: before long the enigma will be explained. Adieu, my friend, I have need of believing that you spoke the truth last night in expressing your friendship for me. But it is necessary to prove it to me in having in me one sister more. . .' Balzac only received this letter on his return from Switzerland, and, fatigued and broken by the return journey in a wretched conveyance, he hastened to send her, while they were preparing his bath, 'a thousand witnesses of friendship'.

They continued to communicate, she to send him her books as they were published, on special China paper and specially bound, and he in return sent his. They wrote and saw each other frequently, the fraternal love becoming at length almost maternal: 'Don't think about business. Complete your beautiful books, and love her who will always love you as a son of whom she is very proud!'

In the month of August 1833 Laure gave up her house in Versailles and her flat at the Abbaye-aux-Bois, and moved with her family back to Paris, where she took a ground-floor apartment, with a garden, at No. 18 rue de la Rochfoucauld, the same street in which lived the Marquis de Custine.

TEN

The Marquis de Custine

At the end of 1834 Laure wrote to Balzac:

'I shall be at your orders at three o'clock. Is that right, my master? And why, if you please? You know that four o'clock is a solemn hour? But then! Adieu. I wish you that for not having come to dinner. . . Adieu, a thousand tendernesses. You know that I love you *dearly*! but the strangest part of it is that I *ought* to love you. It is comic. My God, it is like a play of Shakespeare: laughter, tears, then laughter, and more tears. The change is only in the diminution of laughter and the progression of tears. As for my friendship for you, it is what ought to be the sentiment which binds us, unchangeable, tender and deep. Such an affection must be measured in a *cubic* way. There is not only surface, but depth, width and breadth. See how I talk nonsense! And to you! You, the most intelligent man I have ever seen . . . you are an *incomparable person*, a person kneaded of intelligence, of talent. . . How to write one *word* like you, one word! Then find a Birotteau, a Grenadière, a Cornelius, a Louis XI, and a regiment of marvels, each more ravishing than the next. I tell you, you are a *perfect perfection. La Recherche de l'absolu* is one of those perfections, and I am vain of you, Honoré, and vain with my heart, do you understand?'

Could she put it more delicately—'vain with her heart'?

She enjoyed her little garden in the rue de la Rochefoucauld, into which she could step through the French window—her lawn, flower beds and roses. At five on a summer's morning she would be out in it. She took her guests there and they talked, while she cut off dead heads with her secateurs; Victor Hugo would go to the pump to fill for her the watering can. And what could be pleasanter than sitting out on warm evenings. She gathered her friends around her, and she re-founded her *salon*, her Mondays, when all literary Paris gathered in her small drawing room or walked in her garden. Once again she found herself in her true métier, the role in which she excelled, conducting her *salon*. Balzac was an assiduous attender, with Chateaubriand, Lamartine, Victor Hugo, Alexandre Dumas, Gavarini, the Musset brothers, Duc Victor de Broglie, who had married Albertine, the daughter of Mme de Staël; M. de Forbin, once the chamberlain to Princess Pauline and now the director of the royal museums; the Comte Jules de Castellane, the Marquis de Custine, and many others. And remnants of imperial society as well: the Duc Decazes, Duc de Bassano, the Comte de Rambuteau, Mme Regnaud de Saint-Jean-d'Angely, the Baronne Lallemand, the Marquise de Bréhan and the Duchess d'Otrante. If they appeared to neglect her, a courteous little note would remind them of her pleasure—and their duty. To M. Berthoud, the director of the *Revue de Paris*, she wrote: 'I no longer see you, Monsieur, and that afflicts me, for I have for you a sincere friendship. . . Why then have you deserted my Mondays?' When Balzac absented himself for some weeks she was distraught. Malicious tongues explained his absence. She wrote to him in January 1835: 'My dear Honoré, they all say that you no longer friends with me! . . . Me, I say that they lie! . . . You are not only my friend, but my sincere and good friend. I have kept for you a profound affection, and this affection is not of the kind to change. Yes, we are attached the one to the other by these links of the spirit, which nothing will ever break. . . My spirit is overwhelmed by this suggestion. But it is false, I hope? Adieu. Shortly, *soon*, isn't it?'

In May she wrote, with her left hand, telling him that she was in bed and had had her right arm operated on. 'Come to see me, my friend. It will do me a great deal of good to see you. I know that you are working on *La Lys dans la vallée*. But I am an exception, as my friend the Archbishop said to me yesterday morning, in coming to see me also, he who never goes to any woman's house.' In this the present incumbent differed markedly from Cardinal Maury under the Empire. And she added that she heard that he had been in prison. It was true. Balzac had been arrested for failing to do his service in the National Guard. He did not come. She wrote again, saying that he was the first she had written to after her operation. 'You have not come. That wounds me, it afflicts me. I have always been a *friend* to you, and I have the right to tell you so. It is necessary for me to hope then to find again a friend in you. *All Paris* has written to my house, and yours is the only one I have not seen. . .' She realized she was fighting a losing battle, for in this same spring of 1835 there is a note of desperation in her letters. The question of her authorship of the *Memoirs* had been raised in some quarters, and Balzac was silent:

'I would like to know if we are still friends, or if we are now only persons about to become enemies, for there is scarcely a middle ground. Look, tell me, and teach me also what sort of friendship is it which lets one remain in the same city for months on end without seeing each other, and without giving a sign not of existence, but of interest. But *we*, my dear Honoré, *we* it is not possible that we are like this: there must be stronger reasons that after days of intimacy there do not follow days of pure and smiling friendship. That which only exists in words is neither bad nor cold, it does *not exist at all*. I have never done wrong towards you. Since I wrote, since I have achieved a literary reputation, owing much more to fashion and to chance than to my real merit, that has made me a name which I owe *only to myself*, I could have been wounded at the rumours that have arisen and have not been given the lie to. But I am content to say nothing, and I have not loved you less for your *speaking-silence* on this occasion. . . My old friendship is not open to doubt—my God, old friendships and young loves, that's life!'

But Balzac was deeply in young love with *l'Etrangère*, and was already out of reach.

In spite of many references in Laure's works and letters to the care which she exercised on the upbringing of her children and the love she bestowed upon them, it seems likely that their home life and education were unsatisfactory, if not necessarily unhappy. The truth seems to be that she had little influence on her children. Latterly, she was too occupied with her pressing debts, too deeply engaged in producing the literary material, the money from which, instead of paying their debts, slipped like quicksilver from her purse. In 1825 Josephine, the eldest, who was then twenty-four, expressed a desire to enter the Society of the Sisters of St Vincent de Paul, but for a time was dissuaded by her mother, who had in mind a marriage for her with Comte Gaspard de Pons. Nothing came of this, and Josephine entered as a sister of charity the congregation of Dijon. It has been thought that she was aware of the irregularities in her mother's household at the time that Balzac put foot in the house. The latter studied the girl carefully and she appears in the characteristics of several of his young women. He may have made allusion to what was passing in Josephine's mind in *Le Lys dans la vallée*, when he has a character say of Mlle de Mortsauf: 'The clairvoyant eye of the young woman had, although tardily, divined everything in her mother's heart.' Balzac asked that Josephine remember him in her prayers as he remembered her in his 'old books' (*bouquins*). Later, in 1832, aware of her mother's financial difficulties and ill health, she left the sisters, on the plea of her own delicate health, and returned to Versailles and accompanied her mother to the rue de la Rochefoucauld. Later still, when she was in her early forties, she married a M.Amet, an official in the postal service, and took to journalism, Balzac assisting her in placing her articles. Constance, the second girl, married, against her mother's wishes, an impecunious army officer, Louis Aubert, and proceeded to have a family, which Laure had to help in supporting. The latter wrote to General Allix that the husband had gone off to Turkey, leaving Constance with two small children and another on the way. Constance, too, engaged later in journalism, writing fashion articles, which were well thought of.

Napoleon d'Abrantès, who inherited his father's title, despite his intelligence and knowledge of foreign languages—he translated and wrote German, and spoke and wrote English and Italian perfectly—was not cut out for a diplomatic career. In fact, he was cut out for no career whatsoever, although he wrote verses and subsequently published some books of amusing reminiscences. He was an intimate friend of the poet Théodore de Banville. Napoleon, who was an ardent Bonapartist, lived away from the family the life of a *bohème*, in a small room in the Latin Quarter. On the first day of each month, when his *majorat* of five hundred francs was paid, he went to his wardrobe, took out his finest clothes and, dressing himself as an exquisite, took himself off to the Right Bank, after paying the few *livres* he owed his room-mate. There he lived for several days among his peers of the *jeunesse dorée* until his money ran out. Then he returned to his dingy garret. One day Armand Marquiset met him in the street. Napoleon greeted him and immediately invited him to lunch. Marquiset, knowing well the family's impecuniousness, tried to excuse himself. 'Come on,' insisted Napoleon, 'take advantage of it, it is the end of the month!' It was the 3rd. His mother wrote of him, for once complacently, 'The poor child has already had five duels, and of the five he has always wounded or killed his adversary. . .' A chip off the Junot block. His witticisms went the rounds of the Parisian youth. One day a friend engaged to meet him in the rue Feydeau. 'No, no, not that street,' he replied, 'they're paving it (*on pave*)!' The truth was that there were shops, including his glover, in the rue Feydeau, where he owed money. Thenceforth, the expression for avoiding doing something that one did not want to do was *On pave*. Laure could do nothing with him. She wrote to Constance Aubert: 'Oh, how your brother is to blame! No heart, no soul! . . . He knows how things are with us, he knows, and nothing comes out of that empty head of his except hot air— nothing, nothing but this cursed hot air. . . When I tell you that this girl. . . Don't breathe a word to him; we must keep quiet! The horizon will lighten, and then. . .'. Alfred, the youngest, 'the sage one of the family', according to Laure, after finishing at the military school at La Flèche, made a steady career in the army. He was to die as a lieutenant-colonel at Solferino.

She wrote on; her labours were immense; she covered sheet after sheet with ink: the *Les Salons de Paris*, *Catherine of Russia*, *Mémoires sur la Restauration*, articles, novels, plays. Since she was only paid on delivery of work, there were times when her creditors besieged the house and went unpaid, others when there was nothing to eat. She would write frantic notes to Ladvocat or Gosselin, her publishers, asking for just the few francs to enable her to go on, to tide her over. Well or ill—in 1834 she was in bed with the cholera—she had to produce copy. True to her tradition, she maintained a stiff upper lip. It required the penetrating eye of the bourgeois Mme Ancelot to pierce her defences. The truth was that she could not resist her extravagances. When the money came, it was immediately spent, disbursed on luxuries, on porcelain, crystal, useless *objets*, and flowers, masses of flowers. One day Armand Marquiset called to find her bubbling over with high spirits. Two old acquaintances had looked her up. She was going out, and asked Marquiset to accompany her. They took a cab, which set them down at the florists, where she bought boxes of roses, bunches of violets, hydrangeas in pots—to the sum of two hundred francs—to send to the friends who had just visited her. Marquiset paid the cab fare home. She had spent all she had. There was nothing mean or paltry about Laure, nothing *mesquin*, she was generous to a fault; the money simply poured away, as though down a bottomless drain. If anyone admired anything of hers, she would press it on them. Mme Ancelot once remarked on a piece of valuable china. Laure wanted her to take it, and she only extricated herself from her embarrassment by admiring a piece of crystal. This she accepted, and treasured.

It was Mme Ancelot who realized the difficulties, the tension, the perpetual strain under which she lived. One evening, she tells us, she had returned from the theatre with Laure, when the latter remarked, 'How pleasant the night is, when one can chat. One has no fear of bores or creditors!' 'I have never seen,' wrote Mme Ancelot in 1836, 'a house, where at the same time there was more gaiety or more sadness. One evening we were laughing, and the Duchess was gay along with us. When the conversation languished, she had some amusing story on the women of the imperial court, and never had a more inexhaustible verve made spring from her lips words of such extraordinary liveliness. Because of this one forgot the time for tea, which was at her house ordinarily at eleven o'clock. On this evening midnight had long struck, and we were still sitting around the table. Why this long wait? It was that, the same morning, the need of money had made itself so imperiously felt that all the silver had been put into pawn, and, at the moment of taking tea, one had perceived that, teaspoons being the first necessity, it was necessary to go to borrow them from a friend. Scenes of this kind were often repeated, but always she continued to receive numerous guests.' Her servants—or her servant, for she was reduced to one, whom she grandly called her *femme de chambre*—stole from her, and could not be trusted to take precious objects, or Laure's own clothes, to the *mont de piété*. Laure was quite incapable of putting a stop to the ingrained squandering of her hard-earned money, to her *gaspillages*, as her friends called it. The more she spent, the harder she worked. She owed money everywhere, to Corriol the chemist as well as to Binet the grocer. Her creditors were continually at the door. If she showed a brave front to the world, as if her gaiety was irrepressible, there were moments, when left to herself, she was in despair. She wrote to her daughter Constance Aubert a letter almost incoherent with misery:

'I suffer, I suffer like the damned in hell, from my teeth, from my head—everywhere! I have not been able to write the letter: for two hours I did not see in front of me. But the most frightful thing is the league—for there is one—which is formed around me, one does not carry me a drop of water,—and that this morning, for the fourth time, it was necessary to send away the postman, not being able to take a letter of thirty-one *sous*. . .:—that I have no water in my house,—that,—that—I have lost my head! I have money from the *Revue* only at the end of the week on delivering the last part—and to cap it all Balzac comes to collect it today.—It is possible that he comes to dine.—Listen. I want taken to Giroux or to Susse, or to someone else like them, the little *objets* in sculptured ivory; it is rare here and is the sort of thing the Petit-Dunkerque want. I will ask 50 or 60 francs for them.—That would let me wait until the end of the week and then I will be a big girl. . . But in waiting I do not know this morning where to place my poor sick head. . . I am put out that last night we did not take my mantle, my black satin dress, and you would have done me a service to take taken them. That would have produced something while awaiting the money due to me.—Never have I found myself, never, never, in such a frightful position.—No water,—and a wretched *femme de chambre* who comes expressly to tell me so;—a letter. . .—Wait, I cannot endure this present life; I must get out of it or throw myself into the water.—It is too much.—Nothing gives me comfort, there's only rest there. . . Send me something—what you can, and come to collect the little ivories. Adeline [her maid] is in the house, but I am frightened to let her take these things: she has stolen so much from me!—I would send her to take the mantle and dress,—but in daylight there is no way to do so. Oh, that I had two or three francs today, and tomorrow I would be tranquil. Ah! my child! my child! . . .'

It was in conditions like these that she looked back at the times when she was *la Gouverneuse* of Paris. Even these recollections were so much grist to the mill. She wrote for publication a piece entitled *La Toilette de la Duchesse d'Abrantès*, referring to herself in the third person. She was preparing to go to the Tuileries in the days of her glory: 'It was ten o'clock in the evening when I arrived at the house of the Duchess of A. . . . . . s. She was in her dressing room, before her looking glass, and Frédéric was setting her hair. She had a comb in the shape of a basket, mounted with sapphires of the most beautiful water and of the most beautiful blue, surrounded by diamonds of an admirable purity and whiteness. On her black hair, that formed a marvellous effect. She had on her bosom a garland of diamonds, whose centre was formed by a large yellow rose made with lemon diamonds, not coloured, but yellow diamonds; they were mounted in gold. The rest of the garland was formed with flowers in diamonds and corn-ears of diamonds. At

the top of the garland were pinned some branches of simple hyacinth
of a ravishing blue, others all white.

'When Frédéric left, the Duchess had brought a pair of stockings,
which had still the crimson silk which attached them. Those stockings
were of marvellous work. . .

' "Has Cop brought my slippers?" said the Duchess to the first
femme de chambre.

' "Yes, Madame; but he fears that he has made the sole still too
thick."

'It was paper thin.

' "Do you know," said the Duchess, putting on her slippers, "the
most amusing thing happened to me the other day with Cop. He had
made me for the country shoes of black prunella. These wretched shoes
split on a quarter-of-an-hour's walk in the park. On my return to
Paris I told Mme Albert to show Cop in the next time he came to
bring me my shoes. "What now," I said to him, showing him my
poor shoe split for having taken two steps. Cop looked at the shoe,
returned it and finished by saying to me, after having noticed a little
damp sand on the prunella:

' "Ah! I see what it is. . . Madame must have walked!". . .'

Laure then proceeds to give a detailed description of her dressing,
of her *lingerie*, made by Mlle Minette, her corset by Mme Coutant
and her dress by Leroy, the most famous *couturier* of the period. 'When
this was finished, Mme Albert opened a magnificent piece of furniture
made by Jacob, and which was placed near the chimney-piece; this
bureau was opened only by a secret known to the Duchess and Mme
Albert alone. It was there that was found, in perfect safety, the
Duchess's jewel-case, valued at more than five hundred thousand francs.

'Mme Albert took out a necklace composed of seven large sapphires
of oriental blue, encircled by brilliants of a water as limpid as rock
crystal, or, to speak more correctly, as the diamond that it was. . .
This necklace was the most beautiful jewel that there then was in
Paris in private possession. The sprigs were formed of a sapphire pear
surmounted by a bud encircled with diamonds like the rest of the set.
Three similar clasps held the folds of tulle on the shoulders and the
bosom. Another clasp in diamonds and sapphires held the bows of
white satin ribbon, whose ends fell rather low, and which formed the
belt. Mme Albert then led her mistress before a glass, and had approach
her the two underdressers with two lamps, to see if there was lacking
a pin in the *toilette* of her mistress. . .'

'Mme Albert went to take from a scented sachet a cambric handkerchief so embroidered that little cambric remained; it was edged with
Valenciennes lace. . . She sprinkled on this handkerchief some essence
of Portugal from Rubin's; then, giving her mistress a magnificent
blond tortoise-shell fan whose studs were formed by large diamonds,
she looked once more at her mistress, then said to her in the most
respectful voice:
' "Madame the Duchess may now go. . ." '
Laure went on to describe the clothes she wore for an intimate
luncheon party on the following day, when Maurice de Balincourt
was present. 'All this *ensemble* was so fresh that the Marquis of B., who
lunched with us and whose taste was infallible, expressed his admiration, telling the Duchess to have herself painted like that—which she
had done the week after. She had herself painted by Quaglia in the
dress I have just described.'

If at times she let her thoughts go back to what must then in her
indigence have seemed a fabulous past, she maintained in her social
activity her customary gaiety of spirit. In the grounds of his hôtel in
the Faubourg Saint-Honoré, in 1836, Comte Jules de Castellane had
built a theatre, in which he, a lover of all things theatrical, put on plays,
which were performed for the most part by amateurs from among
fashionable society. Laure d'Abrantès and Mme Sophie Gay were the
two principal producers of these plays, which they sometimes provided
from their own pens. They formed two independent troupes, even
with some hostility towards each other. The press made fun of these
society actors and actresses, calling them the Society of Pulcinellas,
and Théophile Gautier christened Laure the Duchesse d'Abracada-
brantès. Some of the notices were cutting, particularly those of Comte
Rodolphe Apponyi: 'M.de Castellane recently invited me to a comedy
put on at his house. I went there because the Duchesse d'Abrantès was
playing a role that I am used to seeing Mlle Mars play. Mme d'Abrantès
is very intelligent, but that does not prevent her from being very fat,
very red in the face, from having a large and flat nose and rather a big
mouth—with that she has a vulgar air, does not speak the comedy well
and forgot her words. M.de Custine, author of *The World Such As It Is*,
or rather such as it is not, has also played his part badly. He has a fault
of pronunciation which is very disagreeable. All this makes a discordant and boring *ensemble*. Moreover, the room was extremely small,
and the crowd out of all proportion.'

One day Laure ran into Maurice de Balincourt. She sent him tickets

for the performance at the Castellane theatre, writing to him, 'We
have come to that point, when friendship, which ought to exist
between two beings who have been what we have been, is an obliga-
tion in life, or our hearts would then be bad, and I do not think yours
or mine have that fault.' He accepted and came. Laure enjoyed the
whole atmosphere of the theatre; at one time she had attended it every
evening; she knew it so well as to surprise General Thiébault with her
knowledge at Salamanca. She loved conducting the rehearsals. 'One
day', says Mme Ancelot, 'I went to one. They were acting a piece by
the Duchess of Abrantès, a piece in one act of which the rehearsal
lasted five hours, so much it was intermingled with unexpected things,
stories, anecdotes, and of joyous pleasantries entirely foreign to the
comedy. The Duchess of Abrantès above all was in fine form, and we
amused ourselves wildly. We finished by dancing in the little theatre.
But suddenly the Duchess exclaimed that we had been talking for five
hours and had eaten and drunk nothing. Then the master of the house,
who was like the others so absorbed by the pleasures of the matinée
that he had forgotten the necessities of life for the adornment of it,
sent out with all speed to the nearest *pâtissiers*. . .' In such joyous
gatherings Laure forgot her present scarcely tolerable existence, and
lived again in her imagination.

In coming to one of these rehearsals Mme Ancelot one day took a
cab that Laure had just vacated. There she found a letter addressed to
the Duchess of Abrantès. It was from an irate creditor who declared
his intention of bringing against her the full rigour of the law if she
did not immediately pay him what she owed him. Mme Ancelot
put the letter into an envelope and sent it to Laure. Behind this gay
façade things could hardly be more difficult for her. The duns came
almost daily. Mme Ancelot called and found her one day in bed, with
an escritoire on her lap and the bedspread littered with her writing.
She looked very unwell, and admitted as much. Mme Ancelot tried
to take away her escritoire but she reproved her. 'Come, sit and talk to
me for a minute,' she said. 'That will cheer me up. Then I must get
this off to the publishers.' And she chattered away gaily, as if she had
no care in the world.

On 30 April 1836 Comte Apponyi, on his way to a ball at the
English Embassy, stopped at the Hôtel de Castellane. The Duchess of
Abrantès was not acting, 'happily for us', Apponyi unkindly remarked.
'But she was in the theatre. Her expression struck those who saw her.
She had recently tried to poison herself. Some say from despair at not

seeing shared the feeling that she had for a young man; others, because of her financial situation. In fact she is crippled with debts.' This is the only evidence that remains of this alleged second attempt at suicide. It will be remembered that Comte Apponyi was an unfriendly witness. But, partly by means of letters written by Laure to Alexandre Dumas, the course of her last love affair can be traced.

Laure liked and admired Dumas, and had taken him up. He was a frequent visitor at her Mondays. His successful play *Antony*, which was based on his own former love for the beautiful Mélanie Waldor, another of Laure's friends, had made his name. Laure became first his 'sister'—later the relationship aged to that of 'mother'—and she looked kindly on his growing love for Ida Ferrier, the actress. 'Come then for a moment, come, come when you feel like taking a dinner from me. You will be welcomed by me as a sister, or rather as a mother.'

Another assiduous frequenter at her *salon* was the Marquis Astolphe de Custine. He was the son of the aristocrat turned Revolutionary general—'General Moustaches'—who was, together with his father, guillotined, and of the beautiful Delphine de Sabran, the friend of Chateaubriand. Astolphe de Custine was born shortly before his father's death in 1793. The Marquis was a neighbour, living at No. 6 rue de la Rochfoucauld. He was immensely rich, possessing, among others, the beautiful château of Saint-Gratien. He was highly educated, graced with the fine manners of the *ancien régime*, a *grand seigneur;* he was also a good conversationalist, conveying to those with whom he was talking an air of equivocal charm. Philarète Chasles wrote of the Marquis de Custine that he was 'sufficiently well covered, sufficiently strong, comfortably dressed, without overdoing it. He astonished me by his veiled talk, his timidity of spirit, his admirable *bon ton*, his ability to make himself understood, which revealed the true gentleman, his malice swathed in silk and cotton, his graces of the world of the great which seemed hardly virile, an extraordinary shyness—like a personal feeling of self-abasement and of mortification little in accord with the lively flashes and phosphoric lights, the daring observations springing from this thick mixture of grieving modesty and of melancholy, or mysticism and of base sensuality. . .' Chasles did not like Custine.

But Laure did; she found him not only distinguished but highly sympathetic. They began seeing much of each other, and frequently wrote. The friendship grew, and became on her side something more than friendship. Laure, who, with the passing of Balzac's passion and her acceptance of his friendship, thought that for her the torturing demands and pains of love were over, now found that Custine's expressed feeling for her and their reciprocally growing affection was a renewal of the sentiments of her youth. She felt and showed herself visibly younger. At first she was suspicious of her awakened feelings, distrusting herself and the truth of the sentiments expressed by Custine. Then she gave in to affections become so pronounced and, confessing to herself that she loved him, welcomed his advances. He declared his love for her and asked her to marry him. It seemed that the laborious, anxious, wearing life that she was leading was to be a thing of the past, for herself and for her family. She accepted him, and allowed everyone to see the blossoming and fruition of her happiness. He was often at her house; she dined frequently with him at his, and they saw much of each other in the society that was common to both. Then suddenly, without a word of warning, he ceased seeing her. She was completely and utterly at a loss, when he broke off all relations with her. Her grief nearly cost her her reason. She had no one to whom she could turn to unburden her despair except to Alexandre Dumas, which she did in quite heart-rending letters. She had always from the time of Balincourt felt the imperious necessity of analysing and expressing her deepest feelings on paper. For her it was a kind of amatory confessional. It was the period of excessive *sensibility*, and none was so open to its excesses than Laure d'Abrantès.

She poured out her heart to Dumas. She had encouraged him in his love for Ida Ferrier, and she felt that in the two lovers she would be understood, that her over-loving heart would find a sympathetic response. Dumas wrote to her, came to see her, and sent her flowers. Thanking him for a beautiful bouquet, she wrote:

'Ah well, here I am confined, when I hoped for a peaceful and pleasant day! One of those days which refresh you at one and the same time in the heart and blood by the view of a felt happiness, and one of which one knows the justice! . . . Enjoy it well, my dear child (you have allowed me this name, and I am happy to give it to you), enjoy your happiness! . . . Enjoy it both of you! . . . But keep your treasure well hidden! Oh! guard it with the care of a miser. Do not let the world see it . . . it is not jealous, oh! no, but it is envious . . . basely envious!* That which it sees and does not give is

*Balzac had used almost identical words, spoken by Mme de Beauséant in *Père Goriot*, published in 1834.

immediately anathematized by its despotism. . . What right has one to be happy without having asked it? Oh! the decrees of this iniquitous tribunal, more infamous than that of partisan judges, who at least cite you before their figures veiled in black, and there kill you with their daggers. But the world tortures you and rejects you in life, with a broken heart in your poor breast, with which you are not even able to complain too loud! . . .

'Why this sadness? you will ask. Yes, I know, I ought not to speak to you in this way, but you have friendship for me . . . and you have seen enough, understood enough, you have too often seen me weep, not to know all that I have to suffer. . . I know that it is egoistical of my friendship to let you see the interior of a soul wounded to *death* and whose groans, for being always repressed, must be more distressing when they force a passage! Your young friend will forgive me for distracting you for a moment from Her, to bring by your attention some relief to an afflicted spirit. Without telling her *why* I suffer, *tell her that I suffer;* her heart, which I have judged good because she is intelligent and has a gentle and lively look, her heart will make her indulgent.

'Yes, I need to have a moment to pour all this out to you! You have seen the bottom of my poor soul! You have seen my tears. . . Always tears, you will say! And if you knew that I have not ceased from weeping!

'There are women whose heart is withered and whose reason is destroyed; those women have lovers; those women have all the vices, all that which makes a woman at length an object of horror at the period when youth flees her.

'But this same woman can be a creature to be pitied rather than to be blamed, because her life has run into storms which strike and submerge, but do not leave dirty traces on their victim. I do not make myself out better that I am, I have had many faults in my life, many! . . . but never one for which I have to blush. . .'

'Ah well! this woman—*I* indeed, I must complain. Am I not in fact unfortunate to meet at the moment of my life, when at last I had gained some repose, a man who says to me: "I also, I have been wretched, but my unhappiness can become a profound happiness. Love me and your affection will efface everything. I will begin again another life! And I, in exchange, I will give you all the happiness that a profoundly loving soul can give (this is a literal extract from a letter of his of the month of January 1834). Let me light up radiantly this half-light in which you hide yourself! Let me love you! Have confidence. Live for us two, and you will be grateful to Providence, which has made you meet such a future of happiness at that period of life when one has only regrets!"

'How would I have not listened to such words? I have listened to them. They have undone me. I have lost my peace. . . I could not fear for my future. How suspect a man of such baseness? How believe that a man would come to poison the few days which remain to a woman whose youth has quitted her face to take refuge in her spirit, and who must fall struck by a hand which she ought to believe that of a brother. . . When we are disenchanted at the age I have reached, when at this period of life we come to say to ourselves: the falsity of man has nothing in it of the sacred, all that which would be respected by the savages of Africa is not by the man with the gentle words, by a man who for two and a half years has the courage to deceive a woman, in playing at sentiment as children play at chapel! and is it then in laughing that he says to you: "Of what are you complaining?"

'There are moments when I believe my brain is going to burst! When I read the letters whose number is more than five hundred, containing phrases such as those I have just told you, and stronger still! . . .

'Do you know one thing? It is that in the days of agony I wished to die. I have wished it so strongly that I have in fact said farewell to life. Ah well, I have not been able to die! Unhappiness is ingenious in its proofs of affection, is it not?

'Adieu. I have saddened you, I am sure, and however I have much affection for you. But grief is egoistical. Tell me if you are coming soon. . . Be happy, both of you. I wish it with my heart, and you know if it is true.'

There had been rumours circulating in Paris about the Marquis of Custine's tastes, but they had not come to the ears of Laure. Philarète Chasles knew of them and, like so many others, was unsympathetically disposed. She, who fancied she knew so well the world and the hearts of men and women, had no experience, in the masculine extroverted military world which she had frequented, of homosexuality. For her, sexual attraction was between men and women; had she not experienced fully in her life its pleasures and miseries? No one had opened her eyes to the Marquis's sudden changing of his interest to women at the age in life that he had reached. Balzac criticized Custine's book *Le Monde comme il est* in *Figaro* under the name of his friend Sandeau, but he did not see fit to enlighten Laure on the alleged motives for Custine's attendance on her. Perhaps he felt that he had no right to—that the marriage, had it taken place, might have worked out satisfactorily. No one sought to excuse the Marquis's cruel playing with the feelings of a woman. The world was silent, watching this tragicomedy. The blow he dealt her proved fatal.

Laure tried to pick up again the threads of her work; and she did so. But her creditors still continued to harry her. She had to give up her *rez-de-chaussée* in the rue de la Rochefoucauld, with its garden, and move to an unfurnished flat, recently built, in the poorer Nouvelle-Athènes district, No. 9 rue de Navarin. Of late she had taken to borrowing from her friends, and gradually all but the most loyal fell away. At last the creditors moved into her house. She was ill in bed. They sold up under her eyes all that remained of her belongings, leaving her only a chair and the bed on which she was lying. The shock was too much for her exhausted body; she developed jaundice. Her maid Rosemallen moved her in a cab to a *maison de santé* in the rue des Batailles—the irony in that name. But she was not able to find refuge there. She had not the small sum necessary to be paid in advance. A more hospitable place was found for her at No. 70 rue de Chaillot. There she died on 7 June 1838, in her fifty-fourth year. Mme Recamier came to kneel at her bedside.

Maurice de Balincourt learnt of her death from Napoleon Junot:

'I have wished to be the first, my good Maurice, to give you the frightful news; it is one of those misfortunes that one cannot communicate with indifference to certain hearts. You have already doubtless understood me, and you know that it is a question of my mother.

'We have lost her yesterday, at 4 o'clock in the morning. She had scarcely time to suffer; the illness which had tormented her for a month appeared to be convalescing. She spoke only of getting up and of what she would like to eat, and then last night she is dead!

'It is one of those blows to which one cannot bring consolation. However bitter might have been my destiny until this day, I see that I have not yet undergone the cruellest blow. Poor mother!

'It is not she, however, who must most be pitied, God had made her life so bitter, that there would perhaps be egoism in saying: why is she no longer of this world? But we, her children and her friends, who will console us in having lost her?

'Nothing consoles such a grief; nothing but the waiting for the same end, when it will please God to rejoin us.

'I have no need to tell you that I count on your good and constant friendship on this sad occasion. Tomorrow, Saturday, at eleven o'clock, we render her our last duties. I am certain that I will find you there to shake your hand.

'We shall set out from the house where she died, Grand-Rue de Chaillot, No. 70, at 11.30 precise. Until tomorrow.

'Adieu. I embrace you, heart-broken.

'Napoleon d'Abrantès.'

The mass for the dead was held in the little church of Saint-Pierre de Chaillot, the expenses for the funeral being defrayed by Queen Marie-Amélie. Among those who followed the hearse on foot to Père-Lachaise, with the family, close friends and contemporaries of Junot, were Chateaubriand, Victor Hugo and Alexandre Dumas. It was proposed that a memorial be erected to the former *Gouverneuse* of Paris, to the design of David d'Angers; but when a site was chosen, permission was refused by the municipal council of the City of Paris. In his indignation Victor Hugo wrote the poem that appeared in *Les Rayons et les ombres—A Laure, Duchess d'A.*

Balzac was not in Paris. On 8 August 1838 he wrote to Mme Hanska: 'The newspapers will have told you of the deplorable end of this poor Duchesse d'Abrantès; she has finished as the Empire finished. Some day I will explain this woman to you; it will provide a good evening at the château of Wierzschovnia.'

To Maurice de Balincourt 'C.L.' wrote: 'Have I spoken to you of M. de Custine—there is one who ought to have some remorse.'

From Vienna Metternich was policing Europe. On 19 August 1840 Princess Melanie von Metternich noted in her journal: 'M. de Saint-Aulaire read us a novel of Mme d'Abrantès, then we finished the evening playing faro.'

SHORT SELECT BIBLIOGRAPHY

Abrantès, Duchess of: *Mémoires*, 10 vols, Paris, 1895–7
   Histoires contemporaines, 2 vols, Paris, 1835
   Scenes de la vie espagnole, 2 vols, Paris, 1836
   Histoire des salons de Paris, 6 vols, Paris, 1837–8
   Memoirs of Mme Junot, Eng. trans., 3 vols, London, 1883
   Secret Memoirs of the Duchesse d'Abrantès, ed. R. Chantemesse, trans.
     E. Sutton, London, 1927
   Memoirs of the Duchess of Abrantès, 1830, trans. G. Shelley, London,
     1929
Chantemesse, R., *Le Roman inconnu de la Duchesse d'Abrantès*, Paris, 1927
Turquan, J., *La Générale Junot, Duchesse d'Abrantès*, Paris, 1902
Malo, H., *Les Années de bohême de la Duchesse d'Abrantès*, Paris, 1927
Rémusat, Mme de, *Lettres*, 2 vols, Paris, 1881
   Mémoires, 2 vols, Eng. trans., London, 1880
Cooper, D., *Talleyrand*, London, 1935
Thiébault, General Baron, *Mémoires*, 6th ed., 5 vols, Paris, 1894
Maurois, A., *Prometheus, Life of Balzac*, London, 1965
Ancelot, Mme, *Foyers éteints*, Paris, 1850
   Salons de Paris, Paris, 1858
Balzac, H. de, *La Comédie humaine*, Pleiade ed., Paris, 1951–9
   Correspondance, 2 vols, Paris, 1877
Bourrienne, L.-A. F. de, *Mémoires*, Paris, 1829
Masson, F., *Napoléon et sa famille*, 13 vols, Paris, 1930
   Napoléon inconnu, Paris, 1895
Giradin, S. de, *Journal et souvenirs*, Paris, 1828
Arnault, A. V., *Souvenirs d'un sexagenaire*, Paris
Caulaincourt, L. de, *Mémoires*, Paris, 1933
Las Cases, E. de, *Le Mémorial de Saint-Hélène*, Paris, 1822
Stendhal (Henri Beyle), *Vie de Napoléon*, Paris, 1929
Boswell, J., *An Account of Corsica, etc.*, London, 1768

INDEX